Ellen Roseman

MONEY 201

More Personal Finance Advice for Every Canadian

E L L E N   R O S E M A N

National Library of Canada Cataloguing in Publication

Roseman, Ellen, 1947-
    Money 201 : more personal finance advice for every Canadian / Ellen Roseman.

Includes index.
ISBN 0-470-83401-3

    1. Finance, Personal--Canada. I. Title. II. Title: Money two hundred one.

HG179.R675 2003   332.024'00971   C2003-906464-6

John Wiley & Sons
Canada, Ltd
22 Worcester Road
Etobicoke, Ontario
M9W 1L1

Production Credits
Cover & interior text design: Interrobang Graphic
    Design Inc.
Printer: Tri-Graphic Printing Ltd.
Printed in Canada
10 9 8 7 6 5 4 3 2 1

To Edward, Charles and Richard,
with love and gratitude for your endless patience.

Contents

Contents

Contents

Contents

Introduction

Welcome back. You've picked up this book because you want to learn more about handling your personal finances. *Money 201* is the second instalment of a basic course in financial literacy for ordinary Canadians.

This project began as a series of weekend columns in the *Toronto Star*. My goal was to take a step-by-step approach to money management, writing in a style that was crystal clear and easy to understand. I also wanted to use real-life examples to which everyone could relate. There's nothing like a precautionary tale to alert you to mistakes you shouldn't make.

I knew I was running the risk of talking down to those with more sophistication and business smarts. But I was covering such a wide range of material I figured I'd always find some topics where people's knowledge was a little shaky or out-of-date.

Even if you know the RRSP rules inside out and how to do your own tax return (lucky devil), you may not have the same inside scoop on other subjects. How familiar are you with all the new investments, such as income trusts and exchange-traded funds? And how informed are you when you shop for insurance for your house or car?

The Money 101 columns were a big success and soon became a mainstay of the Sunday business section. There was so much email from readers that I spent at least a day a week trying to find answers to questions or respond to requests for personal advice. And along with the fan mail came the occasional insult: "You think you're an expert, yet how can you imply that RRSPs are not the best idea for everyone?"

I'm not an expert, just a journalist with 30 years of experience writing about business in daily newspapers. I talk to experts all the time, but I try to filter what they say through the lens of common sense and plain language. Too many people have told me they can't figure out what their financial advisers say because they speak in jargon.

As do many readers, I have a mortgage I'm still paying off. I have two children in the education system, one in university and one finishing high school. I've always been employed but I live with a self-employed writer who has no benefits or pension plan and a fluctuating income. Freedom 55 is a dream, since I plan to work as long as I can.

I also realize that being good with money isn't only about absorbing information. You have to get a grip on your emotions: Fear and greed when it comes to investing; indifference and guilt when it comes to spending money; intimidation and defeatism when it comes to saving.

With jobs and families and jam-packed lives, most people just don't have time to keep up with everything. You wouldn't believe how often I hear from those who have never bothered to check a bank statement, credit card agreement or insurance policy. Only when things go wrong do they read these documents and see what a mess they've got themselves into.

There's always something new to learn when it comes to your personal finances. That's why I decided to update my *Toronto Star* columns and turn them into a book. *Money 101: Every Canadian's Guide to Personal Finance* was published in late 2002. It did so well— at a time when sales of such books were painfully slow—that we came back with a sequel a year later.

Money 201 has a similar structure to *Money 101*, but deals with different topics and in more depth. You can read this book first if you like, but at some point you should read the other one as well. The chapters are short and bite-sized, so you can zero in on what matters most to you and come back later for more.

The first section deals with spending money more carefully on big-budget items, specifically transportation and housing. If you can cut your spending here, you're more likely to have something left over to save and invest.

In the second section, I look at how to be smarter with your everyday banking and credit arrangements. I've thrown in lots of stories about how you can fight back when a financial institution does you wrong. That's a lesson many people still have to learn.

In the third section, I investigate saving for retirement and alternatives to using a registered retirement savings plan. Contrary to what the financial service industry wants you to think, RRSPs are not a panacea. You need to keep some of your assets outside a tax-sheltered plan, because the taxes catch up with you eventually.

In the fourth section, I look at investment strategies that work in bad markets as well as good ones. When stocks slump, you become more conscious of preserving capital and taking fewer risks with your investments. You also want an adviser who keeps in touch and allays your fears. Too many flunked that test in recent years.

Finally, I work through some financial planning issues. How can you ask your employer for more flexibility on the job? How do you make sure your parents tidy up their business affairs as they get older? These are difficult conversations, but you can tackle them in ways that are more likely to succeed.

I take pains to include as many great Web sites as I can find. There's a world of help online, if you know where to go and how to use the handy tools that are provided.

I want to thank the *Toronto Star* for all its support. Business editor Ken Kidd deserves special credit, along with assistant managing editor Phil Bingley and communications manager Brad Henderson. And I can't forget the readers, who are my best source of ideas. They make my job fun and rewarding.

part one

Cutting Costs of Transportation and Shelter

You want to save and invest for the future. But you have no money to spare because you spend everything you earn (and then some). Sound familiar? You're not alone. Many people have trouble coping with the high cost of living, let alone finding a few extra dollars to put away.

It's a familiar predicament, one I heard about a lot as I travelled across the country promoting my earlier book, *Money 101*. Most of the media interviews focused on the chapters in which I talked about saving money on food, banking, insurance and utilities. I found there was a huge appetite for tips on trimming expenses—and rightly so. You can't get into good financial shape unless you learn to live below your means.

Since cutting costs is the foundation on which financial fitness is built—the key to everything else that follows—I decided to do an in-depth series in *Money 201*. But I wanted to stay away from the traditional penny-pinching hints that take too much time for too little savings, such as those found in *The Complete Tightwad*

Gazette: Promoting Thrift as a Viable Alternative Lifestyle by Amy Dacyczyn (Villard Books). Who's going to follow her advice to turn margarine tub lids into playing card holders, old credit cards into guitar picks and six-pack rings into a hammock or volleyball net? I think most people are too busy to keep detailed price logs, save and sort their cents-off coupons and hunt for lost treasures left out at the curb.

Don't sweat the small stuff. That's my motto. Focus on areas where you can chop your spending in significant ways. I'm not a fan of sacrificing small luxuries. That puts me at odds with David Bach, author of two recent personal finance bestsellers, *Smart Women Finish Rich* and *Smart Couples Finish Rich* (Doubleday Canada). Bach's advice: Stop spending $5 a day for a fancy coffee, a couple of Diet Cokes and a candy bar—and you can retire a multimillionaire.

"I never realized my double non-fat lattes were costing me $2 million," says a not-so-smart woman, age 23, quoted in his book. I'm bothered by the overly optimistic $2 million payoff, which assumes she'll invest all the money saved from foregoing her fancy snacks into stocks and earn 11 per cent a year until she's 65. Come on, get real.

I'm also irritated by the idea of giving up the little things that can make a big difference in your quality of life. Why not stick with your morning cup of coffee, or evening glass of wine, if that's what it takes to get you through the day? The "latte factor" in Bach's books seems like an unworkable solution.

You don't need to feel pain in order to save money, but you wouldn't know it if you look at the most common money-saving advice. A financial plan won't work if it forces people to avoid what makes them happy—just as a radical diet that cuts out all sweets is destined to self-destruct.

I found support for my views in a new book, *Second Acts: Creating the Life You Really Want*, by Stephen M. Pollan and Mark Levine (HarperCollins Canada). It's a guide to reinventing your life, changing careers, starting a business or dropping everything to pursue a life dream.

"There's a reason people will pay more to go to a movie rather than rent a videotape: It's a better sensory experience," say the New York-based authors, who also wrote the bestsellers *Live Rich* and *Die*

Broke. "There's a reason people will pay a service charge at a nearby ATM: It will save them time. And there's a reason people will pay for someone else to mow their lawn: They don't like mowing their lawn."

It's human nature to prefer pleasure to pain and look for the path of least resistance. Asking people to go against these tendencies only sets them up for failure, says Pollan: "If there weren't painless, big-picture savings to be had, I'd be the first to hop on the bulk-buying, brown-bagging bandwagon. But there are quite a few ways for you to save considerable sums of money without making sacrifices."

In this section, I'll help you get ready to pare down the two biggest areas of household expenses—transportation and shelter. Get these costs under control and you'll be well on your way to having a surplus to invest for the future. It's not as easy as cutting out a daily coffee or glass of wine. You have to make an up front investment in under-standing what you're paying on cars and housing (and affiliated expenses) and figuring out how to pay less. But it results in bigger savings down the road.

When I looked at ways to cut my own costs, my first priority was the automobile. Having two cars is a luxury when you live in central Toronto close to buses and subways. But I think it's the secret to stay-ing married for 29 years. It lets my husband and me run our lives on different schedules—and decide which car to let our two sons drive.

But when the cost of parking near the *Toronto Star* building went up to $8 a day, I said that's enough. I started leaving my car at home and taking the subway to work, which helped me slice my commuting expenses in half—to $3.80 a day. That's not counting gasoline, main-tenance and the other costs of auto ownership. Who knows? Maybe this is the first step toward giving up the second car altogether.

Know what it costs to drive your car

Most people are shocked to hear exactly how much it costs to own a car. Maybe they prefer not to know, because driving is so darned convenient. But getting a handle on driving expenses can help you make some crucial decisions. Do you need a car at all? Maybe you can rent when needed or take taxis for the same annual cost. If you drive your car to work, is there a cheaper way to commute? Do you buy a used car rather than a new one? With the soaring cost of automobile insurance, you can save a bundle in premium costs by keeping your car longer and replacing it with a used model.

The Canadian Automobile Association publishes an annual survey of driving costs for new cars. The latest survey, posted at the CAA's Web site, www.caa.ca, shows it costs 13.75 cents a kilometre to operate a compact car (a 2003 Chevrolet Cavalier Z-24 four-door sedan) and 15.25 cents a kilometre to operate a minivan (a 2003 Dodge Caravan SE), based on annual driving of 18,000 kilometres a year. The total annual operating costs—fuel and oil, maintenance and tires—are $2,475 for the Cavalier and $2,745 for the Caravan.

Then there are the fixed costs of car ownership, such as insurance, licence and registration, depreciation and financing expenses. They add up to $7,050 a year for the Cavalier and $7,241 for the

Caravan. The CAA assumes you're financing 90 per cent of the car's purchase at 6.5 per cent interest over four years, then trading it in for a new car with 72,000 kilometres on the odometer.

When you combine the operating and fixed costs, the total annual driving cost is $9,525 (or 52.9 cents a kilometre) for the Cavalier and $9,986 (or 55.5 cents a kilometre) for the Caravan, based on driving 18,000 kilometres a year. The shocking statistic is the daily cost, which works out to $26.09 for the smaller car and $27.36 for the larger car—whether you drive that day or not. This would pay for many taxicab trips and car rentals.

A *Toronto Star* reader calculated his daily driving cost at $18.68, "whether I took my car out or left it in the garage." He'd talk to people who'd say, "You've got to be kidding," until he showed them his daily logbook and meticulous tax records. He had bought a 1992 Mercury Marquis for $28,000 and disposed of it 10 years later after driving 151,000 kilometres.

I'd advise downloading the CAA's survey of driving costs and printing it out. You'll find instructions on how to calculate your own vehicle expenses and a chart that helps you keep track. You can even find out how to estimate your maintenance costs if you haven't kept a record (2.9 cents a kilometre for the Cavalier and 3.01 cents for the Caravan). The data comes from Runzheimer International Inc., a management consulting firm that helps companies decide how much to reimburse employees for car expenses.

The CAA used a gasoline cost of 80.1 cents a litre, the average national price in December 2002. Gas prices go up and down, so here's a formula to use in your calculations: A 10-cent increase in gas incurs a 1-cent increase in operating costs. If gas goes down 10 cents, your operating costs go down 1 cent.

The formula is based on use of a mid-sized Canadian car, which consumes an average of 10 litres of gas per 100 kilometres (or 28.5 miles per gallon). That translates to 0.1 litre of gas per kilometre driven. For the larger sport-utility vehicles, the incremental operating cost is between 1.5 cents and 2 cents per kilometre.

If you find the CAA's driving costs inflated, think again. Dennis DesRosiers, a respected Toronto-area automotive consultant, came up with similar figures in late 2002. For an average-priced compact car, he calculates the cost of ownership at 41.57 cents a kilometre in the first year (based on 20,000 kilometres of annual driving). But that drops to 27.4 cents a kilometre in the second year and 25.5 cents in the third year, because of falling insurance and depreciation costs.

Dispelling the myth that it costs more to own a car as it ages, DesRosiers says the cost of repairs remains stable and any increase is more than offset by the lower cost of insurance and depreciation. You pay dearly for the thrill of buying a new product.

Canadians are fairly conservative in their vehicle buying and ownership habits, his research shows. The most common vehicles we buy every year are economical compacts such as the Chevrolet Cavalier, Honda Civic and Ford Focus. We buy twice as many practical minivans as Americans do (on a market share basis) and half as many sport-utility vehicles, often viewed as more expensive to own and operate. Yes, leasing is popular. But about half of Canada's leased vehicles are purchased by the consumer at the end of the lease and driven for another five to six years.

When it comes to length of ownership, the average car bought new is kept for more than eight years. About a third of consumers keep their cars for 11 to 15 years. In Canada, there are more than six million vehicles on the road and 30 per cent of these cars are more than 10 years old, DesRosiers figures. Not surprisingly, luxury cars (such as Mercedes Benz and BMW) are the winners when it comes to long-lasting vehicles. Toyota and Honda lead the non-luxury car makes in longevity and survival rates.

How to drive down your car's operating costs

If you drive an average car, you only see 44 per cent of the total associated costs. There are other costs incurred when we decide to get into our vehicles, costs borne by society as a whole and not borne by the individual. These include air and water pollution, road construction and maintenance, costs of car-oriented urban development, crash costs imposed on others, policing, lights, emergency services, congestion, subsidies for parking, noise and delays caused to non-motorized travel.

You can help yourself and your fellow citizens by choosing the right car, maintaining it properly and driving it more sensibly. Here's how to cut your driving costs and reduce greenhouse gases at the same time, with tips from Natural Resources Canada's Office of Energy Efficiency (www.oee.nrcan.gc.ca) and the Pembina Institute for Appropriate Development (www.climatechangesolutions.com).

Choosing the right car

Almost all new vehicles have an EnerGuide label, which shows city and highway fuel consumption ratings and estimated annual cost of fuel for that vehicle. Look for this label and use the information to compare different models. Call 1-800-387-2000 to order a free copy of the 2003 fuel consumption guide or download it from Natural Resources Canada's Web site, where you can also compare fuel consumption ratings for new and older vehicles.

Think carefully about buying four-wheel drive or all-wheel drive vehicles, which can increase your fuel consumption by 5 to 10 per cent, compared to two-wheel drive vehicles. How often do you need to use this option and is it worth the extra fuel costs for as long as you own the vehicle?

Opt for the space-saver spare tire instead of a standard-sized tire (it reduces weight and saves on fuel). And instead of a permanent roof rack, which increases fuel consumption because of aerodynamic drag, look at an add-on rack that can be removed when not needed.

Operating an air conditioner can increase fuel consumption by 20 per cent in city driving. Most vehicles leak coolant and must be recharged an average of three times during their lifespan. Try to minimize use of your A/C system and look at cooling options such as a sunroof and tinted glass.

Maintaining your car

Keeping your vehicle in top shape will save fuel and money. Read the owner's manual carefully and follow the maintenance schedule. Virtually all of your car's mechanical systems can affect fuel efficiency in one way or another. Use the grade of gasoline recommended by the manufacturer. Subcompact and compact passenger cars require only regular gasoline, yet many owners buy mid-grade and premium gas.

When buying motor oil, look for a brand rated as "energy conserving." This can improve fuel efficiency by up to three per cent.

Check your tire pressure regularly, especially after temperature changes. Each five per cent of under-inflation translates into a one per cent decrease in fuel efficiency.

Maintain your brakes. Dragging brakes can decrease fuel efficiency by up to 40 per cent. A clogged air filter can increase fuel consumption by 10 per cent.

Driving more sensibly

Drive at the posted speed limit. The optimum highway cruising speed for most vehicles is 90 kilometres an hour. Avoid aggressive driving, with rapid acceleration and quick stops. Practice defensive driving, which means anticipating what's ahead and reacting earlier rather than later.

In winter, idle your car for a maximum of 30 seconds. The most effective way to warm up a cold vehicle is to drive it. On really cold mornings, use a block heater to help your engine start more easily. Lighten your load by removing roof boxes for skis and heavy bags of sand or salt carried around in the trunk when they're not needed.

Plan your trips and combine errands. Avoid short trips of less than five kilometres, which don't allow the engine to reach its peak operating temperature.

Use public transit, if it's available, or try car-pooling. Investigate urban car-sharing services, which are good for occasional drivers and those who want to avoid buying a second car. To find an alternative that can work for you, check the growing list of van-pool, rideshare and car co-op programs across Canada at the Web site www.climatechangesolutions.com/individuals/transport/tools/cpool map.html.

"The average car in Canada is driven just 66 minutes a day, and that includes commuters," says AutoShare (416-340-7888, www.autoshare.com). Members pay $10 to $20 a month for access to cars parked across Toronto, plus an hourly rate of $4 to $6 and a per-kilometre charge of 15 cents. Insurance, maintenance and gas costs are included. Access to cars is limited to 24 hours on weekends, but AutoShare members get a reduced rate on weekend car rentals with a partner agency.

Ali and Vandana Rahjiv joined AutoShare and found they changed their driving habits, making fewer and more-efficient trips. They typically drove about 12,000 kilometres a year, mostly within 15 kilometres of their home. With the pay-per-use system, the Rahjivs no longer felt compelled to "get the most out of their investment" by using their car more often. Instead, they discovered the freedom to take whatever transportation mode was most convenient. As a result, the Rahjivs are now saving about $2,200 a year, while reducing their greenhouse gas emissions by about 50 per cent—a number that is common for people who join car co-ops.

The Climate Change Solutions Web site has a wonderful collection of success stories, showing what can be achieved by changing your habits—both in dollar savings and cutting pollution. The Rahjivs' story comes from there, as do many others you might enjoy reading, with titles such as "Active Transportation: Kwan takes up cycling," and "Tele-commuting: Eli gives up the rat race."

Parents who normally drive their kids to school may be interested in reading a story (with photos) about a "walking school bus" in Toronto. Nine families at the Maurice Cody Public School, all living within a half-kilometre of the school, stopped driving their young children and now take turns walking their children to and from school. The children prefer walking, since they can hang out with their friends instead of sitting in the back of the family vehicle and listening to their parents' boring music.

After the first year, the nine participating families saved a collective $230 in fuel costs and cut greenhouse gas emissions by 1,000 kilograms. And there are other benefits, such as increased physical fitness, less congestion around schools, fewer child traffic injuries and more streetwise kids. To bring the walking school bus program to your neighbourhood, contact Go for Green, a national non-profit charity whose mission is to encourage outdoor physical activity that protects, enhances or restores the environment. Call 1-888-UB-ACTIV (822-2848) or check the Web site, www.goforgreen.ca.

How to comparison shop for car insurance

Your car insurance policy comes up for renewal and you gasp at the higher premiums. After several years of stable rates, the average cost of car insurance went up 30 per cent across Canada in 2002. New Brunswick and Nova Scotia have seen huge hikes, up to 70 per cent. Those with lower increases include Manitoba and Saskatchewan, which have public auto insurance systems.

Premiums are going up because of an influx in non-serious injury claims, the private insurance companies say. They also blame the current investment climate of low interest rates and poor stock market returns, which hurt firms' ability to cover their underwriting losses.

Is it time to start shopping the market to see if you can find a better deal? Yes, if—and only if—you have a good driving record. However, if you and your family members have made several claims in recent years (even if the accidents were not your fault), you may find the rates quoted are much higher than what you currently pay. The effort is still worthwhile, even if you discover you're better off staying where you are.

The Internet is a real boon to comparison shoppers. Many Web sites will give you access to real-time quotes in minutes, even if you don't buy insurance online. It's much faster than spending hours on the phone trying to contact brokers and insurers directly. Online quotes usually come from two sources: Kanetix (www.kanetix.com), which quotes car insurance prices from about 10 large Canadian companies; and the Consumer's Guide to Insurance, which offers quotes from more than 30 companies online (www.insurancehot-line.com) and by phone (416-686-0531).

Before you get going, call your current insurer to get information about your driving history. How many claims have you and other drivers in the family made in the past six years? Ask for details of any accident or claim during that period (including claims under your comprehensive coverage, such as theft or windshield damage).

When you shop for new auto insurance coverage, you will also have to provide information about your conviction record in the past three years (offenses related to the operation of your car, such as speeding tickets and seat-belt infractions). You can obtain your motor vehicle record from the provincial transport ministry, but insurance companies require a three-year history. If you're not sure of dates, check with your current insurance provider.

It's a good idea to keep your own record of the dates of any tickets, accidents or claims. "If you're not sure of the date of your last ticket or accident, tell your prospective insurer you can't remember when it was," says insurance expert Sally Praskey, whose advice is posted at the Insurance Canada site (www.insurance-canada.ca). "If you say you haven't had any tickets in the last three years and the insurer discovers otherwise—and it will—it may refuse your application or charge you more for your coverage."

Some insurance companies will forgive one at-fault accident, especially if you're a long-term customer with an otherwise good record. Full accident forgiveness is an option that typically costs about $30 a year. It's worth the money. However, your chances of being forgiven are much less if you are a new client. Ask what the new company's forgiveness policy is for an at-fault accident before you make your decision.

The insurance company with the lowest price may not be the most generous in settling claims. "Likely one of the reasons it can afford to be priced so much lower than its competitors is that it takes a very tough stance at claims time," Praskey says. Ask your friends and colleagues who've had a recent claims experience how they were treated and whether their claim was settled promptly and without hassle.

A *Star* reader who's an insurance broker offers this advice to clients: By all means shop around, but make sure your prospective company won't cancel you or penalize you for an early accident. Get it in writing. If it won't do that, consider at length the accident forgiveness benefits you're giving up for the money saved.

You can also check the Financial Service Commission of Ontario's Web site, (www.fsco.gov.on.ca), a helpful resource even if you live in another province. There you will find an annual survey, which asks customers of 46 insurance companies and the Facility Association how happy they were with the claims settlement procedure. While the overall satisfaction rate is 86 per cent, the satisfaction rate for individual companies ranges from 61 per cent for Kingsway General (a company that insures high-risk drivers) to 95 per cent for State Farm Mutual.

Alas, my own record is a tad tarnished. I had a minor collision, a fender bender, in 1999. It was my fault, since I failed to notice a car coming through an intersection when I was at a stop sign. My insurance company paid $889 to fix my car's front bumper (over and above my deductible). As a result, I lost my preferred rating, given to drivers who have been licensed for 15 years or more with no claims or accidents. It cost me about $200 a year in higher premiums.

But when I started comparison shopping with the help of Lee Romanov, who runs the Consumer's Guide to Insurance, I found that 1999 claim would hurt me much more if I switched. She told me I already had a decent rate with Liberty Mutual Insurance Co., which charged $2,554 to insure our 1998 Toyota Sienna van and a 1997 Ford Escort. (We get discounts for having our two cars, plus home insurance, with the same company.) She promised to get me a slightly cheaper $2,300 annual rate from Lombard Insurance. But that soared to more than $4,000 when I mentioned the 1999 accident claim.

My next stop was Kanetix, whose Web site I found very easy to navigate. But I was disappointed to get only three quotes—ranging from $3,979 with Direct Protect to $6,625 with York Fire & Casualty—all much more than my current rate.

Later I did an experiment to see the dollar impact of my single accident claim. When I said I had a claims-free record, Kanetix gave me insurance quotes for the Toyota from 10 companies, ranging from $1,277 with Lombard to $2,272 with Direct Protect. But when I included my accident claim, just four companies wanted my business. And their quotes ranged from $2,702 with RBC Insurance to $4,517 with Allstate Insurance Co. of Canada.

Of course, I didn't go elsewhere after finding out how good a deal I had. This is a tough time to be switching companies. Insurers blame the terrorist attacks of Sept. 11, 2001, for making them skittish about accepting new customers with spotty records. But, in effect, they're penalizing frequent users—those who try to collect on the insurance for which they've paid premiums for years. It's the opposite of a loyalty program.

If you have multiple claims, forget about shopping around. In the current tight insurance market, no one will want your business. One *Toronto Star* reader told me he couldn't get a single company to quote him a rate when he tried to shop the market. With four vehicles insured, he and his family had made had seven claims in the previous five years (two at-fault accidents, three not-at-fault accidents and two comprehensive claims). That's the kind of record insurers don't like to see.

Make sure you get an early start on your insurance shopping. Don't wait until a week or two before the policy's renewal date. Give yourself three months, since that's how long it can take to get several quotes and do the paperwork.

You may have to shop around for brokers until you find one who can place your business. Many are so busy that they're not quoting rates over the phone. You have to see them in person in their offices. Don't agree to pay a fee for a broker to quote you a rate. If they don't find insurance for you, they may keep the fee (say $50) for their efforts.

If you can't get coverage from private insurance companies and you live in a province without a public insurance system, you have to go to non-standard insurers (companies that specialize in insuring high-risk drivers) or to the Facility Association, an industry-sponsored pool of last resort. The Facility's rates are very high, reflecting the degree of risk.

Take, for example, a 19-year-old male who's had one accident. He's the primary driver of a Chevrolet Cavalier and lives in Ajax, Ontario (outside Toronto). The lowest rate we found after shopping the market was $4,648 with Lombard Insurance. The highest rate was a whopping $16,470 with the Facility Association. For a 19-year-old female driver with one accident, the lowest rate we found was $3,365 with Lombard and the highest was $8,564 with the Facility Association.

If you have teenagers in your household, don't forget to tell your insurance company if they will be driving your car occasionally. "They should be added to your policy as soon as they get a G1 licence," says Dave Stauffer, a partner with DeHart and Stauffer Insurance Brokers in Oshawa. (Ontario has a graduated licencing system, where beginners start by driving under supervision at all times.) "There's no extra charge when they have a G1 and it gives them some insurance history."

Encourage your kids to take a driver's training course, one with at least 25 hours in the classroom and 10 hours behind the wheel. This will give them a lower rate later on. And if they live in Ontario, taking a driver's training course will let them proceed to the next licensing level (G2) in eight months, instead of one year, after passing a road test.

After shopping around, we found the driver's training credit would reduce the car insurance premium from $2,444 to $2,311 (a saving of $133 a year) for a 19-year-old Toronto male with a G2 licence and no accidents. It would mean a $26 annual saving (from $1,390 to $1,364) for a 19-year-old female driver in Toronto.

Some insurance companies even give a price break to young people who have good marks in school. The idea is they'll be better drivers if they apply themselves to their high school or university studies. So, if your child has a good report card, ask the insurance company whether you can submit a copy and get a lower rate.

Suppose you decide to change insurance providers after shopping around and finding a lower rate. Don't cancel your old policy until your new insurance company confirms your coverage in writing. Otherwise, you could be left stranded—for example, if information turns up later that causes the new insurer to increase your quoted rate.

Also, try to make the switch right before your renewal date. If you wait too long and notify your insurer after the renewal date, you will be charged a penalty. One *Toronto Star* reader was told he had to pay $245—about 10 per cent of the cost of his premium—because he was *one* day late in getting his paperwork done. The ombudsman at his former insurance company agreed the penalty was excessive for a one-day delay and waived it after we appealed his case.

You must notify your current insurance provider in writing if you decide to move. Don't think you can simply refuse to pay the renewal bill. If you don't provide written notification, you are still committed to that insurance and on the hook for the payment, Praskey says.

Adjust your car insurance coverage to cut costs

You don't have to switch to save money on car insurance. Try raising the deductibles, the portion you pay out of your own pocket before the insurance company covers the claim. I went through the exercise and got a $640 reduction in premiums for our two cars, amounting to a 25 per cent discount.

When I checked the policy (which I confess I hadn't done regularly), I found we had $300 deductibles on our collision and comprehensive coverage. I raised them to $1,000; that was where the big savings came in. Collision and comprehensive pay for repair or replacement of your car if it's stolen or damaged in an accident, or hit by a storm or natural disaster. The standard advice is to keep the deductible as high as you can afford. For me, $1,000 was an amount I felt comfortable paying out of pocket—not out of line with what I would pay for major mechanical repairs not covered by insurance.

More than our collision and comprehensive deductibles were woefully out of date. The third-party liability coverage, for example, was only $500,000. Every province requires a minimum of $200,000 (except Quebec, where the minimum limit is $50,000). Liability pays for property damage and bodily injuries caused by you or your vehicle to others. If there's a claim against you for more than your level of coverage, you can be held personally responsible for the balance.

I doubled the liability coverage on both cars to $1 million, figuring that was the key part of the policy. And it's not all that expensive to do. It costs an average $45 a year to raise your liability coverage from $500,000 to $1 million, says Lee Romanov, who runs a company that helps people shop for insurance (www.insurancehotline.com). To go from $1 million to $2 million costs an additional $45 a year.

Some people drop their collision coverage altogether for older cars. (This coverage is optional in all provinces except Manitoba and Saskatchewan.) That's because relatively minor damage could cost more to repair than what the vehicle is worth. But if you do so, be prepared to pay out of pocket to repair or replace your vehicle if you're hit by an unidentified driver—whether it's your fault or not.

Consider, too, that if your car is damaged in a hit-and-run accident, the only way for insurance to pay for that damage is through your collision coverage. "If you don't carry collision insurance, you will be stuck with the entire bill for an accident that wasn't even your fault," says Sally Praskey in *The Insurance Book: What Canadians Really Need to Know Before Buying Insurance* (sold through the Insurance Canada Web site). "Your only other recourse would be to track down and recover the money yourself from the driver who hit you—a challenge for even the most intrepid P.I. And don't look to your insurance company to help you. You're on your own."

Remember that if you lease your car or you've taken out a bank loan to buy it (which you haven't paid off), you have no choice. You must carry collision coverage. This protects the leasing company or bank lender from having to shoulder the cost of repairs if you don't. Another possible saving: Remove the coverage for rentals if your car is damaged. You can get by if you live near public transit or you have several cars in the family. (That's another cut I made to our policy.)

Leave your car at home during the day. You'll save about $145 a year in insurance costs by not driving to work, assuming you commute 10 to 20 kilometres, Romanov says. You can save $275 a year if you give up a 30-kilometre daily commute.

Use the same company for both your home and car insurance. That can get you a loyalty discount of 5 to 10 per cent a year.

Driving safely saves you money. Your rate probably won't go up if you get a ticket for speeding, making an illegal turn or not buckling up. But with two tickets, your annual costs can rise from $250 to $1,000. One at-fault accident can increase your rates by $1,000 to $5,000 a year. Two accidents can increase your rates from $3,500 to $6,000 and stay on your record for six years.

Taking a driver's training course can improve your skills at the wheel and get you an insurance discount, too.

Where you live often makes a difference in what you pay for car insurance. One of my readers discovered that when he changed addresses in Toronto, the insurance went up $1,000 a year for him and his wife. He went online to compare insurance rates and found he always got higher quotes when he put in his new postal code. "For moving 10 minutes away, I have gotten punished on insurance rates," he says about his new home, which is closer to the busy and accident-prone 401 highway. This means he's more likely to get into an accident and make a claim.

The Ontario government has promised new legislation outlawing this practice, but price discrimination based on location is legal when it comes to car insurance. Drivers in larger cities pay more. There are more cars on the road and more accidents—and also a greater likelihood of getting your car stolen.

Take, for example, a married couple, age 35 and 38, who own a 1998 Ford Taurus and drive less than 16,000 kilometres a year. They've had no accidents or driving convictions in six years. They'll pay about $1,430 a year for car insurance if they live in Toronto, compared to about $937 a year if they live in London, Ontario. This couple could try driving the car only for pleasure (and not taking it to work). This would save them $75 a year.

Short of moving to a safer area, there are a few other ways to cut costs. Reducing your annual mileage can help. The more time you spend on the road, the greater your chances of getting into an accident.

Ask for discounts. Brokers often give you a break if you insure several cars or family members with them. It helps to bundle several types of insurance (auto, home, life and business). You might get a premium reduction of 5 to 15 per cent if you've installed a theft deterrent system in your car or if you're a low-mileage driver or an older driver.

Drive a car that's less expensive to insure. The Vehicle Information Centre of Canada (www.vicc.com) looks at the claims history of different makes and models—including accident frequency, repair costs, theft, vandalism and safety ratings.

Keep your insurance provider informed of major changes in your life. Some things that might improve your insurance profile and cut your premiums, says Praskey: You move to a less populated area; you change jobs and commute fewer kilometres to work; you buy a new car that has a better insurance rating; you start a home business and no longer drive to work; you reduce the number of drivers in your household.

Finally, don't make small claims if you can avoid doing so. Police must be informed if you're in an accident that causes $1,000 or more in damage to your car or to another vehicle. Then, once you have notified the police, you must report the accident to your insurance company within seven days. But if the damage to your car is less than $1,000—as long as you haven't damaged someone else's car or injured anyone—you're probably better off not to claim for the accident. That way, it won't go on your record and your premiums won't go up.

You'll have to pay the deductible on your collision coverage anyway. How much extra will it cost to pay for all the repairs yourself? You'll save more in the long run by keeping your insurance record unblemished so your premiums won't increase.

Here's the key point many people don't realize: It's not the amount paid out by the insurance company that counts against you, but the question of fault. "Therefore, an at-fault claim of only a few hundred dollars will count against your insurance record in much the same way as a catastrophic at-fault accident would," says Praskey.

Insurance is there to cover the big losses you couldn't afford otherwise. So pay for the minor repairs yourself and keep your insurance for when you really need it.

Negotiate a good price when buying a new car

The average price of a new vehicle has climbed to more than $30,000 (excluding taxes). This represents almost six months' income for the average Canadian household. Though a new car loses 25 to 30 per cent of its value to depreciation once driven off the dealer's lot, many people still prefer to buy new. They like the comprehensive warranty and attractive financing rates.

Buying a new car is all about negotiation. Only Saturn has gone to a nationwide system of giving full price information up front, with no negotiating. Its no-haggle pricing policy, launched in 1990, has been a winner for parent General Motors of Canada Ltd. Women, who often hate the way they're forced to bargain with new car dealers, make up more than half of Saturn's market.

In the last few years, Toyota Canada Inc. has also picked up on the humiliation many people feel when dickering with car dealers. Its Access program, rolled out in western Canada and in Montreal, allows dealers to get together in a region and submit a suggested selling price for each model, usually discounted from the manufacturer's suggested list price. Then they come up with an average price for every model, which becomes the Access price that's quoted to customers whether they visit the showroom or buy on the Internet.

Toyota hit a minor roadblock when critics made allegations of price-fixing. The federal Competition Bureau launched an 18-month investigation, which concluded in March 2003. The bureau decided that Toyota could continue the Access program and extend it across Canada, as long as the company made clear to dealers there would be no retaliation for discounting below the Access price. As part of the settlement, Toyota made $2.3 million in donations to charitable groups across Canada.

Access Toyota is exclusive to Canada. There's nothing like it in the United States or other markets. "It was developed because of what we were hearing from consumers, that there was a need for greater transparency in the purchasing process," says Toyota vice-president Stephen Beatty. People told the company they didn't like being forced into an adversarial relationship with a car salesman. Nor did they like feeling they could have paid less if they had been a better negotiator or had the courage to walk out if things weren't going their way.

So how do you deal with new car dealers if you lack confidence in your bargaining skills? We asked a few veteran negotiators for tips. Robert LoPresti runs the AutoBuy service for Metro Credit Union in Toronto. At a cost of $175 for members and $199 for non-members, he shops the market and locates the best prices. Paul Timoteo runs Car Cost Canada, which provides consumers with new car dealer invoice prices online (at a per-quote cost of $25 to $95). Invoice prices include rebates and incentives from the manufacturer. With this information, you can determine the price spread from the manufacturer's suggested list price and make a fair and reasonable offer above the dealer's cost on the car you want to buy.

LoPresti's advice: Start with a realistic idea of how much profit the dealer makes on a new car. Many people think it's in the 20 per cent range—say $5,000 on a $25,000 vehicle. "That's a big misconception," LoPresti says. "Margins have been coming down for years. They're under 10 per cent for most vehicles, which means $2,500 on a $25,000 car if it sells for list—and they can be as low as 5 per cent (or $1,250)."

Timoteo's advice: "Dicker up" from the dealer invoice cost, rather than down from the manufacturer's suggested retail price.

Most new vehicles can be purchased for between five to seven per cent over the dealer cost. Canadians can't get free dealer invoice costs on the Internet the way Americans can. The closest thing is Timoteo's new service, at FreeInvoicePrices.com, which charges a $50 fee that is refundable when the customer completes the car purchase.

Don't go shopping until you have an idea of the vehicles and options you want to consider and how much you can afford to pay. "People often say they don't know what they can afford till they go into the negotiations," LoPresti says. "But you can base affordability on the list price."

Instead of visiting showrooms, do your research in the comfort of your home.

Books such as the annual *Lemon-Aid* new car guides by Phil Edmonston (published by Viking Canada) tell you which inferior models to avoid. So does *Consumer Reports* magazine's annual April issue. For information on what cars are perceived as reliable and unreliable in Canada, check out the Canadian Automobile Association's Autopinion, an annual survey of more than 20,000 members (www.caa.ca), with analysis by Dennis DesRosiers.

Don't narrow down your options to a single vehicle. "If you become set on buying one particular car, you may lose a lot of potential negotiating power," says Timoteo. Have two or three possible cars in mind.

Negotiate the new vehicle price first. Only then should you talk about trading in your old car through the dealer. Check the *Canadian Red Book* (available in libraries) or *Canadian Black Book* (www.canadian-blackbook.com) to find the wholesale price of your trade-in. "People think their trade-in is worth much more than it really is," LoPresti notes. "Dealers pay the book value, minus what it takes to refurbish the car."

Keep the financing or leasing option separate from the price negotiations, as well. Low-interest financing programs are very costly to car manufacturers. Often there's a cash incentive for buyers who arrange their own financing through a bank or credit union.

Know your insurance costs before you buy a car, since they can fluctuate greatly from one model to another. Car Cost Canada (www.carcostcanada.com) has a link to the Consumer's Guide to Insurance (www.insurancehotline.com), which lets you compare rates from up to 35 insurance companies. Another good resource is the Vehicle Information Centre of Canada's booklet, "How Cars Measure Up," which gives the 10 best and worst models for theft frequency and collision repair costs (www.vicc.com).

Once you agree on a new car price, you're not done with the negotiating process. There are also freight and pre-delivery inspection charges, which can add up to $1,000 or more, plus administration fees for the dealer of $200 to $400. Try to avoid paying these administration fees, as Metro Credit Union does, or at least bargain them down. "They're very common and provide extra profit for doing paperwork, contracts, maybe a credit application," LoPresti says.

Car Cost Canada provides the dealer's invoice cost for freight charges—but not pre-delivery inspection costs, which tend to fluctuate across the country. And there's no price data for parts and accessories installed by the dealer. "Consider a markup of 20 per cent to be average for after-market parts and accessories," says Timoteo. That explains why dealers tend to push services such as rustproofing once the sale is completed.

If you can't bear to do your own negotiating, you can rent an expert at a reasonable cost. Car Cost Canada, which has 30,000 members, offers a service that will negotiate with up to four dealers in your area for $125 to $145. Dealfinder Inc., based in Ottawa, charges $149 up front to negotiate a deal on a new car and will return the consulting fee if you find something better. Recommended by *Canadian MoneySaver* magazine, it's at 1-800-331-2044 or www.dealfinder.org.

When asked about his best car-shopping tip, here's the reply from George Iny, president of the Automobile Protection Association, a consumer group: "Take an advertisement (from a specific dealership) to another dealer. They get so frustrated that they'll lower their price to below what they'd normally ask, because they know your fallback is to go someplace else that's trying to take you. It's a very, very powerful tool that we've only recently learned."

What if your dream car is a lemon?

Your car needs an expensive repair and the warranty is up. Don't despair. Before doing the work, check to see whether your problem is covered by an extended warranty from the manufacturer. Automakers quietly put these warranties in place when enough complaints come in from customers about factory defects.

"Few car owners know that secret car warranties exist," says Phil Edmonston, author of the *Lemon-Aid* new and used car guides. "Automakers are reluctant to make these free repair programs public because they feel it would weaken confidence in their products and increase their legal liability."

The closest automakers come to an admission, he says, is sending a technical service bulletin to dealers or a letter to the original owner. And instead of using the term "extended warranty," the manufacturers prefer to talk about their after-warranty assistance, goodwill policy or product-improvement program.

Here's a good news story about a goodwill program that affects 1997 to 2002 Toyota and Lexus vehicles (including the one I drive, a 1998 Toyota Sienna minivan). The tale involves a nasty condition known as "oil sludge," which may require the engine to be rebuilt.

Edmonston claims credit for getting Toyota to extend its engine warranty to eight years, which is the longest in the auto industry, with no mileage limit. He hears about vehicle problems from readers who write or send email through his Web site, www.lemonaidcars.com.

"I started looking at all these engine-sludge complaints from Toyota owners," he says. "Then I looked at Toyota's Web site and found a memo to dealers about making a sludge claim. I said, bingo!" He wrote to Toyota Motor Sales USA Inc. in Torrance, Calif., asking what the company would do about engine sludge.

At first, the company agreed to deal with complaints on a case-by-case basis under a goodwill program that lasted 12 months. Owners had to show they had maintained their vehicles. But Edmonston pushed for more. In April 2002, Toyota decided to extend the engine warranty to eight years from the date of the first sale or lease. The U.S. company moved first, quickly followed by the Canadian company.

Engine sludge is less common in Canada because the harsh climate here requires servicing cars more frequently. Two-thirds of Toyota and Lexus owners go to their dealers for routine maintenance. "Although there has been a lower incidence of these maintenance problems in Canada compared to the U.S., Toyota Canada feels that it is important that Canadian customers receive the same benefits as their American counterparts," said Toyota Canada vice-president Stephen Beatty.

In his books and on his Web site, Edmonston lists problems that are covered by manufacturers beyond the original warranty period. His advice to motorists: Maintain your vehicle regularly. Keep your receipts. If you have a problem once the warranty is up, ask your dealer for after-warranty assistance. "You have to sensitize your service manager to the fact he should be applying for goodwill treatment of your claim," he says.

Alldata LLC provides free summaries of automakers' technical service bulletins by year, model and engine option at www.alldata.com. For more information, you can subscribe to Alldata DIY, which provides access to the complete technical service bulletins for $24.95 (U.S.) a year, or a little less than $40 (Canadian). One caveat: BMW and

Honda have refused to allow Alldata to distribute their service bulletins to customers.

Manufacturers and importers in Canada rarely replace new cars, no matter how defective they are. If your vehicle is plagued with problems, you can try suing the manufacturer in court. This takes time and money (lots of it). Or you can use the Canadian Motor Vehicle Arbitration Plan, known as CAMVAP, which provides an alternative to going to court. CAMVAP handled 693 cases in 2002. In the cases that went to a full hearing, the consumer was reimbursed for repairs or offered free repairs 49 per cent of the time. But in only 17 per cent of cases were manufacturers ordered to buy back cars.

In Canada, there's no "lemon law" that forces companies to provide replacements for vehicles that don't meet certain standards of safety and reliability. Rob Sampson, a Tory Member of Provincial Parliament in Ontario, took up the cause after a constituent showed him a purchase agreement that included rights under the lemon law in California. He soon found that all 50 U.S. states had similar laws. A lemon is generally defined as a car that has been repaired four or more times for the same defect during the warranty period.

Sampson introduced a private member's bill, which died on the order paper, giving manufacturers three chances to fix a car before declaring it a lemon. The deficiency would have to substantially impair the use, value or safety of a motor vehicle, or cost more than $1,000 to rectify. "I had a tremendous response from the public, more than on any other issue in the past," says Sampson. Far from replacing CAMVAP, the industry-financed arbitration program, he thinks the lemon law would add a tool to the consumer's arsenal.

Stephen Moody, executive director of CAMVAP, opposes a lemon law because he prefers arbitration to litigation. "The option of being able to go to court would be seldom used because consumers would be putting everything at risk," he says. The Sampson bill wouldn't protect complainants from picking up the manufacturer's legal costs—as well as their own—if they lost their cases.

U.S. lemon laws have created a more adversarial environment, in Moody's view. Dealers refuse to do repairs and write misleading work orders so they don't get caught in the three-strikes-and-you're-out legal trap. "Manufacturers tell us warranty costs are higher in Canada than in the U.S.," Moody says. "Here they take chances trying to resolve problems, even if they can't find a cause."

If you have a dispute about your vehicle and you've given the maker a chance to resolve it without success, then you can ask CAMVAP for help. Whether you've given the company one, two or twenty-two opportunities to resolve it, you're eligible. From start to finish, the CAMVAP process takes about 70 days. If the car requires a technical inspection, the process takes 90 days—still faster than most court cases. Best of all, the plan is free to the consumer. It is paid for by automakers through a formula that reflects each company's market share and past case experience.

You're eligible to ask for CAMVAP's help if your dispute is about manufacturing defects or you feel the manufacturer is not honouring the warranty. The vehicle must be a current model or one from the previous four model years and must have travelled fewer than 160,000 kilometres at the time of the hearing. You don't have to be the original owner.

CAMVAP is governed by an independent board and has a record of coming down on the customer's side. "Generally, manufacturers go to arbitration only if they think they have a strong case," Moody says. "Otherwise, they try to settle beforehand." Once the CAMVAP arbitrator makes a decision, both the customer and the manufacturer are bound by it. There are only very limited rights to have the decision examined by a court under judicial review. You can find details of past awards at the Web site and you can search for cars that have been bought back by manufacturers under the program since Jan. 1, 1999.

Public awareness of CAMVAP, however, is low. With more than four million vehicles eligible for the program in any given year, why are there less than 700 cases? Volume actually fell in 2002, despite the fact that service was extended to Quebec for the first time. It's a sign of the quality built into today's vehicles, CAMVAP says at its Web site (www.camvap.ca). But maybe there are too many hurdles for consumers to navigate.

We steered Paula, a *Toronto Star* reader, to the arbitration program when she told us her 1997 red Saturn coupe burned more oil than usual. "In the last 1,300 kilometres, it has burned 1.5 litres of oil. This is extreme," she said. She reported the problem to her Saturn dealer in Kitchener, Ont., when the car was still under warranty. Nothing happened.

After driving 130,000 kilometres, she was told the three-year-old car needed a motor job at a cost of $2,000. Checking the Internet to see if others had the same problem, she found "letters upon letters of unsatisfied owners. When I read how many other Saturns were burning oil, I couldn't believe it." Paula asked Saturn to fix the car for free, attaching a list of Web sites with owners' complaints of engine failure. Saturn said no.

With 144,000 kilometres on her Saturn, Paula qualified for arbitration. At her hearing, arbitrator Brian Hinkley said the Saturn's engine showed premature wear because of a manufacturing defect. But since Paula had gotten a lot of use out of the vehicle, he ordered the manufacturer to pay one-third of the repair cost. The Saturn dealership initially said the repair would cost $3,500 at most. But so much damage had been done that Paula ended up with a brand-new engine. She had to pay $3,535, just for her two-thirds portion of the cost.

CAMVAP refused to reopen her case and Paula couldn't go to court. "You may go to court or you may use CAMVAP, but you may not do both," the organization advises motorists. It's a good idea to find out what the court process involves, since you may find litigation works better for you (especially if you go to small claims court, where you can argue your case without a lawyer). To get more detailed information on CAMVAP, call 1-800-207-0685 or, in Toronto, 416-596-8824.

Watch out for curbsiders
when buying used cars

In their bestselling book, *The Millionaire Next Door*, authors Thomas Stanley and William Danko point out that most wealthy people drive older cars and only a minority ever lease their vehicles. Used cars are easier to buy than you think. There's no reason to stay away just because you're afraid of getting stuck with someone else's problems.

"Given the high quality of most new vehicles, this certainly is not true any more for most used vehicles," says analyst Dennis DesRosiers, referring to the myth that you're buying someone else's problem. "For the most part, vehicles less than five years old will have relatively few problems and indeed are still covered by manufacturers' warranties that may last up to eight years on certain components."

A good place to start your search for a used car is to check the reliability ratings from 20,000 Canadian owners in Autopinion, published annually by the Canadian Automobile Association (www.caa.ca). Overall, 79 per cent of people said they were very satisfied with their vehicles. That's fairly high. Toyota, BMW and Honda had the best scores, with the Big Three still lower than average.

Say you want to buy an Acura Integra from 1994-2001. You'll find frequency of repair data for the major components (mixed), average repair cost in 2002 ($973), satisfaction with vehicle (8.82 out of 10) and the number of owners who would buy the same car again (94 per cent).

Then cruise over to *Canadian Driver* magazine, www.canadian-driver.com, which carries used car reviews. "Not just a fun car to drive, but with any luck it'll also be a trouble-free ownership experience," says the review of the 1994 to 1998 Acura Integra models, giving the used car prices for each year.

To find out about safety-related problems and recalls, go to Transport Canada's Web site (www.tc.gc.ca) and the U.S. National Highway Traffic Safety Administration (www.nhtsa.dot.gov).

Once you pick a model, the next decision is whether to buy from a car dealer or a private seller. Phil Edmonston thinks private sellers are your best source. "You're on an equal bargaining level with a vendor who isn't trying to profit from your inexperience," he argues in *Lemon-Aid Used Cars and Minivans 2004* (Viking Canada).

But when buying cars privately and checking the ads, you should be aware of curbsiders. These are impostors who pose as private individuals, but are actually in the business of selling stolen, rebuilt or odometer-tampered vehicles. If you live in Ontario, you should insist on getting a Used Vehicle Information Package from the transport ministry. The law requires private sellers to pay $20 for the Ontario government package, which has a vehicle history and lien search, and show it to any interested buyers.

Check the registration and make sure the car you're buying is registered in the seller's name. If it's not, ask why not. And have the car inspected by a mechanic you trust. "If a car is less than two years old or more than $10,000 and someone is selling it privately, chances are it's a wreck," says industry veteran Paul Timoteo, president of Car Cost Canada.

People with late-model vehicles generally trade them in to a dealer when buying a new car. By doing so, they save on the sales tax. For example, Joe, who lives in Ontario, is buying a $25,000 new car and trading in a two-year-old vehicle worth $10,000. He pays the 15 per cent GST and PST on $15,000, the difference between the selling price and the trade-in, rather than the full $25,000—thus saving himself $1,500 in sales tax.

Why would Joe sell his two-year-old vehicle privately? It makes no sense. He has to charge 15 per cent more to cover the sales tax saving he missed, while also paying for emission tests, certification, advertising and the used vehicle information package.

Here are other red flags that may alert you to curbsiders:

- They don't meet you at their homes, but suggest another location.

- They don't have the original owner's manual in the glove compartment.

- They don't have a bill of sale with their name on it.

If you buy privately and end up with a damaged or rebuilt car, you have nowhere to turn if things go wrong. There's more of a safety net if you buy a used car from a new-car dealer. You can take complaints to the Canadian Motor Vehicle Arbitration Plan, which covers cars from the current and four previous model years with less than 160,000 kilometres. And in Ontario, you can apply for compensation of up to $15,000 from the Motor Vehicle Dealers Compensation Fund, administered by the province.

"New-car dealers are the best place to buy used vehicles, without a doubt," says Bruce Lloyd, who runs a no-haggle used car referral service for Metro Credit Union in Toronto ($50 for non-members). Most dealers have an unwritten rule that they stand by their products for 30 days. That's the time when defects are most likely to show up.

Lloyd thinks it's worthwhile to buy an extended warranty on a used car. Some dealers sell used vehicles with a manufacturer's warranty for three to six months, which you can extend for up to three years. A warranty is worth buying if the price is the same as, or less than, a single major repair (such as replacing the transmission, air conditioning, anti-lock brakes or air bags). " I would buy the extended warranty for a used car if it met that criterion—since most of us will have to pay for at least one major repair during the period we own a car—and if I had enough money to pay for it," a *Star* reader says.

Another tip from Lloyd: Buy North American models that depreciate quickly, since you'll get a good deal. He compares two cars that sold for almost the same price when brand new in April 1999:

- The Honda Accord sold new for $24,000 and should sell for $15,400 used in 2003. In four years, it has depreciated by 37 per cent.

- The Chevy Malibu LS sold new for $24,170 and should sell for $11,300 in 2003. It has depreciated by 53 per cent over the same period.

"When purchasing a new vehicle, you should consider the Accord because of the slow rate of depreciation," he says. "But when purchasing a used car, you may want to consider the Malibu. It will sell used for $4,100 less than the Japanese-made Accord, which gives you better value for your dollar."

If you buy a used car from a dealer in Ontario, you have access to free complaint mediation from the Used Car Dealers Association of Ontario, a not-for-profit trade group. It was involved in more than 500 mediations in 2002, most of which were settled in one day. Call 416-231-2600 or toll-free at (800) 268-2598, or check the Web site at www.ucda.org.

The Ontario Motor Vehicle Industry Council, the self-managed body that administers the Ontario Motor Vehicle Dealers Act, also offers mediation to consumers. Its membership consists of all registered dealers and their sales staff. The toll-free phone number is 1-800-943-6002 (416-226-4500 in Toronto) and the Web site is www.omvic.on.ca.

Own or rent a home: Which is better?

About 70 per cent of Canadians are homeowners. We think of our homes as a good investment and the cornerstone of our future retirement security. But there will be times in life when renting is a more sensible option. It's important to know when to buy and when to rent.

My husband and I had been married for five years and were renting the main floor of a semi-detached house in west-end Toronto. We had a big back yard that only we used, a great place to entertain guests in the summer and plant a vegetable garden. Suddenly one day, we were evicted. Our landlords wanted to move their daughter into our flat.

While angry at the time, we now feel the landlords did us a favour by kicking us out. We were so happy renting we may have waited quite a while longer to buy a first home. Without a push, we probably wouldn't have been able to buy a gutted and renovated three-bedroom townhouse in central Toronto for $72,500. It was attached on both sides and too narrow to accommodate a double bed in the guest bedroom—we made couples sleep on a living room sofa bed. But the house won us over with its exposed brick walls, brand-new oak kitchen cabinets and finished basement that became our son's playroom when he was born two years later.

Seeking more room, we moved again when our second son came along. We sold the townhouse for $149,000, doubling our money after a holding period of seven years. We were lucky. I always tell people they should count on owning a house for 10 years in order to break even. Real estate is highly cyclical and goes through extended periods when values decline.

This time, we bought a semi-detached house in a nicer neighbourhood for $257,000. It had three bathrooms and six bedrooms and seemed incredibly roomy. Now, of course, it's cluttered and crowded after 17 years of ownership. But it's been assessed for property tax purposes at twice what we paid. And we know we could sell it for more if we took the time to gussy it up (and put half our stuff in a storage locker).

Now that we're in our fifties with our kids almost grown, we're fantasizing about a second home. We know just the place to buy a recreational property on Georgian Bay, close to ski hills and golf courses, bike and hiking trails, charming shops and restaurants, a two-hour drive from home. Instead, we rent a house there for two weeks each summer. It feels like ours, but we don't have the burden of maintaining it and paying taxes and commuting on weekends. Renting suits us just fine at the moment.

If you're undecided, sometimes it helps to make a checklist. Let's look at the pros and cons of owning a house and renting.

Advantages of owning:

- You get a big tax break, since you never pay capital gains tax on the increase in value of your principal residence.

- You can borrow up to $20,000 from your RRSP (up to $40,000 for a couple) for a down payment. And you don't have to pay tax or interest, as long as you make the required repayments over 15 years.

- You can buy a home with little money down, as little as five per cent. If prices go up, as they invariably do over longer periods, your gain is magnified because you're using leverage.

- You have a forced saving. A rental payment goes entirely to the landlord, but some of the money you pay on a mortgage goes toward building your equity. The longer you stay, the more your equity grows. You can take out a loan against your home equity and get back the equity when you sell.

■ You can live in and enjoy the house while it's growing in value. This is the "imputed rental income," the profit a landlord would make from renting you similar accommodations. It's difficult to pin a number on this non-cash return, but there's an estimate it fluctuates between five to eight per cent of the home's value each year.

Advantages of renting:

■ You have lower expenses. The landlord pays at least part of the cost of home insurance, property taxes, utilities, maintenance and upkeep.

■ You're more flexible. When you want to leave, you simply give your notice and take off. Homeowners have to sell, or rent to someone else, before they can uproot. It's hard to break even, let alone make a profit, when you have owned a home for a short time and you have to pay all the costs of buying and selling.

■ You have more money to invest for the long term. Instead of renting and spending the difference, you can use the money saved from not owning a house to build an investment portfolio for retirement.

■ Renting helps you diversify your investments. By putting a large chunk of your budget into housing, you could be relying too heavily on the fortunes of not just a single asset class, but a single property.

York University finance professor Moshe Arye Milevsky is a well-known critic of home ownership as an investment. "Nobody in his right mind would incur large debts to invest in a single stock, mutual fund or other form of investment," he says. "Yet people routinely concentrate the largest share of their funds in the real estate market.

"Moreover, people tend to buy houses in areas they (and their spouses) work, thus exposing their real estate holdings to the same economic factors that influence their job prospects." For example, many people working for Enron—the bankrupt U.S. energy trading company—had invested all their retirement savings in company stock and also had to sell their homes at the same time, depressing prices.

Home ownership encourages you to overspend on discretionary household items you wouldn't normally acquire, Milevsky argues. "You might never have bought the extra sprinkler or put down that new carpet if you were renting. Home ownership is a form of forced consumption."

The leverage argument is faulty, too, in his view. You can buy not only houses but almost any traded financial asset on margin. "Those investments are liquid; they don't have closing costs, deposits, six per cent commission or driveways that need shovelling," he says.

If you compare returns over the past two decades, stocks have done better than houses as an investment—despite the bear market in stocks since 2000. House prices in Canada went up about five per cent a year from 1980 to mid-2002, says the respected *Economist* magazine. Stock prices in Canada went up about seven per cent.

In the Greater Toronto area, house prices rose 5.7 per cent a year from July 1982 to July 2002. The average house price almost tripled, from $95,496 in 1982 to $274,711 during the first seven months of 2002. But stocks grew even more quickly in that 20-year period. The annual increase in the TSE 300 index was 8.3 per cent.

Of course, you can live in a house and you can't live in a mutual fund. So the Greater Toronto Home Builders' Association sponsored a study comparing an average homeowner with a renter who invested the difference in stocks. The research, by independent housing analyst Will Dunning, found the following results:

- The homeowner has higher monthly costs than the renter in the first 15 years. Then the renter pays more and has to take money out of the investment portfolio.

- The homeowner builds equity more quickly in later years, as the property value grows and the mortgage debt is repaid.

- After 25 years, the renter's portfolio is worth $755,000. But the withdrawals attract capital gains tax, so the after-tax value is

$608,000. Meanwhile, the homeowner's equity has grown to $1.1 million and there are no capital gains taxes to pay.

Home is where the wealth is. Just over one-third of Canadians' household wealth is in land and buildings, says a June 2003 report by the TD Bank's economists. That far exceeds the 23 per cent in life insurance and pensions, the 18 per cent in bond and stocks, the 14 per cent in cash and bank deposits and the 10 per cent in other assets.

What's the outlook for the future? The TD report, "Profiting from Home Ownership," estimates that over a 10-year span, stocks will deliver an average annual return of 7.75 per cent, bonds 5.75 per cent and money market funds 4.6 per cent. That compares with a 3.2 per cent average annual increase in home prices and a two per cent annual increase in inflation.

Yet, "while the expected average annual increase in resale home prices may sound meagre," the report says, "home ownership offers several significant advantages." With no taxes on capital gains from the sale of a principal residence, a 3.2 per cent annual increase in home prices is equivalent to a pre-tax return of 5.8 per cent from another financial asset.

Home ownership is growing (the percentage was only 65 per cent of Canadians a few years ago) because of the low-inflation, low-interest-rate environment created by the Bank of Canada. This has reduced the risk of bust and boom cycles that characterized housing markets in the past. By historical standards, a home has become more affordable for more families. The lowest mortgage rates in nearly 50 years have helped offset the recent rise in prices.

So what does this prove? If you're a renter, you should consider buying a house, if you plan to hold onto it for at least 10 years. But don't take on more than you can comfortably afford. Even if you can buy a house for five per cent down, try to borrow enough from friends or family to boost your equity to 10 per cent. You need a cushion to protect you in case interest rates rise or house prices fall when you renew your mortgage. If you have to sell, you don't want to owe more than the house is worth.

If you're already a homeowner, think twice about investing in a bigger house with a bigger mortgage. Many people overstretch when they trade up. They haven't budgeted for all the costs that go with home ownership—such as property taxes, maintenance and utilities—which often rise faster than inflation.

Buying too much house means you may have to give up other things you want, such as saving for retirement and your kids' education. Or you may go heavily into debt to buy clothes and take vacations. If you're lucky, you will have paid off the mortgage by the time you retire. Otherwise, the payments will take a big bite out of your reduced income after work.

Even if you're mortgage-free at retirement, you have to remember that a paid-up house does not produce retirement income if you continue to live in it. You have to sell it and trade down, or take out a new mortgage.

No matter how much you pay for housing, it's important to keep saving for retirement in a tax-sheltered plan (and to replenish your RRSP if you borrowed from it for the down payment). That could make the difference between being comfortable in your later years and being overstretched and house-poor. You never want to buy as much house as lenders are willing to lend you.

Here's a good rule for renters: Figure out how much more money you would be paying each month for your new home and start living as if you were already shelling out that amount. If you can pull this off comfortably for six months or more, you can proceed, with some confidence, to buy a home. In the meantime, you can save the difference between what you're spending now and what you'll be spending in the future. This will bolster your emergency fund and give you an even greater zone of comfort.

Suppose you don't ever want to own a home. Here's advice from a *Star* reader: Take the money that would have been tied up in the down payment and invest it in high quality REITs (real estate investment trusts). The REITs will pay a tax-advantaged income stream that can be used to subsidize the monthly rent. Depending on the fortunes of the real estate market, the REITs might also be able to be sold for a capital gain down the road. "I wish I had thought of this when I was renting," he says.

The pros and cons of setting up a "second suite"

They used to be called basement apartments. Now they're called second suites. Whatever term you use, setting up a rental unit in your home can subsidize the cost of ownership. You can afford to buy more quickly or move into a bigger property in a better neighbourhood.

First you have to check with your municipality to see if second suites are allowed under the zoning laws. In Toronto, a bylaw came into effect in July 2000, allowing second suites in detached or semi-detached houses (not row houses) that are at least five years old. The second suite must be self-contained, with its own kitchen and bathroom, and the floor area must be smaller than the rest of the house. As a homeowner, you can reduce your liability if you meet all fire, building and housing safety standards. You should also tell your insurance provider and mortgage lender about the second suite.

Will your property taxes go up? In most cases, a second suite won't increase the value of a home enough to make a significant impact on your property taxes. But if you build an addition to accommodate the rental unit, this could result in a reassessment.

What kind of return can you expect on the cost of building a second suite? Landlord's Self-Help Centre, www.landlordselfhelp.com, is a non-profit Toronto agency, funded by Legal Aid Ontario, which gives free information and advice to small-scale landlords. Accountant Mukesh Kshatriya did a sample calculation that shows a healthy 41 per cent return on a $15,000 investment.

Here are the assumptions he used:

- You have a $200,000 mortgage at six per cent. Your mortgage interest is $1,000 a month or $12,000 a year.

- You rent out your basement, which takes up 30 per cent of your house's floor space, at $700 a month.

- You spend $15,000 on converting your basement into an apartment—the cost can range from $3,000 to $40,000—and pay for half of it yourself. The other half is financed through a bank line of credit, also at a six per cent rate.

- Your marginal income tax rate is 40 per cent. And your property tax goes up by $187 a year because of the conversion.

Under the *Income Tax Act*, you must declare all the rent you collect as income. But you can write off both the direct and indirect expenses of operating a second suite.

Direct expenses, which relate directly to the rental unit, are 100 per cent deductible. These include interest on the line of credit ($450), interest on the last month's rent ($42) and incremental property tax ($187).

Indirect expenses, which are shared with the whole house, are partially deductible. You can write off the 30 per cent portion that applies to the rental unit, including mortgage interest ($3,600), maintenance and repairs ($750), heat ($600), hydro ($600), water ($180), insurance ($150) and property tax ($1,050).

Adding it all up, you're collecting $8,400 in annual rent and you have deductible expenses of $8,209. Therefore, your rental income is $191 before tax, $115 after tax. That's a slim profit—hardly worth the work—but it's not your true bottom line. What you declare on your income taxes is not what comes out of your pocket.

Return to your calculations and add back the $3,600 in mortgage interest, $750 in maintenance and repairs, $600 in heat and $1,050 in property tax. These are fixed costs of home ownership, which you would be incurring even if you had no tenants.

Once you do that, you're left with an after-tax positive cash flow of $6,115, which works out to 41 per cent of your $15,000 conversion cost.

"My only regret is that I didn't do this years ago, when house prices were lower," says a *Toronto Star* colleague. "It costs me less to have a house than it did to rent an apartment." She has a monthly mortgage payment of $1,600 and collects $1,400 in rent from her tenants.

Do you need an accountant to prepare your income taxes if you have a second suite? Not necessarily. But it's advisable to hire an accountant in the first year to help you set up a documentation system. You need receipts for everything you claim. Any claims not supported by receipts will be disallowed if there's an audit by the tax department.

You should not claim depreciation (also known as capital cost allowance) on your home against your rental income. Once you claim CCA, the part of your home that is rented out stops being your principal residence. This means that when you sell the home, part of your proceeds will be taxable. Normally, the sale of a principal residence attracts no capital gains taxes. The tax exemption is too important to waste.

Becoming a landlord has its challenges. You have to screen tenants carefully and respect their rights to enjoy their home. Your tenants probably won't get into as much mischief if you're living right on the premises. But you have to act quickly when tenants fail to pay the rent. You should give them a notice to move as soon as the rent is late or after a three-day grace period (according to laws of the province where you live).

Procedures and paperwork are very important in cases where the rent is not paid, says an online guide to renting a home published by the Canada Mortgage and Housing Corp. at www.cmhc.ca. If a landlord has a valid reason to terminate a tenancy but makes a minor mistake in the paperwork, the provincial rental tribunal may not uphold the eviction.

Mukesh Kshatriya, who rents out the basement of his own home, has a tip for screening tenants. "Speak to the current and the previous landlord," he says. The current landlord may give a glowing reference to get the tenant out of the building, while the previous landlord is more likely to tell the truth.

Getting the best deal on home insurance

Both tenants and homeowners need insurance to protect their possessions from theft or fire damage. Property insurance also gives you legal protection if someone gets injured on your property and sues you, or if you accidentally injure someone or cause damage to a person's property.

"At the beginning of the tenancy, it is a good idea to inform tenants that it is their responsibility to purchase contents insurance," says the CMHC online rental guide in its advice to landlords. "This insurance will cover damage to the tenant's belongings resulting from a problem in the residence."

Many of the cost-cutting tips outlined in the previous chapters on car insurance apply to home insurance as well. For example, review your deductibles, the amount that comes out of your pocket to cover a claim before the insurance kicks in. The higher the deductible, the lower your premiums.

Remember that insurance is designed for catastrophic losses. You have to be careful about filing too many small claims in the $1,000 to $3,000 range, including your deductible. "With insurance companies, the size of the claims doesn't bother them as much as the frequency," says Donald Stewart, a consumer information officer at the Insurance Bureau of Canada.

Filing two or three claims within a few years is dangerous. Your insurance rates could increase dramatically—or even worse, you could get cut off as a customer. Switching companies usually means you will pay more, if you can get covered at all.

"Insurers are calling the shots in this really hard market," says Sally Praskey, author of a book on insurance and a principal at the Insurance Canada site, www.insurance-canada.ca, a helpful portal for insurance buyers. "A lot of consumers are writing to me, saying their home insurance has been cancelled or not renewed, and they can't get another policy. It's hard to find another company after one refuses you. People are getting desperate."

Home insurance is not mandatory for homeowners—as is car insurance for car owners. Nor are home insurance rates regulated by provincial governments. This makes homeowners vulnerable if they're cut off, since most lenders insist you provide proof of insurance as a condition of getting a mortgage. They want to know the property is covered in case of a big loss, such as fire or tornado. There's nothing for homeowners similar to the Facility Association, which is required to take on drivers who have been refused car insurance elsewhere. The Facility is a non-profit organization funded by the industry as a whole and regulated by the province.

Customers whose insurance has been cancelled should check out "non-standard insurers," Praskey says. These are companies that take on customers who don't meet the normal underwriting criteria and charge higher rates, reflecting the higher risk involved. One well-known company is Kingsway General Insurance Co. (traded on the Toronto Stock Exchange). If you're turned down for home insurance, you can also try choosing a more stripped-down policy. Instead of getting comprehensive coverage, you can exclude certain risks (such as water damage) or get coverage for only certain perils named in the policy. "Ask what you can do to make this risk acceptable," Praskey says.

This could mean replacing an oil tank more than 15 years old or getting rid of your knob and tube wiring (typically found in homes more than 50 years old). Other things that could be a red flag to home insurers: galvanized plumbing (instead of copper), electrical systems too small to handle today's heavy loads (60-ampere service instead of 100 to 200 amperes), a roof or a furnace that is 15 to 20 years old. A *Toronto Star* reader had his insurance cancelled once the company found out he had aluminum wiring in his home. He called 15 other insurers and was told he'd have to replace it with copper wiring, a $3,000 a cost he couldn't afford. The other option was to pay $300 for an inspection to see whether he qualified for home insurance.

Some companies are reluctant to insure homeowners who use wood-burning stoves for heating. They may want to inspect the woodstove to make sure it's properly installed and maintained. People who own rental properties may also have a tough time getting home insurance, if they don't live there. Companies think there's not as much care taken of the premises.

Installing protective devices, such as smoke and carbon monoxide detectors and monitored burglar alarm systems, can reduce the risk of fire or theft and lower your insurance premiums. Ask your insurer or broker how much you stand to save and what kind of systems they recommend.

Besides avoiding small claims, you should be careful about even calling an insurance company to ask whether it's worth filing a claim. The agent is supposed to report your inquiry to the company and you can get penalized even if you don't go ahead with the claim. Independent brokers have more discretion in reporting claims.

When should you make a claim against your homeowner's or tenant's insurance? How much of a loss do you need to make the claim worthwhile? "I have a $1,000 deductible on my home insurance policy," says Praskey. "So any claim I would make would have to be significantly more than that." Making small claims is dangerous in today's unsettled insurance markets, since your insurer could raise your premiums or even cancel your policy. "A couple of months ago, I phoned my insurance company to put in a claim for water damage caused by a leaky pipe," says Carla, a *Toronto Star* reader. "I was told if I proceeded with the claim (which would have amounted to about $400, after a $500 deductible) that my insurance coverage would either double in cost or that I would be considered a 'high risk' and my insurance would be cancelled totally." It makes no sense to get a $400 insurance settlement if you pay it back—and more—through higher rates. Carla should think about raising her deductible to $1,000 (from $500) and making a claim only if her loss is in the $5,000 to $10,000 range.

This sounds terribly unfair. You pay insurance premiums year after year and never make a claim. Finally, you have a loss from theft or property damage and you think you're entitled to collect. But unless it's a larger claim, the money you're awarded could be eaten up by increased premiums within a year or two. Insurance is designed for catastrophic losses. Your house burns down and you lose your possessions. A visitor falls down your stairs and has a serious injury. An expensive bracelet, covered by a floater that beefs up your insurance coverage, is stolen from your car. (Yes, a homeowner's or tenant's policy covers items stolen from your car that are not part of the car. Items that are part of your car, such as the stereo system, would be insured under the comprehensive coverage on your automobile policy instead.)

Suppose you lose a $2,000 item to theft and you have a $1,000 deductible on your home insurance policy. You file a claim and get a $1,000 payment from the insurer. Your premiums may not go up, especially if you're a long-time customer with a squeaky clean record. But that small claim could come back to haunt you. Let's say a tree falls on your roof in the next year or two, causing $75,000 worth of damage. You can't pay for a loss of this size out of your pocket, so you file another claim. This time, your rates will probably go up sharply or your policy won't be renewed. You'll be seen as a poor insurance risk, even if these losses are not your fault.

Praskey, co-author of *The Insurance Book: What Canadians Really Need to Know Before Buying Insurance*, published in 1999, was warning about insurance companies cancelling property coverage long before the current market tightness. "Don't think of your insurance as a cumulative payment that adds up over the years," she says. "Think of it as buying protection for a one-year period against a large loss. If you ever experience a devastating loss, that's when insurance really pays its way."

In the case of a theft, you should inform your insurance provider as soon as possible. Many companies have a 24-hour hotline for reporting claims and can help you with immediate temporary repairs, such as fixing a patio door pried open in a break-in. Be prepared to supply reasonable evidence to support your claim, such as receipts, photographs or a video inventory. The more information you have, the easier it is to settle your claim.

If you decide not to replace an item that has been damaged or stolen, you will receive only the "actual cost value." That's what it costs to replace the item, less depreciation. Most homeowner's policies sold today pay "replacement cost" on lost or damaged property. That means you must use the insurance money to replace what you lost with something that is as similar as possible in function and quality.

"The advantage of replacement cost is that it doesn't take depreciation into account when paying a claim," Praskey says. "Whatever it costs to replace the item today will be the amount you receive, as long as you do replace it."

Let's say your five-year-old camera is stolen and you're not sure you want to replace it. If you opt for the cash, you will be paid only what a five-year-old camera is worth. If you replace it, you will receive a new camera that is as similar as possible to the one you lost. You can't get something better than what you had or something different, even if the replacement cost is the same. Similarly, if you decide to replace an item with a cheaper one, you're not entitled to the cash for the difference in cost. Insurance is intended to put you back to the way you were before the loss.

Avoid pitfalls when refinancing your mortgage

Mortgage rates are at their lowest levels in years and continue to fall. This can be frustrating to borrowers who locked in at higher rates. You can renegotiate your mortgage at a lower rate, but be prepared for penalties. And make sure you ask—and understand—how the penalties are calculated.

Suppose you start with a $100,000 mortgage at an eight per cent rate. You have three years left on your five-year term and your outstanding balance is $97,218. You want to break your mortgage contract and take out a new loan to benefit from falling interest rates.

First you have to see what it says in your original mortgage document or a recent renewal agreement. Some contracts don't allow for a mortgage to be renegotiated, but most do. If your agreement lets you get out of the mortgage early, you normally have to pay a penalty. Why? Because financial institutions use fixed-term deposits to fund mortgage loans. They can't reduce what they pay on a five-year deposit because you want to renegotiate your mortgage after two years. The penalty is set to compensate the lender.

Most likely, your mortgage contract will specify that the penalty is the greater of two amounts:

- Three months' interest on the current mortgage balance.

- The difference between your current mortgage rate and the new lower rate, multiplied by the number of months left on your five-year term and your mortgage balance. This is known as the interest-rate differential (or IRD).

In your case, a penalty of three months' interest works out to $1,944. That's not too bad. But the IRD penalty is $5,833—or three times as much—probably enough to make you back off the whole idea of renegotiating.

This example comes from a fact sheet published in May 2002 by the Financial Consumer Agency of Canada (www.fcac.gc.ca), which was set up to educate and protect customers of federally regulated financial institutions. It assumes a six per cent interest rate for the three years remaining on your original five-year term. Using a mid-2003 rate of just over five per cent, you would have to pay an even stiffer IRD penalty.

Lenders calculate IRDs in different ways. There are no rules for how they do it. (It's unfortunate there's no legislation, but the politicians never get around to enacting it.) Some financial institutions use their posted mortgage rates. Others use the discounted rates given to their best customers. Make sure you ask which rate they're using.

There's a calculator on the Internet, which estimates the rate at which it makes sense for you to consider breaking your mortgage. Sponsored by a mortgage broker, Mortgage Alliance Co. of Canada, the calculator is at www.quickenmortgage.ca.

Here's a way to minimize the IRD penalty. Most financial institutions let you prepay 10 to 20 per cent of your mortgage in any given year. Ask them to deduct the prepayment before you renegotiate, so you'll have a lower interest penalty. "Most lenders won't do it unless they're forced to," says Jim Rawson, regional sales manager for Invis Financial Group, one of Canada's largest mortgage brokerage chains.

Check to see if you have a mortgage insured by the Canada Mortgage and Housing Corp. that dates back to 1999 or before. The rules in place back then allow you to get out of a mortgage after the third anniversary by paying a three months' interest penalty and not the interest-rate differential, which usually is costlier.

Rawson has a client who paid a $3,226 penalty to get out of a CMHC-insured loan at 6.2 per cent for 10 years. He arranged a new five-year loan at 4.55 per cent, saving the client $16,254 in interest over the next five years. That's a pretty good return.

Rather than charging a high penalty up front, some financial institutions let you get out of your mortgage before the term ends and sign up for a new mortgage at a lower rate. Say, for example, you have one year left on a five-year mortgage term at eight per cent. If the current five-year rate is six per cent, your new rate will be 6.4 per cent for the next five years with the so-called "blend-and-extend" option, which is not necessarily cheaper. The rate you're quoted may be higher than if you had paid a penalty up front.

A *Star* reader, who's a financial adviser, told me about clients who were charged a $3,400 penalty to break the mortgage when they sold their house. They could waive the penalty if they took out a new mortgage at 5.65 per cent with the same lender. "They were under the impression that by accepting the higher rate, they would save money compared to paying the penalty and taking a rate of 4.85 per cent with another lender." The adviser did the math and found their mortgage payments would have been $2,100 higher with the higher interest rate. Also, the principal at the end of five years would have been $800 higher. They would pay interest on the higher mortgage amount when they renewed. In the end, this would have cost the clients more.

Make sure you get amortization schedules from your lender, showing what happens to the mortgage balance before and after you renegotiate. Do this whether you pay a penalty or use the blend-and-extend option. A financial institution should supply an amortization schedule without cost. It's the only way to check the lender's math and see if you're further ahead. (Ron Cirotto, who sells mortgage software, has an excellent article, "Top 10 reasons why you need an amortization schedule," at his Web site, www.amortization.com).

If refinancing isn't a viable option, read the prepayment clause in your mortgage. Most lenders allow you to prepay 15 to 20 per cent a year, raise your monthly payments or, in some cases, double up your monthly payment without penalty. Take advantage of these prepayment privileges to get rid of a high-rate mortgage more quickly. And if your finances permit, look at reducing the mortgage amortization to 10 or 15 years (from 25). This, again, will help you pay off the loan more quickly.

Refinancing also gives you the chance to increase your borrowing to pay for home renovations. The interest rate will be lower than on an unsecured line of credit, but you may have to pay about $1,000 to cover legal and appraisal fees for writing a new mortgage.

As long as rates remain low, it's sensible to explore the idea of refinancing to see if it can save you money. Ask your bank about penalties and blend-and-extend options, or let a mortgage broker lay out some options. You should do better by comparison shopping and letting lenders bid against each other.

The pros and cons
of being a floater

Why do I follow the rate moves by the Bank of Canada and the U.S. Federal Reserve when I never paid much attention before? Because I'm a floater, that's why. For the first time in two decades of home ownership, I switched to a variable-rate mortgage a few years ago. Now I worry about locking in each time interest rates go up.

What's it like to be a floater? So far, so good. When our mortgage came up for renewal on Sept. 1, 2001, my husband and I were paying 6.4 per cent for a three-year term. Rates were at historic lows and CIBC was heavily promoting its better-than-prime mortgage, which would give us 1.01 percentage points off prime (then 5.75 per cent) for the first nine months and one-quarter point off prime for the remaining five-year term.

Our floating mortgage rate, initially 4.74 per cent, slipped to 4.24 per cent after the Sept. 11 terrorist attacks. It fell to 3.49 per cent, then to 2.74 per cent on Jan.16, 2002, where it stayed for three months. Then, it started rising again. By April 16, 2003, it was back to 4.75 per cent. In the summer, it went down to 4.5 per cent.

The way it works is that you pay the same amount each month. But more of your payment goes to principal and less to interest as mortgage rates fall. Interest is calculated monthly, not in advance—unlike a fixed-rate mortgage, which has interest calculated semi-annually, not in advance. If interest were calculated semi-annually, our equivalent mortgage rate would be slightly higher (about 5/100ths of a point).

If we were nervous about rising rates, we might lock into a five-year mortgage at 6.4 per cent. But that's just the posted rate. These days, bankers are keen to give discounts to good customers ranging from half to a full percentage point, depending on how much they value your business. We could probably negotiate a five-year rate of 5.3 per cent, not much more than our current 4.5 per cent variable rate.

I confess I've been thinking about locking in. But interest rates seem fairly stable these days. And after 17 years living here, we have a lot of equity in the house. It's not as if we're stretched to the limit. (I'd love to say we've paid off our mortgage, but that's not the case, alas.)

Moshe Milevsky, a respected academic, has written a paper about the wisdom of choosing a variable-rate mortgage over a fixed rate. The 35-page study, called "Floating Your Way to Prosperity," is posted at his Web site, www.milevsky.com. He concludes that Canadians are generally better off borrowing for a one-year term at the prime rate, as opposed to the five-year rate, as long as they can tolerate moderate fluctuations in monthly mortgage payments.

In the 50-year period from 1950 to 2000, he estimates that a consumer with a $100,000 mortgage—that was to be repaid over the course of 15 years—would have spent an average of $22,000 more in financing costs by borrowing and then renewing at the five-year rate, compared to borrowing at prime and renewing annually. "The main message is quite simple," he says. "Long-term stability has its price."

Floaters have the option of locking in future financing if they desire. The reverse is not true. Consumers who borrow long, but decide to terminate their mortgage to refinance at a lower cost, face interest penalties. The lack of symmetry, he says, is another reason to go short instead of long.

What if you don't qualify for a conventional mortgage?

For most people, the hardest part of buying a first home is saving for the down payment. If you have less than 25 per cent of the purchase price to put down, you'll have to buy mortgage insurance through your lender. This protects the lender against default if you can't keep up the payments.

Canada Mortgage and Housing Corp., the major source of mortgage insurance, charges a one-time premium of one per cent to 3.25 per cent of the loan for a high-ratio mortgage, depending on the size of the down payment. You can pay this premium in a single lump sum, or include it in your mortgage and add it to the monthly payments.

The following conditions apply if you want CMHC mortgage insurance:

- You have a down payment of at least five per cent of the purchase price of the property (7.5 per cent for a two-unit property). This can be a gift from an immediate relative, as well as from your own resources.

- Your home-related expenses do not exceed 32 per cent of your gross household income.

- Your total monthly debt load does not exceed 40 per cent of your gross monthly household income.

- You can pay closing costs equivalent to at least 1.5 per cent of the purchase price.

If you can come up with just five per cent of the purchase price as a down payment, the CMHC requires you to buy a house with a purchase price of $125,000 to $300,000. The maximum price ceiling depends on where you live. Ask your mortgage lender about the limit in your area.

GE Capital is another source of high-ratio mortgage insurance in Canada, with premiums and lending policies similar to those of CMHC. For information, check the Web site, www.gemortgage.ca, or call 1-800-511-8888.

However, you're not out of luck if you can't come up with five per cent down. There's now a national mortgage lender, Xceed Mortgage Corp. in Mississauga, Ontario, which lends 100 per cent of the purchase price to buyers who have no down payments. You can get a good overview of the company at its Web site, www.xceedmortgage.com.

Consider Todd and Maria, who thought they had saved enough for a five per cent down payment on the $155,000 home they hoped to buy in Hamilton, Ontario. But the bank rejected their mortgage application, saying their $7,000 in savings was needed to pay the closing costs on the house purchase. "We liked this house because it was new," says Todd, 35. "We could have gone to an older home, but we didn't want to worry about things breaking down."

The bank referred them to Xceed Mortgage, which charges a high-ratio fee of four per cent. This compares to a 3.25 per cent fee charged by CMHC or GE Capital to high-ratio borrowers who have a five per cent down payment. Todd and Maria used their savings to pay Xceed's high-ratio fee of $6,200, plus other costs, so they have a first mortgage of $155,000 (the same as the house price).

How much will you pay for closing costs? It depends on the purchase price of your home and the services available in your area. But

GE Capital provides an example at its Web site showing total costs of $8,215, broken down as follows:

- Mortgage application fee (to cover the cost of processing): $150.

- Appraisal fee (to ensure the home's value supports the mortgage): $150.

- Inspection cost (to assess the property's condition and identify problems): $300.

- Property survey (to verify the measurements and boundaries): $1,000.

- Home insurance: $450.

- Land transfer tax (levied in some provinces when property changes hands): $2,000.

- Interest adjustment (to cover any gap between closing date and first payment date): $100.

- Prepaid property tax and utility adjustments: $1,100.

- Legal fees and disbursements: $1,100.

- Moving expenses: $1,000.

- Service charges (to hook up utilities such as telephones): $50.

- Decorating: $800.

Xceed insures its own mortgages, selling them to private investors. It charges interest rates that are about one percentage point higher than those of the major banks. Started by the Bank of Montreal, which still has a 10 per cent ownership stake, Xceed is an alternative lender; it approves deals other financial institutions may turn down. Alternative lenders have more flexibility than banks and trust companies, which aren't allowed to lend more than 95 per cent of a home's value for high-ratio financing. It's against the law.

The Bank of Nova Scotia has a promotion, called the Free Down Payment Mortgage, which appeals to buyers with good incomes but limited savings. The word "free" is misleading, since customers must pay the bank's posted five-year rate (with no chance to negotiate). They also pay a high-ratio insurance premium.

Say, for example, you were buying a house for $250,000. Scotia-bank would "gift" you the five per cent down payment, worth $12,500, which would bring your mortgage amount down to $237,500. The bank then would go to a mortgage insurance company, GE Capital, which charges a high-ratio fee of 3.9 per cent (or $9,262.50). This fee would raise your total mortgage to $246,762.50.

Your monthly payments were $1,652.87 at Scotiabank's five-year rate of 6.5 per cent in mid-2003, when the promotion was offered. No rate discounts or shorter terms were available under this plan. And to limit the risk of default, Scotiabank and GE Capital capped the price of the house at $300,000 in the Greater Toronto area.

Xceed Mortgage is more flexible. Its no down payment plan applies to houses with a purchase price of up to $400,000. "What can you get in Toronto at $300,000 these days? Not a lot," says Xceed chief executive Ivan Wahl. Both GE Capital and CMHC require borrowers to have a 10 per cent down payment if they buy a $400,000 house in Toronto.

Xceed insures its own high-ratio mortgages with the four per cent premium and higher interest rates. It also insists on an appraisal to make sure the buyer hasn't overpaid. "There's the odd time when someone literally pays too much in the heat of battle," Wahl says. "If our appraiser says you paid too much, this can be difficult if you're counting on 100 per cent financing and you haven't presented a conditional deal. So there's some real risk for individual borrowers. Thank God this happens only infrequently."

Suppose you buy a $400,000 house. You have little saved for a down payment, so you opt for Xceed's First Purchase 100 plan. The total mortgage amount is $416,000 once the four per cent high-ratio premium is added. This is spread over 25 years. You can choose a three-year or five-year mortgage term.

Wahl thinks there's an untapped market of middle-income Canadians who can easily carry a mortgage but can't save for the future. "We're doing about $40 million a month in mortgages," he said in

April 2003, "and almost half of them are 100 per cent mortgages." Xceed's 100 per cent mortgages are also used for refinancing. They appeal to existing homeowners who want to consolidate other debts at a lower rate.

Consider, also, the case of Projna and Sarbajit, recent newcomers to Canada with two young daughters. They want to buy a $180,000 house and they have a $20,000 down payment, plus $5,000 for closing costs. But mortgage insurance from CMHC or GE Capital is not an option. They're too new to Canada, with little credit or employment history.

Also, they don't meet the requirement that home-related expenses not exceed 32 per cent of gross income. With a guaranteed income of $40,000 (plus commissions, which aren't guaranteed), they would be paying 46 per cent on home-related expenses. The only way they could get financing is through a mortgage broker, who has access to private funds for second mortgages.

"Most mortgage brokers wouldn't put this deal together. They're really non-qualified applicants," says Jim Panasiuk, a principal in The Mortgage Department Corp. in Oakville (www.themortgagedepartmentcorp.com), who prides himself on doing the tough deals.

Panasiuk found a way to make it work. The couple would put down $18,000, or 10 per cent of the purchase price, and get a conventional first mortgage of $135,000. The interest rate would be 6.35 to 6.95 per cent, with monthly payments of $925. And a second mortgage of $27,000 from a private lender would have an interest rate in the 14 to 17 per cent range, with monthly payments of $394.

"The private lender is giving a high-ratio mortgage with no insurance," Panasiuk pointed out. The steep rate reflects the risk of the transaction. A home appraisal is crucial in such a deal, since the property would be sold to recoup any losses if the borrower defaulted.

Panasiuk told the couple to find at least $8,000 for closing costs, which would include his $3,500 fee. Mortgage brokers don't usually charge for their services, since the lenders pay them. But borrowers who need extra help may have to pay fees directly. "This is not a deal I can get pre-approved," he explained. "They would have to go out and buy first, then put in an offer subject to financing."

Why go through the hassle? Projna and Sarbajit want to buy soon. If they wait too long, they fear that rising interest rates and property values could price them out of the market. The deal arranged by a mortgage broker would get them into a first house, with monthly payments they could carry, while they wait to qualify for a conventional mortgage. In two years, when Projna is working again (she's now a homemaker) and Sarbajit has a higher income, the family can refinance at better rates.

If you're anxious to buy a home and don't qualify for a high-ratio mortgage, you can check out alternative lenders and mortgage brokers. But make sure to look ahead and try to protect yourself against possible setbacks.

What if interest rates go up when you renew the mortgage? Can you handle the higher payments? What if one of you becomes unemployed or can find only part-time work? What if you and your spouse split up? Do you have disability insurance in case you get sick? Do you have life insurance that covers the mortgage if one spouse dies? Can you set up an apartment in your home to help pay the operating costs?

None of this is nice to contemplate, but it's necessary if you live on the edge. Buying a house may be a good move, but only if you have a measure of job security and good health. Don't let a lender force you into a bigger commitment than you feel comfortable with or can afford. And put a contingency plan in place to deal with the consequences of bad luck or adversity.

Do your homework before renovating your home

Lenders are keen to let you borrow up to 75 per cent of your home's value to fix up kitchens and bathrooms, add a family room or become more energy-efficient. Low-priced loans are great. But you will defeat the purpose if you hire the wrong contractor and pay too much for sloppy work.

Everyone has a horror story about home repairs and renovations. My blood still boils when I think about Dave, the guy we hired 20 years ago to fix up a bathroom, who often failed to show up or call. I knew it was time to fire him when he missed yet another appointment and told us he had tripped over his dog and broken his thumb. Could he have come up with a sillier excuse? Clumsy Dave had to go, even if the bathroom was half-finished.

The Ontario Ministry of Consumer Services gets 2,000 calls a year about home repairs and 240 written complaints. Lack of communication is a common concern, along with poor quality of work, failure to live up to a warranty or failure to do what was promised after taking a deposit.

Ontario's new Consumer Protection Act will let you cancel a contract if the work hasn't started within 30 days of the promised date. And you can refuse to pay more if the final price is 10 per cent higher than the estimate. If you have problems, you can call the consumer ministry at 416-326-8800 in Toronto or toll-free at 1-800-889-9768.

Until the law takes effect, there are ways to stay out of trouble. Get all details spelled out in the contract before you sign, keep deposits to a minimum and check your invoice to make sure all repair work is clearly identified. A written contract is your best protection, especially if you have to take someone to court for doing shoddy repairs.

Don't fall for an offer to pay cash "under the table" and save the seven per cent GST, with nothing in writing. The deal could turn into a real nightmare, exposing you to lawsuits, financial liens or liability for workplace accidents or injuries. The Canadian Home Builders' Association has launched a campaign to keep homeowners away from handymen who work in the underground economy. "A professional contractor always carries liability insurance and workplace compensation coverage (when required) and complies with municipal building permit and licencing rules. This protects you," says the association at its Web site (www.chba.ca).

Without a written contract, you may be liable if a contractor goes bankrupt or fails to pay for materials and labour that go into a project. You could face liens and have to pay the suppliers, even if you had already paid the contractor.

Make sure your written contract spells out who is responsible for getting building permits and approvals, the CHBA warns. "And because most homeowners' fire and liability insurance doesn't cover construction-related risks, contact your insurance company before construction begins, inform them about your renovation project and make arrangements for any additional coverage needed."

So how do you find a reliable contractor? Start by getting recommendations from friends, relatives and neighbours. Questions to ask: Have you recently hired a contractor to do building, renovation or repair work? Would you hire the contractor again? Was the work done properly? Was it completed on time and at the agreed price?

Make sure any contractor you hire gives you a list of customer references. A good contractor won't refuse your request. Call the customers and ask the same questions as before, plus others. Did the work crew arrive on time with all the necessary materials? Were there any problems during construction and did the renovator take adequate steps to resolve them? Was the follow-up work under warranty done satisfactorily?

Check out the 100 or so local renovation firms that have joined the Greater Toronto Home Builders' Association. They have agreed to use standard contracts and live up to a code of conduct. GTHBA contractor members must offer a minimum two-year warranty on all work (except minor home repairs), carry $2 million in liability insurance, maintain a safe work site and upgrade their knowledge and technical skills. For information about the Renomark quality assurance program launched three years ago, call 416-391-4663 or check the Web site (www.renomark.ca).

While there's no formal mediation program, the GTHBA tries to help unhappy customers. Too many complaints and the firm's membership will be revoked, which happens about once a year, says spokesperson Suzanna Cohen. I love the rule that contractors return phone calls within two business days. That's a real winner to customers who deal with the non-communicative Daves of this world.

Don't feel bad if you're intimidated—and scared off by real-life stories of nervous breakdowns and marriages falling apart after a delayed and over-budget reno job. That's a normal reaction. I'd recommend reading a free online guide to home renovation at the Canadian Home Builders' Association's Web site. You can also find worksheets to download that help you manage the process.

part two

Getting Your
Finances in Order

Canadians have a love-hate affair with our banks. We admire them for being big, solid and profitable. But we also distrust them for being big. We believe they care far more about corporate clients more than about individuals.

One of our big beefs about banks is that they nickel-and-dime us to death with service charges. Nearly half of us (46 per cent) don't feel we get a lot of value for the fees we pay. That comes from a survey of 1,500 Canadians sponsored by the Public Interest Advocacy Centre, a non-profit group that provides legal and research services on behalf of consumer interests. "Canadians are ambivalent about banks, despite their embrace of new technologies," says PIAC counsel Sue Lott (www.piac.ca). We're keen on electronic banking, for sure. The survey found 33 per cent of Canadians do some of their personal banking through the Internet alone; 85 per cent use a bank machine at least once a month; and 49 per cent have used a debit card 11 times or more in the previous month.

Banking in person still matters, however. When surveyed, 52 per cent said they had visited their bank one to four times in the previous month. A majority (61 per cent) said it's important to be able to be able to do their banking in person, while a slightly lower majority (55 per cent) indicate a preference for bank machines over dealing with a bank teller.

I'm conflicted, too. I rarely go to a branch, preferring to withdraw cash from bank machines and pay bills by phone. But when the CIBC closed my home branch and my work branch—both in the same year—I felt orphaned. Switching to an online bank with lower fees was mighty appealing. It's an option I may not resist much longer.

At least, I'm aware of the service charges I pay my bank and what I get in return. Many people aren't paying much attention. The Public Interest Advocacy Centre's survey found a distressing lack of awareness:

- About two-thirds (64 per cent) of Canadians are unaware that some major banks in Canada own no-name machines that charge more than a bank's own machines.

- A majority of Canadians (56 per cent) are not aware that financial institutions have their own ombudsmen to help deal with customer complaints.

- Almost three-quarters of Canadians (72 per cent) are unaware there is a federal agency that assists customers in their dealings with financial institutions.

- A majority of Canadians (52 per cent) are unaware of their financial institution's policy on the use of customer information.

When you don't pay attention, you get into trouble. You miss the mistakes that show up on your statements. You settle for what you get, without negotiating for more. You take no for an answer, instead of appealing to a higher level or organizing a protest. Why let the banks get away with their games?

In this section, I'll talk about protecting your interests when you entrust your finances to a large institution. My advice rests heavily on stories from *Toronto Star* readers that show the mess you get into when you fail to take precautions against error. We'll look at how to escalate your complaints when you're facing opposition and how to turn no into yes.

Financial institutions are more accountable than they once were. They have to answer to internal and external ombudsmen and a variety of complaint-handling agencies. That's good for customers, but you have to know who does what and where to go. Otherwise, you get frustrated and exhausted.

I'll give some tips on what to do if you dig yourself into a deep hole and can't find your way out. Bankruptcy is not the only solution and I'll explore other ways to keep your creditors at bay. Finally, I'll talk about how to maintain your credit rating and how to rebuild it after getting into financial trouble.

Find the lowest-cost banking package for your needs

We all need a personal banker, someone who lends a friendly face to the giant financial institutions that dominate our lives. I'd have switched a long time ago if not for Voula, the banker who keeps me loyal to CIBC.

With a banker on your side, you can get discounted loan rates and better repayment terms, I've learned. And if you ask for a duplicate tax receipt, she'll call and tell you where the original is. So, I'm fairly insensitive to the lure of lower prices elsewhere. But if you're not getting the service you pay for with your service charges, it's worth shopping the market to see what other banking packages are available.

There's a terrific online "Cost of Banking Guide" to help you do just that. Launched by the Financial Consumer Agency of Canada (www.fcac.gc.ca), it leads you through a series of questions and points you to the accounts that suit your needs. You'll find helpful information on credit-card interest rates, the cost of withdrawing cash from an automated bank machine and how to prevent identity theft.

You don't have a computer hooked up to the Internet? Use one at the office or at the local library. You're not going to change banks that often in your life. Try out this comparison-shopping tool for banking packages, even if you're happy where you are, to find the deals you could get if you decided to switch one day.

The search for the best service package starts with where you live. You click your province on a map, since not all financial institutions are licensed to operate everywhere. Then you're asked if you qualify for a special account. These are offered to seniors (59 years old or older), young adults (under 18) or registered full-time students at a post-secondary institution.

The next question deals with your ability to maintain a minimum balance in your account at all times. Many banks waive the monthly service fees for those with a monthly balance of $1,000 to $2,000. If you're paying off credit-card balances or loans, it's probably not cost-effective to keep money sitting idle in your bank account to avoid service charges. But you can save much more by maintaining a minimum balance than you'd earn if you bought a guaranteed investment certificate.

The FCAC gives two examples of how the math works in your favour if you bypass GICs in favour of having a minimum balance in your account:

- Mr. Smith can waive his $6.50 monthly service fees—saving $78 a year—if he keeps a $1,000 balance. The same $1,000, invested in a one-year GIC at two per cent, would yield $20 a year (before income tax). It's to his advantage to keep a minimum monthly balance in his account until he finds an investment with after-tax returns higher than 7.8 per cent.

- Ms. Doe earns five per cent on her $5,000 investment, giving her an annual return of $250 (before tax). But with a $5,000 balance in her account, she qualifies to waive service fees of $24.75 a month, for an annual saving of $297 a year. It's to her advantage to keep a minimum monthly balance in her account until she finds an investment with after-tax returns higher than 5.94 per cent.

In the fourth step, the key part of the exercise (and most time-consuming), you have to haul out your monthly bank statements and figure out how many transactions you do—withdrawals, bill payments and transfers—both at a branch and self-serve by phone, Internet, bank machine or with a debit card. Online banking, if you've tried it, can help with this calculation. I checked a recent month and found 60 self-serve transactions. That's high, but I'm a big debit card user.

Then you indicate what specialized services you use: certified cheques, money orders and bank drafts, overdraft protection, cheque returns, safety deposit box. The guide comes up with a list of service packages that suit your profile.

In my case, I was given a list of eight service packages that had overdraft protection—a deal-breaker for me—and unlimited monthly transactions. I found I could pay anywhere from $20 to $25 a month for a similar package of services I'm getting now for $24.50 with CIBC's Premier Service Account. All throw in perks such as free stop payments, personalized and certified cheques, money orders, traveller's cheques and discounts on safety deposit boxes.

The newest inducement to sign up for high-cost packages is to get refunds on Interac network fees. Many financial institutions give four refunds a month, but the Bank of Montreal's Unlimited Plan gives 10 a month, the National Bank's Virtuoso plan gives a 50-cent rebate on each one and HSBC's Peak Performance Package gives unlimited Interac fee refunds.

If you choose a service package that requires you to keep a minimum monthly balance, take care not to let it drop below that amount, even for one day. Otherwise, you'll be charged the full monthly fee.

And if you have a service package with a limit on monthly transactions, find out how much each transaction costs once you reach the maximum. Check your statements to see how often you exceed the limit. You could be paying more than if you had a higher-priced account with a greater number of transactions or an unlimited amount.

To save money on banking, remember to use your institution's bank machines as much as possible. Keep a list of the ones most conveniently located to your home or work. Take out enough money to avoid paying high service fees at another bank's machine or a no-name machine. Also, try to withdraw cash at the same time you make a debit card purchase, if the store allows you to do it for free.

Three levels of fees
when you use an ABM

I am feeling cranky about the cost of automated banking machines. The CIBC has closed so many branches near my home that I no longer find it convenient to take out cash on the weekends. I wish I could do my withdrawals by telephone or Internet.

Meanwhile, non-bank machines are popping up everywhere. These no-name ABMs are costly because of the surcharges. I'd love to tell you I never use them. I certainly try not to, but sometimes I'm caught short of cash when nothing else (a cheque, credit card or debit card) will do.

There are three types of fees associated with ABMs:

- Regular transaction fees (50 cents to $1). You pay these fees for services provided by your own financial institution. They vary with your service package and the type of service provided. Some service packages offer a fixed number of transactions; others offer unlimited transactions so you don't pay any transaction fees.

- Network access fees or Interac fees ($1 to $1.50). You pay these fees to get access to your account when you use an ABM not owned by your financial institution.

■ Convenience fees ($1 to $1.50 for financial institutions, $1.50 to $3 for private operators). You always pay these fees when you use an independently operated, or white-label, cash dispenser. And you often pay these fees if you use an ABM operated by a financial institution that's not your own. The ABM will display a message telling you the amount of the convenience fee and asking you if you want to proceed. Some of the money usually goes to the owner of the premises where the machine is located.

The financial institutions that have introduced convenience fees for non-clients at both their in-branch ABMs and the ABMs located outside their branches include Bank of Montreal, CIBC, Laurentian Bank, National Bank, Royal Bank, Scotiabank, TD Canada Trust and Desjardins. If you're not a customer, you might have to pay total fees of up to $4 per transaction (your regular transaction fee, the Interac fee and convenience fees).

If you withdraw money from a white-label ABM, the three levels of fees could add up to $5.50 (a $1 regular transaction fee, $1.50 in Interac fees and $3 in convenience fees). It's absolutely insane to pay such high fees for a $20 cash withdrawal, amounting to 27.5 per cent of the transaction.

Many people don't realize that the white-label machine they use in a store, subway or other public location could belong to their bank. In 1996, the federal Competition Tribunal forced financial institutions to open up the ABM market to outsiders. Banks now own fewer than half of all Canada's ABMs (41 per cent), compared to 76 per cent in 1994.

When I told my personal banker Voula there weren't enough ABMs in my area, she told me to use a white-label machine at a nearby grocery store. She said it was part of CIBC's Amicus network, which does back-office processing for other companies (including President's Choice Financial and Investors Group). The Interac fee and convenience fees wouldn't apply because I was a CIBC client.

Why are banks putting white-label machines in stores? They have to protect their turf. Faced with the prospect of having their ABMs ripped out unless they shared the convenience fees with merchants, banks developed new cash dispensers that look like no-names.

Of course, the banks explain it a little differently. They're putting ABMs into stores and gas stations for our convenience. While willing to absorb the extra cost for their own customers, "some banks may choose not to subsidize non-customers who use these locations," says the Canadian Bankers Association at its Web site (www.cba.ca). "The customer can avoid convenience fees and network access fees altogether by using an ABM operated by his or her financial institution."

Maybe so, but banks are operating fewer ABMs than they once did. The number of bank-owned ABMs in Canada peaked at 17,174 in 2000, going down to 16,806 in 2001 and 16,546 in 2002. Meanwhile, the number of non-bank ABMs grew to 39,996 in 2002 (from 31,922 in 2000).

These statistics, which come from the bankers themselves, tell a story. At the same time they're advising customers to use ABMs operated by their own institutions, Canada's banks are closing branches and devoting their efforts to putting white-label machines in non-bank locations. They should blame themselves for the fact that many clients pay too much in ABM fees. Convenience is a red herring.

Check your monthly bank statements

Do you scrutinize your monthly bank statements? If you don't, this story should change your mind.

A Toronto business owner approached me and said he didn't normally check his statements. But he went over all the entries after a cable TV cheque went astray and found two withdrawals he didn't recognize: One for $850 on March 1 and one for $700 on March 2. He was suspicious because the money had been withdrawn in person from his CIBC branch in mid-town Toronto. "I haven't been in the branch for years," he said.

The man asked for copies of the withdrawal slips and saw the signatures were almost identical to his own. Someone had impersonated him to get money out of his account. How could this happen? Didn't the branch ask for identification?

"If a customer is known in their home branch, then our staff will typically not require a bank card as identification before performing a transaction," said CIBC spokesman Rob McLeod. "If the customer is not known in their home branch, then CIBC staff are expected to ask for a bank card in order to confirm identity and check the signature if necessary."

The man hadn't visited the branch for years, so was obviously not known to the staff. Yet no one had asked the impostor for identification. The branch manager promised to flag the man's account. Whenever he went into any CIBC branch to withdraw money, he would be asked for his card and other identification. As an extra precaution, the branch manager would be notified each time and would have to authorize the withdrawal.

The branch manager was proud of the beefed-up security system and asked the man to try it out. "To my horror, the teller handed me the $250 I'd asked for without checking," he says. No one had asked him for ID, swiped his convenience card or alerted the branch manager. The new layers of protection hadn't worked. The fail-safe measures had failed.

The branch manager later apologized and said she was working with her team to make sure procedures were understood and followed to prevent any future client impersonations. "Despite our efforts to assist you with the investigation of the fraudulent activity on your account," she wrote, "our process for identifying our account holders was not followed when you personally made a withdrawal to 'test our process.' I must tell you that I was equally if not more disappointed in this experience you encountered at our branch."

CIBC reimbursed the business owner for the missing $1,550 after he submitted a sworn affidavit prepared by his lawyer. But the bank didn't tell him to notify the credit bureau about the fraud, he says. That advice, which is basic for fraud victims, came from the police.

But that's not the end of the story. While checking his bank statement, the man noticed something else. He wasn't earning any interest on an average monthly balance of $70,000 to $80,000. "I would never have kept so much money in the account if I'd known," he said, somewhat sheepishly.

He had his money in a Money Multiplier account, a funny name for a vehicle that pays nothing. (CIBC no longer offers it.) The interest rate on the account had slipped to zero across all tiers in line with the Bank of Canada's rate cuts, says McLeod. CIBC used a statement insert to tell him (and other customers) the interest rate had been cut to zero.

"Is it my fault I didn't pick up one of the flyers in my statement?" the man said. "I don't read junk mail." He'd have preferred a personal letter.

After I got involved, the branch manager gave him $1,500 "as a goodwill gesture" for the interest he would have earned on his account if he had moved his funds to CIBC's Premium Growth account introduced the previous spring. That account was paying 0.9 per cent on balances of $25,000 to $59,999 and 1.65 per cent on the part of the balance that exceeded $60,000 at the time he complained about his zero-interest Money Multiplier account. While happy to be compensated for the lost interest, the man decided to leave CIBC. He opened an account with another bank, where he told us he was getting more personal service than he'd had before.

Obviously, customers have a responsibility to check their monthly statements to make sure they're getting the best deal. But in this client's case, the bank also had a responsibility to tell him—in a more personal way than with a statement insert—that he was getting a terrible deal. If the bank really had his interests at heart, someone would have noticed the large balance and the lack of interest and would have called him to make sure he knew about the new premium account.

Robert, another *Star* reader, told me that he'd checked his updated bankbook and found two identical entries for a debit card purchase on the same day. After calling the bank, he found out there had been a computer system problem that day and he would get credited for one of the entries.

"Why did I have to be the one to detect this problem and bring it to the bank's attention?" he asked. "As you know, there are many people who never check their accounts to determine the accuracy of entries made by the bank. My experience suggests they could be losing money and never be aware of it. By the way, my call to the ombudsman's office was not returned."

Don't trust post-dated cheques

Frank used to pay all his household bills with post-dated cheques. He wanted to avoid late payment charges, while not tying up his money for too long. Then, he started noticing that more of his post-dated cheques were being cashed before their due dates.

"The biggest offender was Bell Canada," he told me. In a 15-month period, Bell cashed his cheque early six times.

The last straw came on Feb. 14, when he downloaded the previous day's transactions from the Internet. He found two of his cheques (one post-dated to Feb. 21 and the other to March 1) had been cashed early. The total amount was $410.36.

Who's at fault when post-dated cheques are cashed prematurely—the customer's bank or the companies to whom the cheques are addressed? Frank's bank, TD Canada Trust, denied responsibility. "I was told that a cheque was a contract between me and whoever I issued it to," Frank recalls.

His branch agreed to get him copies of the post-dated cheques, but said he'd have to call each of the companies and ask them to put the money back into his account. That didn't sit right with Frank. So he did some research on the Internet and found the Canadian Payments

Association (www.cdnpay.ca), to which all Canadian banks must belong. The association sets rules for the orderly conduct of Canada's cheque clearing and settlement system. Its rules (A1, part III, section 7) say no item that is post-dated shall be introduced into the system.

Yes, that's true, said a spokesman for the Canadian Payments Association. Banks are supposed to reject cheques that are presented for payment before their due date. But there are five million cheques a day going through the system in Canada. Mistakes can happen. "We generally suggest that if there are other payment options open, you may want to consider them instead of post-dated cheques," he said.

The Canadian Bankers Association gave a similar answer. Millions of cheques are processed every day and errors can occur. The CBA's advice: If a post-dated cheque is cashed early, tell your bank. It will reverse the transaction and cancel any service charges for insufficient funds. Consider paying bills electronically, since there's less likelihood of premature payments. TD Canada Trust spokesman Jeff Keay advised setting up automatic bill payments. "Using the electronic system eliminates the need to track cheque copies and provides control over when payments are made," he said.

Frank felt the banks were trying to force people to stop writing cheques. But there's a problem only with post-dated cheques, Keay emphasized. "Strictly speaking, post-dated cheques are not allowed. Customers aren't supposed to write them, companies aren't supposed to accept them and banks aren't supposed to settle them. But they still exist and there is always a risk they will be settled prematurely. The enormous number of transactions in Canada any given day requires a degree of automation, making it difficult to verify the date of every cheque."

What about the companies that cashed Frank's cheques early? Bell Canada spokesperson Catherine Hudon said the company's policy was to store any post-dated cheques until the billing date and then send them to the banks. She promised to have customer service investigate Frank's complaint about having his post-dated cheques cashed early by Bell on a number of occasions.

Enbridge Gas Distribution's spokeswoman Lisa McCarney said post-dated cheques go into a "bring forward" file, to be deposited on the due date. But errors can slip in because this is a manual process. "We encourage customers to use other options, such as pre-authorized payment plans, current cheques or money orders," she said.

Get the point yet? Post-dated cheques can't be trusted. Use them sparingly. Keep a photocopy of each post-dated cheque you send, so you'll have proof if disputes arise. And don't let your bank branch give you the run-around, as Frank's did. It should fix the mistakes, then wrangle with the companies that cashed your cheques early. That's not your job.

After this article was published, I heard from many *Toronto Star* readers who still used post-dated cheques. They told me about circling the date or highlighting it with a fluorescent marker to make sure the date would stand out and get noticed.

Charges often reversed if you complain

Financial institutions are more flexible than they once were in handling complaints. If you dispute a charge on a statement or bill, and can provide proof there was a mistake, the bank will reverse it right away. That's what three readers found when they confronted a financial institution about fees that were applied incorrectly or not communicated properly. Their stories show the need to remain vigilant in your everyday banking affairs.

Steve had a U.S. dollar account at the Royal Bank of Canada, with a balance of about $50 (U.S.). Early in the year, he got a notice saying he would no longer receive monthly statements unless there was activity in the account. A new fee schedule arrived with his statement in June. And the following January, he opened his statement and was surprised to find his account had been debited $15 (U.S.) because it was inactive.

Why didn't the bank announce the new fees closer to the date of imposition? The law requires 60 days' advance notice of a change in fees, said a Royal Bank spokeswoman. The publicity effort (with statement inserts and signs in the branches) began in May, seven months before implementation. Since many clients said they hadn't been notified in a timely fashion, those who protested had the charges reversed.

The Royal Bank's call centre wasn't authorized to give refunds, so customers had to visit their branches to complain. "Fortunately, I'm a self-employed consultant, so I could make the time," said Steve, who closed his U.S.-dollar account and withdrew the $50. He wondered how many customers swallowed the inactivity charge because they couldn't get to their branches.

Glenda had an experience with the Bank of Montreal that made her realize the shortcomings of a "stop payment" order. She had asked the bank to hold off on a withdrawal from her account that was scheduled for the following day. The reason for waiting: She had started a new job and her employer didn't process her direct-deposit paycheque in time.

"I thought the stop payment was a great idea, even though it cost a $10 fee," she said. "I was assured I had caught it in time and my creditor (Dell Computer Corp.) would be fine with this arrangement." Imagine her annoyance to find the money had been taken out of her account on the following day, a Friday, despite the stop-payment order. That meant she was broke, with nothing to spend on the weekend.

The Bank of Montreal's call centre told her it was standard procedure with a stop-payment order to withdraw the money first and return it to the account later. The federal Bills of Exchange Act forces all financial institutions to operate that way, says Ralph Marranca, a bank spokesman. They have to debit an account first and credit it later on items that have a stop-payment order.

The credit usually appears the next business day. Because Glenda's account was debited on Friday, she had to wait until Monday for the money. "We contributed to the confusion by giving her wrong information," Marranca admitted. "It's a coaching opportunity for us. We'll talk to our staff to make sure they understand the rules and can explain them clearly to customers."

The bank refunded her $10 stop-payment fee, a $22 fee for a cheque that bounced and her $14 monthly bank service fee. But

Glenda still felt embarrassed and angry and wanted to warn others about stop-payment orders. "They have to explain things. Otherwise, it can be very confusing," she said.

David had an American Express Air Miles credit card. He called Amex to ask about buying insurance to cover his balance, in case he got sick and couldn't pay. He was told he had to subscribe to get any written information. If he didn't like the plan, he could cancel in the first 30 days and get a refund.

He accepted the insurance and then decided it was too expensive. Though he cancelled promptly, he was billed $96 for the premiums and was told the charge might not be reversed for two more billing cycles. But I contacted American Express on his behalf and made sure the charge was reversed immediately.

"We do expect our cancellation turnaround time to be quicker, and we're looking into the delay in this case," said Amex spokeswoman Tara Peever. She added that the insurance underwriter, American Bankers Life Assurance Co. of Florida, had a policy of not releasing the insurance certificate without a cardholder's commitment.

Requiring customers to purchase a product before getting information about it "seems backwards," David responded. He felt that Amex shouldn't blame another company when the Amex name and logo were all over the insurance documents.

Bank ombudsmen are at your service

If you have a complaint, how can you get it taken seriously? Escalate, escalate, escalate. Always appeal to a higher level when you're dealing with a large organization that has a well-defined chain of command.

Banks have a four-layer system to deal with unhappy customers. First you talk to the branch; then to the telephone banking centre or customer service department; then to the bank's ombudsman; then to the Ombudsman for Banking Services and Investments. Don't stop after the first step. You should never take no for an answer from a mid-level employee.

Garry, for example, contacted me after TD Canada Trust temporarily misplaced the shares he wanted to sell. He had walked into a branch with a certificate for 132 shares of BCE Inc., worth $4,758.60 at the time. A customer service representative said it would take two to four days for the shares to be deposited into his TD Waterhouse trading account.

"Although in the past it has never taken more than two days, I was okay with this," he said. "I planned to sell the shares on the following Monday." But the shares hadn't arrived by the following

Monday. Every day he made calls and sent faxes and emails to the branch and to TD Waterhouse.

They still hadn't arrived by the Monday after that and he was desperate. He left a message for the branch manager, saying he would write to the *Toronto Star* if the shares weren't in his account. "I was immediately called back and told they would be in my account the next day for sure. They were." But the shares had dropped $270 in value during the time they went missing. The bank manager promised a letter of apology and compensation.

Five weeks went by and nothing arrived. Garry was told the letter had been sent to the wrong address. It took two more weeks till he received TD's goodwill gesture, a $25 restaurant gift certificate. He was insulted. After he took my advice to escalate, he got a slightly better offer. TD's telephone banking centre said it would refund the $29 commission for sale of the shares. A representative apologized that they were held over for "one day" at the branch. (In fact, they were in the branch for nine days and took another week to get into his brokerage account.) She said TD Waterhouse was not aware of his desire to sell the shares. "I was in regular phone contact with them through this," Garry protested.

Then he contacted TD ombudsman David Fisher. Within 10 business days, he got a much improved offer of $145. "I accepted," Garry said. "It wasn't what I asked for, but at this point I just wanted it to be over."

Banks are sensitive to communication. They're concerned when a customer has not been informed verbally, as well as in writing, about important product details. Banks also have ombudsmen, who investigate complaints after they're turned down by lower-level staff. Unfortunately, customers often give up the fight without being told about the ombudsman's existence. I always tell bank customers to appeal to the ombudsman. I wish bank staff would do the same.

Carol, a widow, appealed to me after her claim for a refund of the $7,800 outstanding balance on her late husband's life-insured line of credit was turned down. She had spent more than two years fighting with the Bank of Nova Scotia and Canada Life Assurance Co. about the life insurance coverage, which ended on her husband's 70th birthday. He had died two months after he turned 70, so the insurance was no longer in force.

Scotiabank said the time limit had been spelled out in the insurance application. But Carol and her husband had not been notified when the coverage was about to end. And, to make things worse, the bank had continued taking money from her husband's account for two insurance premiums after his seventieth birthday and another premium after his death.

"It was an error on the part of the bank that insurance premiums continued to be charged to the ScotiaLine," said the bank's ombudsman Bill Bailey, who reviewed the case (at my urging) and wrote it up in his 2002 annual report. Carol's husband had signed the application more than 10 years earlier and believed the coverage was in place, since the premiums were clearly shown on his statement every month. So Bailey decided to refund the ScotiaLine balance.

In another case I mediated, Tai and his wife had bought their first home, a condo, in 1999, taking out a mortgage with the Bank of Montreal. They had been using the bank's MasterCard that allowed them to earn First Home Dollars, which could be applied to the down payment on a first home. Customers could get up to $2,500 under the credit card program, which is no longer offered, if they kept their mortgage with the bank for five years.

The couple got a $2,500 subsidy from the bank and devoted themselves to paying off the mortgage more quickly than required. After just four years, they had saved enough to retire the loan altogether. But before making their final payment, they went to their branch to ask what would happen to their First Home Dollars. "The BMO representative assured us that the original $2,500 was ours," Tai said.

To their surprise, they found their First Home Dollar down payment had shrunk to $2,083 once the mortgage was paid off. The branch representative said there was nothing she could do. The manager didn't return their calls. So Tai called customer service and said he had bought a new house—but would not likely go back to BMO for a mortgage.

I suggested calling the bank's ombudsman. The office acts as an intermediary to resolve complaints from customers who are unhappy with a banker's decision.

A week after Tai called BMO ombudsman John Graham, he heard back from the branch manager who hadn't answered his calls before. The $417 cheque arrived soon afterward. "With a baby on the way, I'm sure the refund will go nicely toward diapers or other baby expenses," Tai said.

Under the agreement, said BMO spokesperson Ralph Marranca, customers had to finance, renew or refinance their mortgage with the bank for five years. If they paid the mortgage in full before completing the five-year commitment, they agreed to reimburse the bank by giving back a prorated amount of the FirstHome dollars they had initially received. "We take care to explain to our customers how the program works and the details are clearly stated in the agreement that a customer must sign," Marranca said. "Nonetheless, if there's some uncertainty or concern, as there seemed to be in this case, we're happy to sit down with the customer to explain our position or review our decisions as each case might warrant."

Tai had tried to protect himself. Aware he could be penalized for leaving the bank before five years, he checked beforehand with a branch representative and reread the agreement. (He didn't notice the penalty against too-prompt repayment.) Since there was some confusion, the bank's ombudsman did the right thing to refund his First Home Dollars. That ensures he will come back to BMO when taking out a mortgage for his second house. And isn't that what a loyalty program is all about?

Alice, another *Toronto Star* reader, asked me to help recover the balance on a life-insured mortgage she and her late husband had taken out when they bought a house in Kingston. The Royal Bank and its insurance carrier, Canada Life, had rejected the claim on the grounds he had a pre-existing condition when he took out the mortgage.

Alice's husband had gone to a hospital emergency room on Oct. 5, complaining of dizzy spells and nausea. He was told at the time there was nothing wrong. His illness wasn't diagnosed until Dec. 4—

three days after the couple had taken possession of their home. He died the following September of a type of cancer called glioma.

Alice told me she and her husband had acted in good faith. "The lady at the bank said we should take life insurance because of our age. I was 54 and my husband at that time was 55. There were questions about health, but we were not too concerned as we felt we did not have any major problems."

I sent her to the Royal Bank's ombudsman, Dennice Leahey (now retired), who called to thank me for the referral and to say she wished more customers were told about their right to appeal to a bank ombudsman. Once Alice's case was reviewed, the mortgage life insurance was reinstated.

If your request for redress is turned down, ask about the appeal process. Insist on your right to go to the next level. If you can't get details on the next level, call the ombudsman first and ask for advice on handling your complaint. You can find the ombudsman's telephone number and email address on a financial institution's Web site. Check to see if there's an annual report, showing the numbers and types of cases handled by the ombudsman's office and how they were resolved.

Here's a list of the Big Five banks and where to go when you want to escalate your complaints:

- Bank of Montreal: Vice-chairman of personal banking, 1-800-372-5111. Ombudsman, 1-800-371-2541.

- Bank of Nova Scotia: Office of the president, 1-877-700-0043. Ombudsman, 1-800-785-8772.

- CIBC: Customer care centre, 1-800-465-2255. Ombudsman, 1-800-308-6859.

- RBC Financial Group: Customer relations centre, 1-800-769-2540. Ombudsman, 1-800-769-2542.

- TD Canada Trust: Customer service 1-800-430-6095. Ombudsman, 1-888-361-0319.

If you're unhappy with the bank's ombudsman, you can appeal to a higher level. Contact the Ombudsman for Banking Services and Investments, 1-888-451-4519, www.obsi.ca, within six months of completing the dispute resolution process at your financial services provider. The office doesn't handle complaints about pricing, levels of interest rates, credit-granting policies, issues relating to general industry policies or disputes that are before the courts.

The ombudsman, Michael Lauber, has been on the job since July 1996. He handles complaints about investment dealers, mutual fund dealers and investment fund companies. The OBSI has about 500 members, including foreign-owned banks and most trust and loan companies. (They're listed on the Web site.) Members don't have to accept the ombudsman's recommendations on behalf of a customer, but they have so far. Those that don't agree to a recommendation will be reported publicly.

The OBSI is one of three complaint-handling services that make up the Financial Services Ombudsnetwork. The others are the Canadian Life and Health Insurance OmbudService (1-888-295-8112, www.clhio.ca) and the General Insurance OmbudService, which works with companies offering home, car or business insurance (1-800-387-2880 in Ontario only, www.gio-scad.org). The three industry services are linked by the Centre for the Financial Services OmbudsNetwork, which operates a customer assistance centre at 1-866-538-3766, www.cfson-crcsf.ca.

Once you've gone to the Ombudsman for Banking Services and Investments, you're at the end of the line. There's nowhere to appeal the recommendations. However, you're free to reject them and try other avenues, such as small claims court.

You can also call the Financial Consumer Agency of Canada, 1-866-461-3222, which has a mandate to monitor compliance with federal laws and voluntary codes of conduct. The agency has clout, since it can levy penalties on institutions that don't obey the law. But it doesn't provide compensation to consumers. The biggest concerns it hears about are problems with bank accounts; issues relating to credit cards, loans and mortgages; branch closings; service fees; and quality of service.

Access to bank accounts without a credit check

Why do you need a credit check to open a basic bank account? The question came to me from Susan, who was in a self-employment assistance program offered to those who were unemployed and receiving government benefits. Once her business plan was approved, she went to the bank to get a business bank account.

"Before I even had a chance to specify what kind of account I wanted, they said they couldn't help me unless I consented to a credit check," she told me. "I just want a basic bank account. I don't need a bank card, overdraft or company cheques. If I'm more than willing to have every cheque coming into my account held until it is clear that the funds are available, where's the credit risk?"

Susan went to the Privacy Commission of Canada, looking for help. She found a case on the Web site (www.privcom.gc.ca) that upheld the rights of a customer against a bank demanding a credit check as a condition of opening a basic account. In a ruling on March 12, 2002, former Privacy Commissioner George Radwanski said he was opposed in principle to running credit checks as a matter of course, because they are "an intrusion into highly sensitive personal information."

He wanted to limit the use of credit checks to what he considered their only legitimate purpose—to assess financial risk for an individual who was actively seeking credit. Banks should develop a procedure that would allow a person to open an account if he or she was unwilling to consent to a credit check, but was willing to forgo all forms of credit, Radwanski recommended.

Susan thought she was in great shape once she found the privacy commissioner's ruling in a case almost identical to hers. But her bank still refused to open a basic account without a credit check. She lodged a formal complaint with the bank, as well as with her federal and provincial members of Parliament. Some people she talked to minimized her concerns. "One lady suggested I go to a credit union. When I explained to her that I didn't drive and I wanted a branch close to me, she suggested maybe I should take a bus. Would she take a bus?"

Another reader complained to me about being turned down when she tried to open a savings account at President's Choice Financial. A credit check had revealed she was a bad risk. Other than a record of a credit union loan, she had no credit history at all. "The credit record is all in my husband's name (or the first name on the applications, which must always have been his). I had assumed all along that if we were joint borrowers, I would get the credit for having paid off the loans. Apparently not. To establish a credit rating for myself, I need my own credit card," she said.

While the experience was a wake-up call that her credit rating was below grade, she resented the fact that President's Choice Financial would not open a savings account for her. She wasn't asking to borrow money. "I finally spoke to someone who said it was the credit bureau's decision. I suggested it seemed ironic that my 18-year-old son was not only able to open two PC accounts last year, but was also given a free box of chocolate chip cookies."

PC Financial had given her the wrong answer. All a credit bureau does is to provide information on a person's credit history. It's up to the financial institution to decide whether the person is a good or bad risk. I advised her to escalate to the CIBC ombudsman, who does double duty as the President's Choice Financial ombudsman as well.

(Loblaws, which owns the bank, contracts out services to Amicus Bank, part of CIBC.)

The ombudsman sent her to the customer care centre, which responded quickly. "The decline letter you received is a standard decline and it should not have been generated," she was told. Despite a limited credit history, she was an existing customer and did qualify for a simple savings account. "Please note that PCF is presently working on updating our processes to avoid these types of situations," said the online bank. The woman's account would be credited with the $24.95 charge she incurred to get her credit file information—but no chocolate chip cookies.

When it comes to credit checks for account applications, the policy varies from one financial institution to another. "Banks do reserve the right to deny someone a bank account for that reason," said Shawn Murray, director of communications for the Canadian Bankers Association. The CBA says a credit check helps determine the conditions for the account, such as daily ABM withdrawal limits or hold policies on non-electronic deposits.

In October 2001, the federal government introduced a new Bank Act and said banks had to open low-cost accounts for individuals who met certain requirements. They had to submit two pieces of identification to open an account. One piece of ID would be enough if a person could confirm his or her identity with another client or community member. In the preliminary regulations, published in the *Canada Gazette* on Nov. 30, 2002, there was no requirement that customers agree to a credit check when opening a retail deposit account.

Under the draft rules, banks could deny account access on only four grounds: They believed the account would be used for fraudulent purposes; the individual had a history of fraudulent financial activity; the individual misrepresented such information; the banks wanted to protect customers or employees from physical harm.

The Financial Consumer Agency of Canada will enforce the rules when they become law in fall 2003. Complaints about refusal to open accounts make up one-third of all the complaints received since the agency was set up in the fall of 2001. The agency monitors a public commitment by the Canadian Bankers Association, on behalf of its members, that covers access to basic banking.

In his first annual report, FCAC commissioner Bill Knight said he was concerned about the number of people who were refused personal bank accounts, generally because of their credit histories. He had reviewed 50 cases and found the financial institutions involved, in many instances, "have not respected the spirit of the public commitment." Knight recommended the government develop and put in place specific regulations covering access to accounts by the fall of 2003. "This is crucial if we are to protect the principle of access to basic financial services for all Canadian consumers."

Until the law is passed, you can complain about being asked for credit checks when opening an account. Call the Privacy Commissioner of Canada at 1-800-282-1376 and the Financial Consumer Agency of Canada at 1-866-461-3222.

Don't overpay on credit card interest

When the Financial Consumer Agency of Canada issued its first credit card report in fall 2001, it was critical of the growing spread between the Bank of Canada's benchmark overnight lending rate (then 2.5 per cent) and the average interest rates on credit cards.

For standard credit cards, the spread between the two rates was at a record high of 16.03 percentage points—up from 13.19 points in 1996 and 10.19 points in 1980. Canadian credit card rates used to move up and down with the Bank of Canada rate, subject to a time lag. However, this trend has not been evident in the past few years. "Generally, the interest rates on standard cards have not moved along with the (overnight) bank rate since 1995," said the FCAC's first credit card report.

Spreads are still high, despite intense scrutiny. By spring 2003, the Bank of Canada rate had moved up to 3.25 per cent, while the rates on standard credit cards and regular rate gold credit cards averaged 18.5 per cent. The only deep discounter was the Wal-Mart TD Visa card at 15.48 per cent.

Why are credit card rates so high? Why are they stuck in the high double digits, even when the Bank of Canada rate slips under five per cent? There are a number of reasons given by the Canadian Bankers Association:

- Losses on credit cards because of fraud. For the year ended Oct. 31, 2002, fraud losses totalled more than $128 million.

- High infrastructure costs to operate the system. This includes processing a large volume of transactions both within Canada and internationally, collecting payments and preparing statements.

- The cost of providing benefits such as insurance, reward points and affinity programs.

- A proliferation of low introductory rates for new cards and low-rate balance transfer options, which carry a much lower rate of interest than rates for standard credit cards.

I find all these explanations unsatisfying. Bankers seem to blame high rates on consumers' insatiable demands for benefits. And they don't mention that fraud losses have come down from $142 million in 2001, $156 million in 2000 and $134 million in 1999. This reduction in fraud losses is an amazing achievement, considering that the number of Visa and MasterCard credit cards in circulation in Canada grew from 37.7 million in 1999 to 49.4 million in 2002.

So I went looking for an informed source outside the banks and came up with the Canadian credit card index, a new economic indicator published by Moody's Investors Services (a respected analytical firm that has been measuring the health of U.S. credit card portfolios since 1989).

Moody's Canadian credit card index tracks the performance of $33 billion in receivables, or 76 per cent of the outstanding Visa and MasterCard balances in Canada. It excludes credit cards issued exclusively by retailers, as well as Visa and MasterCard products offered and co-branded by retailers (such as Petro-Canada or Sears Canada). Here are some highlights of the spring 2003 report, which comes out quarterly:

- Canadians use credit cards more for convenience than as a source of credit. That's shown by the fact we repay more of our balances each month. The payment rate in Canada, calculated as a percentage of the opening balance that is repaid during the month, was 32.5 per cent. The payment rate in the United States was 15 per cent in the same period.

- Fewer Canadians fall behind on their monthly credit card payments. The delinquency rate (that is, accounts more than 30 days in arrears) was 2.5 per cent in Canada, compared to 5.5 per cent in the United States.

- Fewer Canadians default on their credit cards. The loss rate (accounts written off as uncollectible) was 2.8 per cent in Canada, compared to 6.8 per cent in the United States.

The surprise here is the difference between Canadians and Americans. We're more than twice as responsible with credit than they are. Maybe it's a matter of character, since Canadians are more risk-averse in their finances and more law-abiding than U.S. consumers are. But the sluggish U.S. economy also plays a role. Canada's robust growth has resulted in a higher employment rate, with more jobs created in 2002 than in any other year on record. In the first quarter of 2003, Canada's unemployment rate fell to 7.3 per cent, the lowest since October 2001.

Personal bankruptcies, which account for half of the credit card write-offs in the United States, hit a high of 1.5 million cases in 2002. Meanwhile, Canadian bankruptcies declined by 1.5 per cent to 78,210 in 2002, the first year-over-year decline since 1999. The U.S. personal bankruptcy rate is roughly twice as great—575 per 100,000 people, compared to 330 per 100,000 in Canada.

"Essentially, it has become acceptable and easy to claim bankruptcy in the U.S., while in Canada there is still a negative, albeit decreasing, stigma attached to going bankrupt," said the first Moody's Canadian credit card index, issued in August 2002.

The conservatism of Canadian banks is also a factor. They've been more selective about the kind of borrowers to whom they extend credit. U.S. financial institutions have been moving down the credit curve—the result of competitive pressures to expand their card portfolios. Many actively target sub-prime borrowers, those with poor credit ratings who normally go to pawnshops and cheque-cashing outlets.

"The U.S. cardholder, in general, is a less creditworthy person, more highly levered, more stretched and more susceptible to economic downturns. We're seeing signs of that now," said Moody's managing director Andrew Kriegler.

Card issuers in the United States began extending credit to higher-risk borrowers 15 years ago. This coincided with the launch of credit card securitizations (essentially, debt instruments traded by investors). They felt comfortable easing up on credit quality, since capital markets were there to absorb the risks. Canada's market for credit-card securitization is small, but growing, which means our financial institutions may go after sub-prime borrowers one day.

But today, Canada's banks are doing very well with their credit card divisions. How well? It's hard to say since they don't break out their credit card profits separately. But Moody's calculations of net yield, a proxy for profitability, shows Canadian credit card portfolios surpassing those of U.S. portfolios (11.2 per cent versus 10.3 per cent). This shows credit card issuers can still make money in Canada because their losses are so much lower—despite customers' tendency to pay more of their balances each month.

FCAC commissioner Bill Knight had this advice for customers: Shop around. "We shop around for gifts," he said. "But we never think about the cost of the card we use to shop with—or we think only about the points."

You don't pay in full and carry a balance from month to month? Don't feel guilty, but do consider switching. You should be using a low-rate credit card with an annual fee. The best deals, according to the FCAC's credit card report of spring 2003, are Scotiabank's Value Visa and MBNA Canada's Low-Rate Gold MasterCard, both with a 9.9 per cent interest rate and a $29 annual fee.

There's also a trend for banks to offer a low-rate line of credit that you access with a credit card that tracks the prime rate. Hallelujah. The best deals here are Scotiabank's ScotiaLine Visa Account (as low as prime plus 2.5 per cent, with no annual fee), TD Canada Trust's Emerald Visa (prime plus 1.9 per cent to prime plus 6.9 per cent, with a $12 annual fee) and National Bank's Syncro MasterCard (prime plus four per cent or six per cent, with a $35 annual fee).

Once you get your low-rate card, figure out what it costs you to carry the debt. According to a survey by Leger Marketing, 41 per cent of cardholders said they didn't know what interest rate they were being charged on their main credit card. Among those who owed $500 or more to a credit card company, 33 per cent didn't know how much interest they were paying.

MoneySense magazine has a credit card calculator at its Web site, www.moneysense.ca, which lets you see how much it costs to carry a balance at different rates. Click "tools" on the home page.

Say you have an outstanding balance of $2,500. With a no-fee credit card that charges 17.9 per cent, you'll pay $447.50 a year in annual charges. But you can cut your costs almost in half—down to $291.50 a year—if you switch to a 10.5 per cent low-rate credit card that has a $29 annual fee (say CIBC's Select Visa or Laurentian Bank's Black Low-Rate Visa).

The MoneySense calculator comes up with an adjusted interest rate. It takes into account the interest rate and converts the annual fee into a rate based on your average outstanding balance. In the above example, when you have a low-rate card at 10.5 per cent with a $29 annual fee, and you have a balance of $2,500, your adjusted interest rate is 11.66 per cent.

With the Royal Bank Low-Rate Select Visa, which also has a 10.5 per cent rate but a slightly lower $25 annual fee, your adjusted interest rate is 11.5 per cent—and your annual cost of carrying a $2,500 balance is $287.50. And with the Scotia Value Visa, which has a 9.9 per cent rate and a $29 annual fee, your adjusted interest rate is 11.06 per cent—and your annual carrying cost for a $2,500 balance is $276.50.

Low introductory rates can mislead

Ted considers himself a smart customer, but he was tripped up by an introductory low rate on a credit card. He asked me to warn others not to be fooled by these popular promotions.

Suppose you're carrying a balance from month to month on a Visa or MasterCard with an 18.5 per cent interest rate. You transfer the balance to a new card that offers a 4.9 per cent rate for the next six months, a decision that can save you lots of money.

But there's a secret to making the low-rate offer work: You have to put the new card away and never use it for purchases. Take it out of your wallet and throw it into a locked drawer, immune from temptation. That's because anything you buy will be billed at the standard credit card rate, which averages 17.9 per cent to 18.9 per cent.

If you read the small print in your cardholder agreement, you will find out in what order your payments will be applied. With most credit cards, the payments are applied first to cash advances (including balance transfers and convenience cheques). Only later will the payments be applied to purchases.

"There's an implication that you can enjoy the 4.9 per cent rate on everything you charge to the card for the six-month period," Ted said. "I think the banks deserve to have their hands slapped for doing that."

Another reader said his son fell for a similar promotion involving a Visa cheque.

"Enjoy this low rate of 4.9 per cent from the day the cheque is posted to your Visa account until July 31, 2003," the bank said—adding in smaller print that it "may apply any payment you make to balances with lower interest rates, including balances subject to special promotional rates."

The son had always paid for his purchases in full each month, thereby avoiding the 18.5 per cent interest charge. When he got his April statement, he again paid for all his purchases in full, thinking he would be leaving his 4.9 per cent loan balance intact.

To his surprise, the bank applied his payment to the 4.9 per cent loan and then charged him 18.5 per cent on all his purchases. "His reaction was that he felt tricked into borrowing money at 18.5 per cent for every purchase," the reader said.

I agree. These credit card promotions trade on most people's inability to read and understand the small print in the cardholder agreement. They should say loud and clear that you must refrain from using your credit card for any purchases in order to get the low rate.

The Financial Consumer Agency of Canada advises finding out which transactions the low-rate offer applies to before you accept a credit card. If the rate applies only to balance transfers or cash advances (not to purchases), then you should limit your new purchases until you pay off the balance transfer or cash advance.

"If you make purchases while carrying a balance, you may reduce the potential savings from the low introductory rate," the FCAC points out. Not only are the payments applied to the lower-interest balance first, but you also lose the interest-free period on new purchases.

Here's an example. Suppose you transfer a $5,000 balance on Oct. 1. Your new card has a 6 per cent introductory rate on balance transfers and an 18 per cent interest rate on purchases. You make no purchases during the month, so your outstanding balance is $5,000 on Oct. 31. You will pay $25.47 in interest at the six per cent interest rate.

But what if you make a purchase during the month? This is what happens if you make a $1,000 purchase on Oct. 5, then make a partial payment of $1,000 a day later to bring the balance back to $5,000.

On Oct. 31, your outstanding balance is $5,000, just as before. But since your partial payment is applied to the balance transfer, you'll pay six per cent interest on $4,000—or $21.21 altogether. Then you'll pay 18 per cent interest on the $1,000 of new purchases—or $13.32 altogether.

The bottom line: You'll pay a total of $34.53 in interest, compared to $21.21 if you don't make any purchases. You'll be paying a penalty of $9.06 (or more than 40 per cent) for buying something and paying back the money a day later.

Since offers vary from one financial institution to another, make sure you ask your credit card issuer to explain how its order of transactions applies to your payments. And if you find the payments are applied first to balance transfers, use another card for all new purchases.

The introductory low-rate deals are spreading. A direct-mail solicitation for the Canadian Tire Options MasterCard showed your savings for the three months the discount was in effect. With a 5.9 per cent rate, you would pay $29.10 interest on a $2,000 balance. With a 19.5 per cent rate, you'd pay $96.16, a saving of $67.06. But once the three months were up, you would be charged Canadian Tire's regular interest rate of 18.9 per cent unless you paid off your balance in full.

How much better off would you be after moving debt from a card with a 19.5 per cent rate to one with an 18.9 per cent rate? Canadian Tire did the math in a small-print footnote on the back of the brochure. With a $2,000 balance, you would pay $93.21 interest at 18.9 per cent (instead of $96.16 at 19.5 per cent). You'd be just $2.95 ahead over a three-month period.

Low-rate credit card offers for a limited time period are similar to what furniture and electronics retailers do when they promise no interest on purchases for 12 months or more, said Perry Krieger, a Toronto bankruptcy trustee. "Credit card companies know that a reasonably high percentage of people won't have the money to pay off the balance at the end. So they'll be stuck with higher interest rates."

Ask yourself whether you can come up with enough cash to pay what you owe after a few short months. Otherwise, leave the credit card balance where it is.

A solicitation from Capital One, a card issuer that relies on low rates for balance transfers, was intentionally vague about the rate charged to those who still owed money at the end of the six-month introductory period. In small print, Capital One said the rate would be 9.9 per cent, 12.9 per cent, 14.9 per cent, 17.9 per cent or 19.8 per cent, "depending on our review of your application and credit information."

In fact, Capital One will often raise the interest rate above 19.8 per cent if you make a late payment or exceed your limit. The Credit Counselling Service of Toronto says some clients are paying 21.98 per cent on their cards. Capital One is shown as charging rates of up to 23.9 per cent in the FCAC publication *Credit Cards and You*.

Before transferring balances to a new card, try to pin down the rate you'll be paying on purchases and cash advances. If you haven't paid off the balance when the offer ends, what rate will you pay later?

You have to read the fine print carefully. Capital One also had a low-rate deal where you would pay 7.9 per cent on balance transfers and never face a higher rate until the debt is discharged. However, there was a one-time fee of three per cent of the amount transferred to the card. That would mean an extra $60 on a $2,000 balance, or $300 on a $10,000 balance. Could you save enough to offset the transfer fee?

A final issue to consider with balance transfers: Once you have a zero balance, will you run up big bills again on the old cards? The temptation may be tough to resist unless you cut them up or take them out of your wallet. Explore other options, such as a loan or line of credit, for consolidating high-rate balances before applying for a new credit card.

After expressing my views on low-rate card offers, I heard from several readers who said I had missed the point. They were in the habit of switching their balances every few months from one card with a low-rate introductory offer to another.

I agree it makes sense to find the lowest interest rates you can if you have a high credit card balance. However, you should always try to whittle down the amount you owe, instead of just moving it around. This behavior could count against you when it comes to your credit rating.

Watch out for currency conversion fees

When you use your credit card outside Canada, you may find the transaction costs more than you anticipated. Banks routinely add service charges (or markups) for converting foreign currency purchases into Canadian dollars. These charges, imposed on top of the exchange rates, go up to 2.5 per cent of the value of the purchases, depending on the bank and the credit card.

Yes, customers do get informed about the service charges on foreign currency transactions. But the details are buried in small print contracts that often go unread. You may only find out if your bank decides to raise the rates.

The Royal Bank bumped up its foreign currency conversion fee to 2.5 per cent (from 1.8 per cent) on July 1, 2003. The increase was widely covered in the media and drew attention to the high cost of these charges, amounting to $25 for each $1,000 of purchases abroad.

Several other financial institutions—Bank of Montreal, Capital One Bank, MBNA Canada and National Bank—also charge 2.5 per cent. You may find that rate prohibitive if you travel a lot outside Canada or use your card to pay for mail-order goods and services from the United States or abroad.

If so, shop around to find a card with lower service charges for foreign currency conversions. You can find information at the Financial Consumer Agency's Web site or in its publication, *Credit Cards and You*, published twice a year. The spring 2003 issue lists a variety of rates for converting overseas purchases into Canadian dollars, such as American Express (1.6 to 2.2 per cent, depending on card), CIBC (1.8 per cent), Citibank (2 per cent), HSBC (1.8 per cent), Laurentian Bank (1.8 per cent), President's Choice (2 per cent), Scotiabank (1.8 per cent) and TD Canada Trust (1.65 per cent).

The relative bargains may not last. In the United States, banks charge foreign currency conversion fees of up to three per cent, a Visa International official told the *Toronto Star*.

Instead of using credit cards, you can also buy travellers' cheques or visit automated bank machines when you're out of the country. (Of course, travellers' cheques and ABMs have hefty service charges, too.)

If you travel frequently outside Canada, another thing to be aware of is the higher fee for taking a cash advance on your credit card. Fees for cash advances generally range from $1.50 to $3.50 for transactions in Canada and from $2 to $6 for cash advances made in a foreign country. These fees are imposed on top of any convenience fees for using white-label ABMs.

Treat your credit cards as if they were gold

There are almost 50 million credit cards circulating in Canada—twice as many cards as adults—so there are lots of opportunities for fraud. Organized criminals can steal credit cards from offices, vehicles, health clubs and golf clubs. They make counterfeit cards or send false applications for cards. Sometimes they promote non-existent or exaggerated goods and services by telephone or on the Internet. You supply your credit card number and, bingo, you get fraudulent charges against your account.

Industry controls are having some effect, says the Canadian Bankers Association. But there's no room for complacency, as the following stories suggest. If you have a credit card, you could be a victim of fraud.

Real, a *Toronto Star* reader, wrote to me after reading a column that criticized a negative-option marketing campaign by Sears Canada Inc. Sears had identified 500,000 Ontario customers with Sears or Eatons cards that weren't being used much. It sent them all a new MasterCard, which had to be activated before use. This wasn't an unsolicited card, Sears said, but a replacement of an existing card. Customers were given written notification first and a number to call if they didn't want the MasterCard.

Real missed Sears' first letter, but cut up the unwanted card when it arrived. Imagine his surprise a few weeks later, when he received a call from Sears MasterCard trying to verify some charges. "You can bet I was hot, as I had not accepted the card," he said. "They went on to ask me about my change of address and phone numbers." It turned out that someone had opened a credit card account in his name, then told Sears he had moved to a different city nearby.

This was Real's second experience of credit card fraud in two months. The first time it happened, his bank notified him about a $4,000 cash advance taken from his Visa account at another bank. Since he and his wife still had their Visa cards (which hadn't been stolen), the bank swallowed the charges racked up by the impostor. "When I was told the crooks had a lot of information about me, including my former address outside Ontario, I became alarmed," he said.

Identity theft is the fastest-growing crime in North America, according to Ann Cavoukian, Ontario's Information and Privacy Commissioner. "An insurance company now offers insurance against identity theft because it's so damaging and harmful," she told me. In their book, *Privacy Payoff* (McGraw-Hill Ryerson), Cavoukian and Tyler Hamilton, a technology columnist with the *Toronto Star*, point out that thieves no longer have to pick through garbage cans and raid mailboxes to acquire identifying pieces of information about a person.

In the digital age, identity theft has gone high-tech. Criminals can use Internet search engines, do-it-yourself hacker kits and online "private eye" search services to do the dirty work for them—for a nominal fee or even for free. "Across all industries, both online and offline, businesses need to do a better job of safeguarding the information they hold about consumers," the authors warn. "Otherwise, identity thieves will thrive, and consumer fears will be heightened."

Credit card fraud isn't always a big-ticket item. Myra contacted me about a $57.50 item debited to her son's Visa card. "I have been running into a brick wall with CIBC Visa representatives," she said.

"The sales draft obtained from the merchant bore no signature of my son. The bank is not willing to investigate this item any further, saying it has passed the 30-day period." A $57.50 loss is a big deal for a university student, she said.

CIBC refunded the money within a week of my passing along the letter. Customer care co-ordinator Cathy Macdonald apologized for the "unnecessary frustration" caused to both mother and son. While Myra was thrilled to get the problem resolved—"without your help, CIBC would never have listened to me, although I spent countless hours trying to get help," she said—the potential fraud item remained a mystery. No sales slip with her son's signature was ever obtained.

To avoid fraud, treat your credit cards as if they were cash. Never leave your cards unattended at work, since (according to the Canadian Bankers Association) there are more card thefts in the workplace than in any other single location. Motor vehicles are the second most popular location for thieves.

Always check your monthly statements and make sure the charges are yours.

Never give your card number over the phone or the Internet unless you know you're dealing with a reputable company. Only give it when you have called to place an order.

Report lost or stolen cards right away. If you're expecting a replacement for a card that's about to expire and it doesn't arrive, track it down and notify the issuer.

Finally, check your card when it's returned to you after a purchase. Make sure it's actually your card.

Check your credit rating on the Web

Want to know how lenders see you as a credit risk? You can get a free copy of your credit report if you can wait for it to come in the mail. You can also get the results delivered in minutes from three Canadian sources of credit information, if you have access to the Internet and a credit card. I tested all three Web sites and found them fairly easy to navigate. But there's a big difference in results.

Equifax Canada Inc., the first to introduce online access in June 2002, sells a basic report for $14.50 (including GST) and a deluxe report for $21.95 that has a numerical score. "We do more than half a million disclosures a year by mail and fax," said president Rick Cleary, "and now we're doing about 35 per cent of that online." A reason may be that the deluxe report, called Score Power—available only on the Internet—explains how you can improve your credit rating.

In August 2002, iQuiri Inc. of Calgary launched an online credit report service through its own Web site and those of affiliates such as Telus Corp., AOL Canada Inc. and Yahoo Canada. You can get a free credit report if you sign up for iQuiri's monthly credit monitoring service, which costs $89.95. "The demographic is 25 to 40 years old, people who are so credit-active they make one payment and everything changes," said Stephen Ufford, vice-president of business development.

Trans Union of Canada Inc., based in Hamilton, Ontario, went online in December 2002, doing a "soft launch" to get the bugs out, said Karen Grant, vice-president of marketing operations. Trans Union sells credit reports (which include a numerical score) for $14.99 each. It also lets customers challenge any errors online.

Here's the lowdown on what I found:

- My favourite is the $21.95 Score Power report from Equifax (www.econsumer.equifax.ca). A third party, Fair Isaac & Co., develops the score, which is widely used by lenders. FICO scores range between 300 and 900, with higher scores better than lower scores. The average Canadian consumer scores 770. Equifax provides great context and explanatory material about how to improve your score over time.

- Trans Union (www.tuc.ca) asked five questions to verify my identity, more than any other Web site, before giving me access to my report. I was momentarily stumped by one question: "Which province were you living in when you were issued your social insurance number?" Only a half-page of the 10-page report dealt with the credit score (developed by Trans Union, not an outside party). The explanation was skimpy—for example, it gave a number but didn't say what was the highest number you could get—and not personalized.

- iQuiri (www.iquiri.com) asks for your social insurance number, saying this is mandatory information, and uses your SIN as your identification to log in later. You don't need to provide your SIN to get your credit report at the other Web sites. (The federal government advises giving out the number only for authorized uses, such as income-tax related transactions.) Ufford says you can omit your SIN if you call and make other arrangements, but this isn't explained clearly. The credit information here is limited since Northern Credit Bureaus is smaller than the other two bureaus. But there's a user-friendly rating system, using an arrow on a colourful sliding scale, ranging from "very poor" to "excellent."

In general, I think this is a real innovation for customers. If you're buying a house or car or borrowing to buy an RRSP, you're racing to meet a deadline. The information on your credit report can mean the difference between getting accepted for a loan or not. It can also affect the interest rate you're offered. If anything on the report is wrong or outdated, you want to be able to tell the lender right away.

iQuiri says 48 per cent of credit bureau reports have errors, quoting a CBC *Marketplace* investigation. They may be small errors (such as spelling), but still should be corrected. "This product, information, was what the Internet was created for," Ufford says. "There's nothing faster or more secure."

To order your report by mail, call Equifax at 1-800-465-7166 or Trans Union at 1-800-663-9980. You can contact Northern Credit Bureaus by fax at 1-800-646-5876.

After I wrote about this issue in the *Star*, Northern Credit Bureaus launched an online service of its own. The cost is $12 for a credit report, available from www.creditbureau.ca. While the company says it's not mandatory to provide your SIN, making it available reduces the chances of their mistaking your files for someone else's with the same name and birth date.

You know there are problems with your credit record when an application for a loan or credit card is refused. That's usually a good time to check your file for errors. Asking why a credit card application was rejected, one *Star* reader found out her bank had put a hold on her fully secured line of credit, of which only a small part was being used. She didn't get a written apology from the branch manager, as requested, but she did get a $50 restaurant voucher, to be redeemed at an East Side Mario's nearby.

Don't trust your kids with too much credit

Donna thought her 19-year-old son could be trusted with credit. Then she found out he had lost more than $4,000 in a single day at a Halifax casino, playing blackjack with borrowed money. She asked me to warn other parents about the dangers of gambling and financial institutions' willingness to give instant credit over the telephone.

"The lending institution immediately doubled the credit limit on his Visa, which he used for cash advances, and then gave him credit lines on two bank accounts, without any proof of the ability to repay the cash advances or credit lines," she says. The story shows the need for financial literacy education in high school, as well as appropriate controls on credit use by young adults.

Donna's son started gambling at the age of 17, using fake identity papers. Casinos in Ontario require proof that customers are 19 years old before allowing them in. Things got worse when he moved to Halifax to study business at Dalhousie University. "I never had a problem before coming here," he told me in an interview from his residence. "The casino is so close, a three-minute cab ride for $6 or $7, that you can't help but go when there's nothing else to do."

He went to the casino frequently and, inevitably, started losing money. He kept going back to regain the money he'd lost. "It got past the point where it was fun. I tried to turn it into a job," he says. He had a Visa card with a $500 credit limit, which his mother had co-signed when he was 17. When he turned 19 (and was working at a summer job), he applied for a Visa card in his own name and had the limit increased to $1,000. With his frequent casino visits, he soon exhausted the $1,000 limit on his Visa and spent all the money in his two bank accounts.

That didn't stop him. Using a pay phone at the casino, he called the bank's 1-800 number at 7 a.m. after a night of gambling to ask for more credit. When the bank asked if he was working, he said yes—though he hadn't worked since August. "I did kind of lie," he admits. "But I was surprised at how easy it was. There was no request for proof or phone numbers."

The bank doubled his Visa limit to $2,000, so he took out a $1,000 cash advance. When that money was lost, he called again and got the bank to put overdraft protection on one account. Then he got overdraft protection on his other account. He maxed out both credit lines (to a total of $3,226.74) over a period of a few hours.

Donna complained to the bank about its willingness to give instant credit to her teenage son. "We're certainly sympathetic to the issues raised," said Rob McLeod, a CIBC spokesperson, adding that he couldn't discuss her son's case without his permission. But McLeod was willing to talk in general terms about access to credit for young people.

CIBC offers a student credit card with a $500 limit to those who have income of at least $1,200 a year. "We rely on students' statement of their circumstances and are prepared to give them a card with a low limit to help them start building their credit record," McLeod said.

Donna's son, however, had applied for and received an adult card, based on his employment income of seven months. When he had asked for extra credit during his marathon gambling session, he didn't tell the bank he had stopped working. Then he lied about his employment status on the telephone. "When any adult customer asks us to approve an increase in credit, we will look at the history of our relationship with this individual and make a decision based on their specific financial circumstances," McLeod said.

Why couldn't the bank have waited 48 to 72 hours before approving her son's credit increase, Donna asked. That would allow time to check on whether he could repay the money, given his age and stage in life. Banks frequently put holds on cheques before releasing the money to customers. Why don't they put holds on credit requests?

"We try to ensure that we meet customers' needs in as timely a manner as we can," McLeod responded. "Instituting deliberate delays would, I am sure, not be viewed positively by most of our customers. As you know, banks have in the past been criticized for being too restrictive on giving credit to individuals or businesses. So we do have to tread a line that hopefully results in the best result for the vast majority of our customers."

Donna and her husband bailed out their son, so he still had a good credit rating. And he still had a Visa card, but he asked the bank to cut the limit to $500. A month after his last visit to the casino, he hadn't gone back. He was getting good marks in his business studies and hoped to become an investment banker.

"Kind of ironic this happened," he said. "I've definitely learned from this. I've learned not to be an idiot."

Secured cards help those with credit problems

Credit card offers are everywhere. Many Canadians don't go more than a week without getting pitches in the mail for gold or platinum cards with up to $50,000 in credit privileges. But some people—new immigrants, women who've just been divorced or widowed, youngsters working at their first jobs, those who have filed for bankruptcy—find credit cards hard to get. No one gives them a break.

That's where a secured credit card comes in. Customers deposit money into a savings account that is used as collateral for a line of credit. There's little risk for lenders, who know they'll get paid in a default. If you don't make your credit card payments, they can use the deposit to pay down your balance. So they can approve borrowers with a troubled or non-existent credit history.

A secured credit card, while more expensive than a regular credit card, can help you build a credit rating or rebuild one that's troubled. If you make payments promptly and faithfully, you'll eventually be eligible for an unsecured credit card.

Mainstream financial institutions have been slow to embrace secured cards. CIBC offers one exclusively for people who have completed a debt management program with the Credit Counselling

Service of Toronto. "It's been a big win for us," said Laurie Campbell, program manager of the non-profit charitable agency. Borrowers put down a $500 deposit and get a CIBC Visa card with a $500 line of credit. If they pay on time, they get their money back with interest after two years and a higher credit limit.

CIBC has now introduced a whole family of secured credit cards. Three have a $500 limit and require a $500 deposit (CIBC Secured Classic Visa, CIBC Secured Dividend Card and CIBC Secured HBC Rewards Visa Card), while two have a $5,000 limit and require a $5,000 deposit (CIBC Secured Gold Visa Card and CIBC Secured Vacationgold Visa Card). The gold cards also carry annual fees ($99 and $30 respectively).

Home Trust Co. launched its secured Visa credit card in September 2000. Response has been limited, the company says, despite the fact that virtually everyone is approved. Maybe it's because the card is rather pricey. There's a monthly service fee of $7.50 (or $90 a year) and an annual interest rate of 19.5 per cent for purchases and 21.5 per cent for cash advances. (These rates rise to 24.5 per cent for purchases and cash advances if your account is in arrears.) Customers also pay a one-time account set-up fee of $39. They put down deposits of $750 to $10,000 and receive two per cent annual interest. (This rate is subject to change.)

Home Trust, which relies on referrals from mortgage brokers, also offers a secured Equity Plus Visa card with an interest rate of 11.99 per cent (available only in Ontario and Alberta). Rather than put down a deposit, customers draw against the equity in their homes. They can borrow up to 85 per cent of the home's value, to a limit of $75,000, and use the money to start a business, do home improvements or consolidate high-interest debts into a lower-rate line of credit. (There's a two per cent set-up fee, along with $571 for title insurance and about $250 for a home appraisal.)

Capital One Bank, another issuer, has a Secured MasterCard that requires a $75 to $200 deposit and has a minimum credit limit of $200. The interest rate is 21.9 per cent for purchases and cash advances and there's a $59 annual fee.

Here are some tips on using secured credit cards from the FCAC:

- Check your credit file periodically with the three credit bureaus in Canada. Correct all errors immediately, since they may prevent you from getting an unsecured card.

- Find out who holds your deposit, whether it's your credit issuer or another financial institution chosen by the issuer. No matter who holds the deposit, check with the credit issuer to see if your deposit is insured with the Canada Deposit Insurance Corp. (CDIC) or a provincial deposit insurance corporation.

- Be cautious about secured credit card offers from financial institutions you don't know. They may be scams. If you have doubts, call the FCAC at 1-866-461-3222.

- Watch out for secured card offers from issuers outside Canada. If you have problems, you may find it hard to resolve them with a company located in another country.

- If the card doesn't have a recognized brand name (such as Visa, MasterCard or American Express), it may be accepted at only a small number of stores.

- Make sure you understand all the terms and conditions associated with a secured card before accepting it.

What to do if you're drowning in debt

Don't think this topic is relevant to you? Think again. Many of us who seem to be managing splendidly are just a hop, skip and jump away from bankruptcy. All it takes is an unexpected reversal—losing your job, separating from your spouse, getting injured or becoming ill—and your financial world can fall apart.

What if interest rates went up again, not just a little but a lot? Canadians have gone on a massive borrowing binge, aided by record low interest rates that make debts cheaper to service. But some households couldn't survive a simultaneous rise in rates and fall in property prices, since much of this borrowing is tied to home equity.

Though consumer bankruptcies went down in 2002, because of the strong Canadian economy, the number of bankruptcies has been increasing exponentially over the last few decades. There has been a shift in the type of bankruptcies, too. In 1966, business bankruptcies made up 60 per cent of total filings. Consumer bankruptcies now make up 90 per cent of total filings.

Who goes bankrupt? Recent studies show it's no longer a remedy used primarily by working-class men. Iain Ramsay, a law professor at York University, did a random sample of 1,150 consumer bankruptcy files in Toronto. He found most bankrupts were 30 to 39 years old, a time of life associated with major commitments such as buying houses and furnishings on credit. Almost half of those filing for bankruptcy were women—up sharply from a study 20 years earlier. And the divorce rate among bankrupts was twice as high as in the general population. Marriage breakdown alone rarely causes bankruptcy, Ramsay concluded. It's when marriage breakdown collides with other problems, such as unemployment, that people may end up staring insolvency in the face.

Almost three in ten debtors described themselves as self-employed, twice the rate of the general population. Those in the skilled clerical, sales and service categories (such as real estate agents) were over-represented. Small business operators are often included in consumer bankruptcies, defined as those in which liabilities from a business venture make up less than half of the total amount owed.

Ramsay said bankruptcy statistics understate the bad news about small business. "There has been much celebration of the role of self-employment and small business in the new economy but, based on this study, individuals pay a high price for business failure."

Another study of consumer bankruptcy, sponsored by Industry Canada in 1997, pinpointed student loans as a major cause of bankruptcy for those under 30. "Many of these debtors borrowed in the pursuit of publicly approved goals, such as obtaining a post-secondary degree," the authors said. "They tried to do what we, as a society, encouraged them to do." But later, they're "accused of abusing the system, or of mismanaging their affairs." Nevertheless, Ottawa passed new rules in 1998 barring the discharge of student loans by bankruptcy for 10 years after a person leaves college or university.

When you're in financial trouble and facing urgent demands from creditors, the natural impulse is to call a bankruptcy trustee. Bankruptcy wipes out most debts—except alimony, spousal or child support, court fines or damages arising from fraud or assault—and gives people a fresh start. You get discharged from bankruptcy after nine months (unless there's opposition from the trustee, your creditors or the federal Superintendent of Bankruptcy). And the bankruptcy stays on your credit record for seven years.

Bankruptcy can have distressing consequences. ACEF, a Quebec consumer group, surveyed 800 Canadians who had declared bankruptcy between Jan. 1, 1996, and Dec. 31, 1998. Almost four out of five of those interviewed said bankruptcy had caused bad changes in their lives: Difficulty in borrowing and rebuilding credit, a feeling of humiliation or loss of self-esteem and the loss of assets such as their home. Only 17 per cent saw bankruptcy in a positive light, saying they had learned to live within their means and were less stressed than before. "The decision to declare bankruptcy requires in-depth consideration," ACEF concluded, "since it can bring about significant changes in the lives of individuals."

For more information, consult *Dealing with Debt: A Consumer's Guide*, a useful publication from the federal Superintendent of Bankruptcy. It's available online at www.strategis.ic.gc.ca. (Click D for "debt" in the index of topics.)

An alternative to bankruptcy is to seek help from a credit counselling agency in your community. These non-profit agencies dole out advice about budgeting and dealing with bill collectors. Many people find that's all they need to get back on track. If that's not enough, you can go on a debt management program. You work out a plan to deposit money regularly with the credit counselling agency, based on your ability to pay, and have it divided up fairly among your creditors. Clients who go for advice generally pay nothing, while those on debt management programs pay fees of up to 10 per cent of the amount disbursed to creditors.

Once you're on a debt management program, creditors agree to stop charging monthly interest. They may lower the interest rate or even reduce the principal owed, so you can pay off your debts more quickly. As well, you get welcome relief from overzealous bill collectors and garnishee orders. Creditors prefer getting some money from debtors than losing it all in a bankruptcy. That's why they subsidize the operations of non-profit credit counselling agencies. Contributions also come from the United Way and provincial governments, in some cases.

To find an agency in your area, check out Credit Counselling Canada, www.creditcounsellingcanada.ca. The Ontario Association of Credit Counselling Services (at 1-888-746-3328, www.indebt.org) can give details of Ontario's 26 non-profit credit counselling agencies, including the Credit Counselling Service of Toronto, an organization with which I've been associated as a voluntary board member for many years (and am currently serving as president). It's at 416-228-3328, www.creditcanada.com.

Some people find it hard to stick with a plan to repay creditors slowly. While a bankruptcy is discharged within nine months, a credit counselling program can drag on for five years or more. And those who complete a program may wind up with the same poor credit rating as people who choose bankruptcy—a slap in the face for all their years of effort.

If your creditors don't agree to a debt management program, the next step may be a consumer proposal. If your total debt is more than $1,000 but less than $75,000, excluding the mortgage on your home, and you can't manage to make your monthly payments, you can file a proposal to your creditors. If you're married or living common-law and you both signed for most of the debt, you can file a joint proposal.

Unlike a bankruptcy, which discharges your debts, a consumer proposal allows you to repay a portion of what you owe over a number of years. It also stops the interest clock. Once the proposal is accepted, creditors can't take legal steps to recover their debts by seizing property or garnisheeing wages.

Bankruptcy trustees, who administer consumer proposals, were initially reluctant to suggest them as an option. But in 1998, the federal government raised the fees they could charge. Today, bankruptcy trustees are talking about alternatives in their advertising. As a result, the number of consumer proposals has gone up sharply.

Here's an example of an actual consumer proposal filed in Toronto:

- The debtor had assets of $2,300 and owed $27,975 to six unsecured creditors (American Express, Trans Canada Credit Corp., three banks and one trust company). When asked to give reasons for his financial difficulty, he said: "Reduced income due to disability and high monthly interest charges."

- His income after tax was $1,041 a month. Once expenses were deducted, he had $125 a month for debt repayment.

- He agreed to pay $7,500 over a five-year period to the bankruptcy trustee, resulting in an expected distribution to creditors of about $4,300.

A proposal to pay 25 cents on the dollar doesn't sound like much. But it's better than nothing. If the person were to have filed for bankruptcy instead, "we expect to generate only $1,350 in gross realizations for the benefit of creditors," the trustee said. Once costs were deducted, the creditors would get "approximately nil."

Creditors have up to 45 days to accept or reject a consumer proposal. If they don't respond, they're considered to have accepted. But if creditors reject the proposal, the person is not automatically bankrupt. It's back to square one. Bankruptcy trustees can make a counteroffer to creditors and try to negotiate a more acceptable arrangement.

Under a proposal, trustees are required to provide credit counselling. The cost is $85 for each of two sessions. The first session examines budgeting and credit management, while the second looks at the causes of insolvency. Bankruptcy trustees may appear to be on the consumer's side but they're legally obligated to represent only the creditor's interests.

"It's against the law for your trustee to give you any advice with respect to the protection of your assets," said Bill Lutton, president of Par-O-Law Canada Inc., an Oshawa, Ontario-based paralegal firm that acts as a consultant to debtors. "Fair-minded trustees struggle with this issue, trying to set a fair and equitable payment that the debtor can afford while still trying to recover the most money for creditors."

A Division 1 proposal is an alternative to bankruptcy for small business owners and self-employed professionals who can't pay their bills. The federal Bankruptcy and Insolvency Act (Part 3, Division 1) outlines how those with more than $75,000 in debts, excluding residential mortgages, can ask their creditors for leniency.

Candidates for a Division 1 proposal are typically doctors, lawyers and other professionals, age 45 to 55, earning $200,000 to

$250,000 a year, said Jay Harris, a bankruptcy trustee with Harris & Partners Inc. of Toronto. The biggest creditor is usually the federal government, specifically the Canada Customs and Revenue Agency. These people know that courts and creditors are taking a harder line. If they go into bankruptcy, they may not be discharged automatically if they have enough income or assets to pay more than a token amount. Unsecured creditors will accept a Division 1 proposal if they're convinced they will get more than in a bankruptcy.

Here are details of an actual Division 1 proposal, filed in Toronto:

- The self-employed debtor owed $101,500, mainly on credit cards. The stated reasons for financial difficulty: "Low income, poor budgeting and the inability to handle high monthly interest charges."

- Under the proposal, the debtor agreed to pay $320 a month, or $19,200 over five years. Professional fees were $6,500, leaving $12,700 for the unsecured creditors.

- If the person were to go bankrupt, the creditors would realize only $2,000, the trustee estimated.

A Division 1 proposal is an attractive option for small business owners looking to reduce personal and business debt. As long as the company is registered as a sole proprietorship, the debts owing by the company can be included in the proposal. It must be accepted by 51 per cent of the creditors who are owed a total of at least two-thirds of the money. This is unlike proposals under $75,000, where only 51 per cent of creditors have to approve. The person is automatically bankrupt if creditors reject the proposal. But what usually happens is that the creditors negotiate a mutually agreeable proposal, either by increasing the monthly payment slightly or extending the payment term.

Why would people agree to pay off debts slowly over a period of years when they could be discharged from bankruptcy in nine months? A proposal allows you to hang on to your assets. "If you can come up with an acceptable plan, you don't lose your retirement savings plans and the equity in your home," Harris said. "You're further ahead than cashing in RRSPs to pay creditors and starting all over again."

When you complete any type of proposals, you are given a credit rating of R7. That's only slightly better than the R9 rating you would have received if you had gone into bankruptcy. Credit bureaus use a nine-point rating scale: R1 indicates that payment was made on time; R2 that payment was made 30 days late, but not more than 60 days. An R9 rating indicates a bad debt or one that has been placed for collection and it also applies to bankruptcy.

Information about a proposal is not purged from your credit record until three years after you have finished repaying creditors (compared to seven years for a first bankruptcy, 14 years for a second bankruptcy). If you want to improve your credit record, call your banker and ask for a meeting, suggests *Dealing with Debt: A Consumer Guide*. Bring your pay stubs, your budget and your discharge papers and ask the banker how you can earn your way back to a good credit record.

Beware of cheque-cashing and payday loan outlets

Your bank account is overdrawn, your credit cards are maxed out and your next paycheque is a week away. How do you get your hands on some money right away? For many low-income Canadians, the answer is a payday loan—also known as a cash advance loan, cheque advance loan or post-dated cheque loan. You go to a cheque-cashing outlet and write a post-dated personal cheque for the amount you wish to borrow, plus a fee. When you get paid (up to two weeks later), you let the cheque be deposited or renew the loan by paying another fee.

A cash advance loan secured by a personal cheque is very high-priced credit. And it's hard to understand what you're paying, because these outlets don't follow disclosure rules laid out for other financial institutions.

In 2001, I went to a few cheque-cashing outlets, as common as pizza and hamburger joints on Yonge St. in downtown Toronto, to ask about a payday loan:

- At Money Mart, you pay a fee of 89 cents per week per $100 for a cash advance, plus a $14.99 item fee and a 2.99 per cent fee for cashing a first-party personal cheque. If you borrow $300 for one week, you would write Money Mart a cheque for $326.33.

- At Unicash Financial Centres, the cost for a payday advance is 2.5 per cent, plus a $14.99 handling fee. To borrow $300, you would write a cheque for $322.49.

- At Cash Money, a payday loan is easy to understand and costs more than elsewhere: $20 for each $100 advanced. To borrow $300, you would write a cheque for $360.

By labelling their transactions as cheque-cashing instead of lending, these companies can avoid credit laws. In Canada, the Criminal Code has an interest-rate ceiling of 60 per cent a year. Anything above that is considered usury.

Cheque-cashing outlets charge more than 60 per cent annual interest for their short-term loans. A 14-day loan with a fee of $10 per $100 has an annual interest rate of 261 per cent. A $15 per $100 fee works out to 391 per cent a year and a $20 per $100 fee to 521 per cent a year.

Money Mart's position is it avoids the 60 per cent threshold for criminal interest by making the $14.99 cheque-cashing fee optional. A borrower who repays the loan in cash before the due date pays only the interest due, prorated to the payment date, and not the cheque-cashing fee.

"The cheque-cashing fee is not a fee that the customer must incur for the advancing of credit," Money Mart president Sydney Franchuk told *Vancouver Sun* business reporter Michael Kane in January 2003. "It is a fee they may incur for the benefit of not having to return in person to the Money Mart outlet." More than 20 per cent of payday loan customers take advantage of the cash repayment option rather than allowing the post-dated cheque to go through, he added.

Cheque-cashing outlets fall under provincial administration. Most provinces, except for Quebec and Saskatchewan, have no regulations and don't require registration. "We get very few complaints about them, in fact almost none," said Ontario consumer ministry spokeswoman Brenda Darby.

In Toronto, the Royal Bank of Canada quietly opened its own outlet in Toronto's working-class Parkdale neighbourhood in fall 2002. Another was opened in Toronto's Regent Park, a low-income housing development, in fall 2003. Cash & Save doesn't offer payday loans or cash advances. Instead, it allows customers to cash cheques, buy money orders, send wire transfers or pay bills without opening an account—and without having to endure the five-day holds common to bank branches. All they need to do is register and show two pieces of identification.

Say, for example, you had a $1,000 cheque from an employer. You would pay $12.50 at Cash & Save for immediate access to your money. That compares to 75 cents to cash the same cheque at a Royal Bank branch on a pay-as-you-go basis, or 27 cents if you had the Signature Plus flat-fee option ($4 a month for 15 debits). Still, you would pay much less at Cash & Save than at rival cheque-cashing outlets.

Informal surveys have shown that two-thirds of the people using Cash & Save already have Royal Bank accounts. They say they prefer to use the cheque-cashing outlet—and pay fees of 1.25 per cent of the cheque's value—for the convenience, long hours and friendly service. The bank has linked up with St. Christopher House, a local community agency, to offers programs in basic financial literacy.

The Public Interest Advocacy Centre, an Ottawa-based consumer group, did a study of alternative banking services from the customer's point of view. (There's an executive summary at www.piac.ca.) "Users feel very comfortable in these places, while they're not comfortable with banks," said co-author and lawyer Sue Lott, who sympathizes with this reaction. "Banks are never very user-friendly. Even I'm intimidated by them," she adds.

With funding from Industry Canada, PIAC did a telephone survey of a random sample of Canadian households, as well as focus group interviews in Toronto, Vancouver and Calgary. Its report focused on payday loans, the most recent and popular alternative service. These are short-term loans in the $100 to $200 range, in return for a post-dated cheque or delayed automatic debit, plus a percentage fee.

Of 4,206 households contacted, 202 had used the alternative banking sector in the previous three years. That's a rate of 4.8 per cent, representing more than one million Canadians. Only four per cent of users were young people under 21, while single mothers and seniors made up less than one per cent each. The common idea that these businesses are preying on the poor is far from the truth. Only 15 per cent of users would fall under Statistics Canada's definition of low income.

(Pawnshop customers are the exception. Their incomes are $20,000 lower than the Canadian average, their employment rate is 20 percentage points lower than average and they're less likely to own their homes.)

Most alternative banking customers have jobs, although they're not university-educated professionals, and they're similar to the Canadian population in age, gender and income. The idea that people go to cheque-cashing outlets because they have problems with credit also proved to be wrong. Only nine per cent of users said they had a poor credit rating, and well over half were carrying less debt than usual.

The reason most people gave for using alternative bank services: Money was tight. They had a shortfall from their pay period or just barely enough to cover expenses. While credit card use was lower— 53 per cent of alternative banking customers had credit cards, compared to 75 per cent of Canadians—this was more likely through choice than lack of availability. People singled out the service aspects of alternative banking, such as confidentiality, friendly staff and a welcoming atmosphere.

This report, a welcome contribution to the debate about cheque-cashing outlets, shattered the myth that people had no other choices. While users could go to banks, they decided to use alternative services, often at a much higher cost. The implication, said the consumer advocacy group, is that "banks are failing a large segment of the market."

I think the Royal Bank is on the right track in its experiment with Cash & Save, which provides the friendly service of a cheque-cashing outlet while staying away from controversial payday loans. If more mainstream banks moved into alternative services, the market could become more competitive and fees would fall.

Meanwhile, it's up to provincial governments to license and supervise this growing financial sector. Why is it almost completely unregulated? British Columbia officials, speaking in confidence to *Vancouver Sun* business reporter Michael Kane in January 2003, gave five reasons for doing nothing:

- The courts are backlogged with more-serious cases.

- Payday loan companies provide a necessary service, which main-stream lenders are failing to provide.

- If payday loan companies were outlawed, it would shift the business to back alley loan sharks with their Soprano-style collection methods.

- While borrowers may be flummoxed by interest rates, they know what they are getting into in terms of dollars, and the amounts involved are relatively small.

- Payday loan companies should be compensated for accepting high-risk clients and wouldn't be able to stay in business if their total charges for one or two-week loans were kept below the 60 per cent annualized interest rate limit in the Criminal Code.

"The nature of payday lending has created a Catch-22 for regulators who want to curb the industry's excesses but can't be seen to be regulating an illegal activity," Kane said.

While cheque-cashing outlets are operating legally and performing a service that's in demand, you should look for alternatives, such as getting an advance from your employer or a loan from family or friends. A payday loan is similar to a third mortgage on your house, said Linda Stern, a bankruptcy trustee with Mintz & Partners Ltd. It's a last resort for desperate borrowers.

The main hazard with payday loans is that you won't have the cash to pay back what you owe on the due date. You may have to roll over the loan and pay another set of interest and cheque-cashing charges. The loan may be extended again and again, until the interest burden is many times the original amount.

In a B.C. court case, an automotive fleet manager from Burnaby lost his 1992 Dodge Stealth after signing it over in return for a loan from Insta-Cash Loans of Nanaimo—a loan he later regretted, according to court documents in which he described the situation. In June 2002, after missed payments, Insta-Cash seized the car, worth up to $18,000.

- Loan received: $2,900.

- Cost of loan over one month: $1,400.

- Total repayable: $4,300.

The man couldn't make his repayment, so he extended—four times over four months, with a payment each month:

- February 2002: $1,200.

- March 2002: $1,200.

- April 2002: $1,200.

- May 2002: $1,200.

- Total additional costs: $4,800.

- Total cost to carry the five-month loan: $6,200.

- Total obligation arising from the loan: $9,100.

You work hard to trim your expenses and organize your finances. Finally, you have some money to invest. You set up an automatic debit from your bank account to buy mutual funds or stocks. You're ready to do some serious saving for your retirement or your kids' education or whatever goal you have in mind.

Then the stock market tumbles and tumbles and tumbles—three years in a row—until your hard-earned savings are shredded like confetti. You wonder what's the point of putting more money into your investments, only to lose it as you did before. And you know you'll barely keep pace with inflation if you switch to guaranteed investment certificates or government bonds, since interest rates are painfully low.

What do you do now? Find other types of investments that are going up in value? Hang on to what you already own but stop throwing new money into the stock markets? Hire a new adviser? Pay off your mortgage more quickly? Or forget investing and saving and spend money on travel, leisure and other things that improve your quality of life?

It's a dilemma. The past few years have been tough on investors, especially those who haven't been through an extended slump before. You learn not to trust the market rallies because you're afraid of getting your hopes dashed again. You read the business pages in your newspaper less often and you click off before the business broadcasts on TV. You may even (horror of horrors) throw out the letters showing how your investments are doing or throw them into a drawer unopened. You've lost the faith that sustained you.

In this section, we'll look at how to invest your money in bad markets (as well as good ones) and we'll try to figure out which investments shine when times are tough. While stocks began to rally in 2003, no one knows whether this is a real recovery or just a pause in an extended decline that will last for many years. Even if stocks stay strong, you still need to know how to survive a nasty bear market—since it can come back at any time.

What to do with your money in a bear market

A bear market is any period when there's a prolonged downturn of 20 per cent or more in stock indexes. Some people say the bear market that started in the spring of 2000 ended in March 2003. Others say this was a short-lived surge in prices and we're in for a much longer siege.

When you see a bear, what do you do? Play dead, say some investment experts. Fighting back can be dangerous, since it's hard to make big gains during a bear market unless you're a short seller. What if you don't have the patience to hold on to stocks as they relentlessly descend? What if a shrinking portfolio imperils your plans for early retirement or your children's education? And what if there's only a temporary rebound and we're mired in this mess for a long, long time?

I recognize that playing dead is not the only survival tactic. If stoicism is not your strong suit, you may prefer to take an active strategy and fine-tune your asset mix. Or you may want to get out of equities altogether. In the next few chapters, I'll look at alternative investments such as bonds, real estate, gold, income trusts and hedge funds.

Where did bear and bull markets get their names? The origins are unclear, says the definitive Investopedia.com Web site. One explanation is that the terms derive from the methods in which each animal attacks opponents. A bull will thrust its horns up in the air, while a bear will swipe down. Another explanation is historical. The middlemen who bought bearskins from trappers would sell skins they had not yet received, hoping that prices would drop. They became known as bears and, since bears fought bulls as a popular sport, the term bull became known as the opposite.

Since 1956, a bear market has occurred, on average, once every five years. The average bear market lasts about 10 months, although about 35 per cent of bear markets have lasted 1.5 to 1.8 years. The 2000 bear market was one of the longest in history. During the average bear market, stock prices decline by 25 per cent. By July 2002, U.S. stocks had fallen more than 40 per cent from their peak in March 2000. But this wasn't the worst bear market ever. In the great crash of 1929, the U.S. stock market lost 87 per cent of its value. And in the bear market of 1973 to 1974, the S&P 500 index fell 48 per cent. For a bear market to end, earnings at most leading companies have to start growing strongly again. But since the stock market anticipates things, stock prices usually recover a few months ahead of an earnings recovery.

Did all the high-profile business collapses depress stock prices? Well, they didn't help. But stocks had been falling for about 18 months before the first big scandal (Enron) unfolded. Big bankruptcies are typical after a big boom cycle, since a rising stock market helps a company mask its problems. When the stock market recedes, weaknesses are revealed at unstable companies that can no longer depend on high share prices to keep investors and debtors happy.

Should you buy falling stocks in a bear market? This can be a good move if you're a value investor who loves bargains. But first, you should pay off any credit card debt and set up a rainy-day fund. Don't put any money into stocks that you will need to withdraw for at least five years. And make sure you can handle volatility. Even when the market is near bottom, you can still experience sharp short-term losses.

Bear markets are also a good opportunity to re-examine what you own and get rid of things that no longer give you confidence. If you bought rashly or you didn't fully understand what you were buying and why, you won't have the strength to stick with your holdings as they fall below the purchase price.

Don't think you can sell everything during a bear market and buy back in later. Even the experts who watch stocks for a living can't predict all the ups and downs. Why should you do any better? When the recovery finally arrives, you may not react in time.

Investors who held on to their stocks through the bottoms of the 12 bear markets since 1945 gained an average 32.5 per cent in the first year of the market's recovery, according to a study by SEI Investments. Those who bought one week after the market began to rebound made a 24.3 per cent return, and those who missed the recovery by three months gained only 14.8 per cent in the same time period.

Strategies for investing during bear markets

What to do if you're blue? Don't be scared to admit you're scared. It's a normal reaction. "When the going gets tough, that's when you start to feel the pain of bad decisions and lack of planning," said Warren Baldwin, vice-president of TE Financial Consultants Ltd. in Toronto. A crisis can be a wake-up call to look at what you're doing and see if you can do better. "If you haven't waterproofed your tent and made sure all the hatches are battened down, you're not going to be a happy camper," he adds.

If slumping stock prices make you nervous and depressed, then you may be a fair-weather investor, less tolerant of risk than you think you are. Fair-weather investors should cut back on stocks if they're uncomfortable. Go through your portfolio systematically and decide whether you still like the investments you've chosen. Consider replacing volatile stocks or mutual funds with something more stable.

Cutting back on stocks may be smart, but selling all your stocks is a bad idea. You need to keep at least one foot in the market to get the best long-term growth. "There's a saying, 'If you can't stand the heat, get out of the kitchen.' But you can't afford to stay out of this kitchen," Baldwin said.

If you cashed in everything to buy bonds or guaranteed investment certificates, you would earn five per cent at most. But your
return would shrink to 2.7 per cent after you paid tax at the top marginal rate. After you factored in inflation of about two per cent, you
would make hardly any money.

There's just one scenario in which selling all your stocks makes
sense. If you hold stocks or mutual funds outside of a registered
retirement savings plan and you have personal loans and credit card
debt, get rid of your debt first. That's the best investment you can
make. "Don't put one cent into investments outside an RRSP unless
you pay off your high-interest debt," advises Jamie Golombek, vice-
president of taxation with AIM Funds Management Inc.

I'm not just talking about high-interest credit card debt at 18.5
per cent a year. Even if you owe money on a low-interest card at 9.5
per cent, you will do better to discharge the balance than to buy
stocks. Since you pay your debts with after-tax dollars, a 9.5 per cent
credit card rate is equivalent to a pre-tax investment return of about 19
per cent. "Unless you find an investment that can guarantee you
19 per cent before tax, it doesn't make sense not to eliminate debt,"
Golombek says.

Does the same advice apply to mortgages at four to six per cent
interest rates? Yes, if you have non-registered investments. You can
sell them and use the cash to pay off the mortgage, then take out an
investment loan and buy back the stocks you sold. This has the effect
of making your mortgage tax-deductible (since you can write off the
interest on your investment loan).

The Supreme Court of Canada upheld the principle of interest
deductibility in a 2001 case. A Vancouver lawyer named John Sin-
gleton withdrew $300,000 from the capital account of his law firm
and used the money to buy a home. He later borrowed $300,000
from a bank to repay his law firm. The Supreme Court said it was
fair to deduct mortgage interest since the borrowed funds could be
traced to a business-earning purpose. Canadians can sleep better at
night knowing their interest claims won't be challenged, unless the
federal government responds by changing the law. (This hasn't yet
happened.)

For a nervous investor, keeping one foot in the stock market means choosing lower-risk mutual funds and trusts that focus on income distribution and capital preservation. Look for funds that invest in large companies, suggests Peter Brewster, editor of the Canadian Mutual Fund Adviser. Large companies have market position, momentum in their businesses and staying power. They can usually survive better than small companies can when times get tough. "Just be sure you have plenty of time—at least five years—to hold even the most conservative of stock funds," he says.

Gordon Pape, author of an annual buyer's guide to mutual funds, has a similar view. Continue to build your holdings in well-managed equity funds, so you're well positioned to benefit from a market turnaround when it comes. Keep your risk to a minimum and choose funds that historically display a better-than-average safety profile. Bear markets are not a time to be overly aggressive.

Funds for cautious investors hold a lot of cash. Their ultraconservative managers stay away from stocks they think are overvalued. Sometimes they sell a holding and can't find anything to buy. A cash level of 5 to 10 per cent is normal for equity funds, since they need to cover redemptions. A cash level of 30 to 40 per cent is considered high.

Mackenzie Ivy Canadian and Mackenzie Ivy Foreign, two funds known as great bear market performers, tend to have cash levels in the 30 to 40 per cent range. The AIC American Focused Fund had just 8 per cent of its assets in stocks and 92 per cent in cash and short-term securities in June 2002. "Most funds in this country are fully invested with an average of only 5 per cent cash," manager Larry Sarbit told advisers. "They are tied to the stocks they own. If prices sink significantly, the value of most of these funds will be likewise pulled under water."

A year later, the $943 million AIC American Focused Fund still had 70 per cent of its assets in cash. The cautious manager had done some buying when markets rallied, but obviously wasn't ready to get fully invested. His results reflected that caution. In the three years ended June 30, 2003, Sarbit had a positive return of 9.1 per cent—compared to a 13.8 per cent loss for the S&P 500 index. But he lagged the market slightly (a 6.3 per cent gain in the fund, compared to 6.4 per cent for the index) in the three months from March 1 to June 30, 2003. Likewise, the two Mackenzie Ivy funds were lagging the market in 2003.

Dividend funds are good investments during a bear market. The average Canadian dividend fund gained 5.7 per cent annually during the three years to June 30, 2003, while the average Canadian equity fund lost 5.1 per cent. Dividend funds also outperformed Canadian equity funds over the longer 5-year and 10-year periods. That's because companies that pay dividends are large and solid and have real earnings. However, once the downturn ends, rising interest rates can hurt dividend funds.

What if you want to pick your own stocks? Where are the blue-chip companies suitable for sissies? I asked a few veteran stock pickers to name companies they could comfortably recommend as an investment for a 90-year-old widow or an 8-year-old child.

The golden rule for tough times: Find stocks that pay dividends. "I look for a dividend yield of three per cent or more," said Tom Caldwell, chairman of Caldwell Securities Ltd. in Toronto. "These companies won't make decisions that will jeopardize the dividend." Banks, telephone companies, pipelines, gas and electric utilities all pay out profits in dividends to shareholders. They're seen as stodgy in high-flying markets and relatively safe when other things collapse.

"The list gets thinner and thinner as we go along," said Douglas Davis, president of Davis-Rea Ltd. Investment Counsel of Toronto. A stock he owns and likes is Enbridge Inc., which distributes natural gas and sells retail energy. "It's well-managed and tends to do well in crummy markets. As long as the market is dropping, this is a defensive stock I'd like to have in my portfolio," he said. He also puts Canada's largest bank on the shopping list. Royal Bank of Canada, unlike some rivals, didn't get too heavily exposed to troubled telecom firms and pays a good dividend yield.

Tom Slee, who writes for Gordon Pape's *Internet Wealth Builder* newsletter, says investors should stick with old-fashioned businesses they understand. Pharmacy chains such as the Jean Coutu Group and Shoppers Drug Mart, he says, are attractive at a time when the

Canadian population is getting older and has greater demand for prescription drugs and cosmetics. Food is also a defensive sector. People always have to eat, no matter what the economy is doing.

Ross Healy, president of Strategic Analysis Corp. in Toronto, couldn't name a single stock suitable for widows and orphans. That was a good thing, in his view. "At the end of every decline, the market always hunts out and finds the last repository of safety and beats the heck out of it," said Healy, a well-known bear. "It happened with utilities when everyone went into them after the high-tech thing folded. When the banks get killed, we'll know it's all over and we can say the market has bottomed."

What about buying stocks you already own as the price falls? This strategy, known as averaging down, is often compelling to those with a keen sense of value. You look for a blue-chip company that has fallen sharply from its peak, because of profit warnings or a shift in investor sentiment.

Say, for example, you owned 100 shares of Bombardier Inc., Canada's premier aerospace company. You had bought them at $15 and you decided to pick up another 100 shares when they fell to $3.30 in June 2002. You were confident the company had a solid future and investors had overreacted. The new purchase would bring your average cost down to $9.25. As a result, your break-even point would be lower than before. You could sell at a profit when Bombardier hit $9.50 or so, not $15. The stock would have to go up three times in value, not five times, before you made money. (Unfortunately, Bombardier was still trading under $5 a year later.)

This behaviour is also driven by psychological factors. You may be reluctant to realize losses. Until you sell, you can convince yourself that your loss was just on paper. Averaging down means you postpone realizing a loss. But experts say you should average down on a stock only if nothing about it has changed except for the price. If some fundamental fact about the company's business has changed for the worse, then it's time to admit your initial mistake and take the loss.

You may also be nervous about buying stocks that have had a winning streak, feeling they're in danger of a fall. Stocks that have already crashed seem safer, and potentially more profitable, since they're "due for a run." The remedy to this flawed thinking is to look at real-world examples. The New York Yankees, a winning baseball team, come out near the top year after year. Some stocks that fall in price stay down and never recover. I'm not saying that will happen to Bombardier, though I have to say I sold my own shares in February 2002 at $12.77. (While I hadn't lost money, I was nervous.)

Stocks often fall in advance of bad news. You could be averaging down, thinking nothing is wrong, while a negative announcement is right around the corner. Nor is it safe to average down after a company releases the first bombshell, since there may be more to come. Bad news comes in clumps, as the ongoing saga of Nortel Networks Corp. has shown. Once there's a sign of vulnerability, investors hammer the company and scrutinize things even more closely, wondering if they'll find something else wrong.

"It is a dangerous fallacy to assume that because a stock goes down, it has to come back up. Many don't. Others take years to recover," said William J. O'Neil, former editor of the *Investor's Business Daily* newspaper, in his best-selling book, *How to Make Money in Stocks: A Winning System in Good Times or Bad* (McGraw-Hill Ryerson).

Letting your losses run is a serious mistake, O'Neil says. "I'd go so far as to say that if you aren't willing to cut short and limit your losses, you probably shouldn't buy stocks. Would you drive your car down the street without brakes?" He recommends limiting your losses on stocks and selling once they drop seven to eight per cent below the purchase price.

Mutual funds are an exception. He thinks it's smart to put a fixed amount of money into funds each month and hold them for the long haul. The difference is that a stock can go to zero. But a widely diversified and professionally managed fund will find its way back when the market gets better.

Bonds excel when times are tough

Don't put all your faith in stocks. That's the lesson to be learned during the bear market when portfolios that included bonds—no matter what the weighting—did better than portfolios with only stocks.

"The reason is simple: Fixed-income traditionally performs inversely to equity," says investment counsellor Richard Croft. When the economy falters and stocks decline, central banks start to cut short-term interest rates. Bond prices then rise, since investors are willing to pay a premium to get higher rates over the long term. Rising bond prices lead to handsome capital gains on top of the interest income.

It's hard to buy individual bonds if you don't have a large portfolio. You certainly won't replicate the Scotia Capital bond index, which is made up of a broad selection of government and corporate bonds across all maturity dates. Mutual funds are the best solution.

Several bond funds can keep up with the bond index, even after deducting their one to two per cent annual management fees. The TD Real Return Bond Fund had an annual return of 8.4 per cent over the three years to June 30, 2003. A real return bond pays a rate of return adjusted for inflation, a feature that safeguards your long-term purchasing power. Other top performers are McLean Budden

Fixed Income (8.2 per cent over three years) and Phillips Hager & North Bond (8.6 per cent).

Instead of an actively managed bond fund, you can also buy a bond index fund. Costs are kept low in order to produce an index-like return. Bond index funds are new and most don't have three-year records. The iUnits Government of Canada 10-Year Bond fund had a 13.1 per cent return in the year to June 30, 2003, while the iUnits Government of Canada 5-Year Bond Fund had a 9.9 per cent return. (The iUnits funds are traded on the Toronto Stock Exchange.) Several banks (TD, CIBC, Scotia and Royal) offer low-cost bond index funds.

Bonds do well during a bear market, but over longer periods of time stocks have beaten bonds by a wide margin. Ibbotson Associates in Chicago compared Canadian stock and bond performance from December 1939 to July 2002. The average annual return was 10 per cent for stocks and 6.3 per cent for bonds. That performance gap of 3.7 percentage points makes a huge difference when translated into dollars. If you had invested $1 in Canadian bonds on Dec. 31, 1939, you would have had $46.85 by July 2002. But if you had invested $1 in Canadian stocks, you would have had $396.13.

Canada Savings Bonds, unlike government of Canada bonds, never go up or down in price. There's no potential for capital gains to supplement your interest income. And if you're not careful, you could lose purchasing power by holding onto your CSBs for too long.

The Series 78 Canada Savings Bonds issued in fall 2002 paid a paltry two per cent interest rate for the first year. That was lower than Canada's inflation rate, then running at 2.3 per cent. I soon discovered that many people who already owned savings bonds didn't realize they would be earning the same two per cent, starting November 1, 2002. "It was my understanding that CSBs had a rate of interest that was maintained until maturity of the bonds," said one *Star* reader. "Thus, you knew what your income would be."

That's no longer the case. Since 1998, Canada Savings Bonds have been sold with rates that are guaranteed for no longer than one to three years. Rates are set according to market conditions. The Series 84 bonds, issued in November 2003, paid 1.75 per cent for one year.

The CSB Series 49, which came out in 1994, had a 12-year term to maturity. "But we priced it for only seven years. The rest of the years were not priced," explained Jacqueline Orange, president of Canada Investment and Savings, the federal agency that markets the bonds. The seven-year schedule ran out on November 1, 2001, when the rate dropped from 5.5 per cent to 1.8 per cent. It went up to two per cent on November 1, 2002.

It turns out that 1994 was one of the most successful years ever for CSB sales. The government sold $7.5 billion worth of Series 49 Canada Savings Bonds. They came out at a time when the stock market was in a slump; people were taking money out of mutual funds to buy them.

CSB sales are nowhere near the 1994 level, though the season is now six months instead of a few weeks. The government sold only $2.8 billion worth of savings bonds from October 1, 2001, to March 31, 2002. And there's a new product, the Canada Premium Bond, which pays higher rates but has redemption restrictions. In November 1994, the government had $32.7 billion worth of bonds outstanding—compared to $24.3 billion on March 31, 2002.

After the Series 49 sales blip, Ottawa had some success with savings bonds that paid escalating rates over many years. Series 51, issued in fall 1996, started at three per cent in the first year and went up to 8.75 per cent by the tenth year. They paid seven per cent for the year starting Nov. 1, 2002. Series 52 and 53, which came out in November and December of 1997, had a seven-year escalating rate structure. They paid 6.25 per cent starting in November 2002.

If you own any of these savings bonds (Series 51, 52 or 53), you should hold onto them until maturity. You won't find anything that gives you this much reward for such low risk. So take out your key and open that safety deposit box to see which CSBs you own. Then check the Web site, www.csb.gc.ca, or call 1-800-575-5151.

If you still hold Series 46 to 50, 54, 60, 66 or 72, which paid just two per cent starting in November 2002, or some later series that paid only 1.3 to 1.35 per cent, you should cash them in and find another interest-paying investment. You can do better elsewhere.

Canada Premium Bonds offer higher rates but less liquidity. Unlike CSBs, which can be cashed any time, the premium bonds are cashable once a year, on the anniversary date and 30 days afterward. Rates are not automatically adjusted each year as they are with most CSBs.

Norman, a *Toronto Star* reader, was unhappy with the lack of rate adjustment. He had assumed he would earn more interest on his premium bonds in future years if interest rates rose. "As I get older, I try to keep things simple," said the 80-year-old retired executive. "You've got to watch these bonds all the time. What if you're down in Florida? It's putting a burden on the family to do the right thing."

Canada Premium Bonds are guaranteed, but no changes are made to the rate after the issue date. In contrast, CSBs have a minimum guaranteed interest rate that is increased if market conditions warrant. "Most customers take the view that if the automatic adjustment was very important, they could buy the original Canada Savings Bond," said a spokeswoman for Canada Investment and Savings.

People buying these bonds may not realize that rates aren't adjusted each year. Norman didn't know. Nor did his investment adviser, who had to call Ottawa for confirmation. The Canada Premium Bonds go on sale each fall (as do CSBs) and can be purchased monthly from November to April.

Premium bonds with a fixed rate have a decided advantage when interest rates are falling. In that situation, you don't want an automatic adjustment. But when rates are going up, premium bonds are less attractive to those who don't want to worry about managing their portfolio. That point should be made more clearly to buyers.

Getting better rates from smaller banks

Guaranteed investment certificates are posting historically low rates, but they offer a form of loss insurance that is very tempting when the financial world goes haywire. A good strategy is to buy five-year GICs each year, using a laddered approach. Some of your money comes up for renewal each year and can be reinvested at current rates.

In August 2003, the big banks were paying 3.05 per cent on a five-year GIC with compound annual interest. Sure, the posted rate is negotiable. You can get an extra quarter or half a point interest if you're a good customer or you can bring new business their way. But there were higher GIC rates (up to 4.26 per cent) at smaller financial institutions, which don't have a costly branch network to maintain across Canada.

You can buy directly from some companies. But you can also get GICs from lesser-known financial institutions from deposit brokers, who shop the market for you without charging fees. Like travel agents, they get commissions from the companies whose products they sell. To find a deposit broker in your area, call the Canadian Federation of Independent Deposit Brokers in Barrie, Ontario (705-730-7599), or search for one near you at www.fcidb.com (click Broker Members).

Do you want to know how much more you would earn with a higher-rate GIC or savings account? Go to the Web site for Fiscal Agents, a big Toronto deposit broker (www.fiscalagents.com), and check the GICs Rate and Return Comparison calculator.

Here's an example:

- You invest $1,000 in Equitable Trust's five-year compound-interest GIC at 4.26 per cent.

- You invest another $1,000 in TD Canada Trust's five-year compound-interest GIC at 3.05 per cent.

- Equitable Trust pays annual interest of $213, while TD Canada Trust pays $152.50. That's a difference of $60.50 a year.

- At the end of five years, you have a total of $6,159.69 (deposit plus interest) with Equitable Trust. You have $5,810.45 with TD Canada Trust. When compounded, that adds up to a difference of $349 over five years.

If you want to hang loose while waiting for GIC rates to rise, you have lots of high-interest options. In August 2003, you could get 2.8 per cent on your savings at Amex Bank of Canada (1-888-453-2639, www.americanexpress.ca) and Manulife Bank of Canada (1-877-765-2265, www.manulifebank.ca). You could get 2.75 per cent at ING Direct (1-800-464-3473, www.ingdirect.ca) and President's Choice Financial, owned by Loblaw Companies Ltd. (1-888-872-4724, www.banking.pcfinancial.ca). You would earn these rates on the first dollar invested, with no minimum amounts required.

Among the Big Five banks, the Bank of Nova Scotia was the first to offer a high daily savings rate (2.4 per cent in mid-2003) with its Money Master savings account. It's a virtual account with online statements and unlimited free transfers if you use the telephone, ABM or Internet. For all other debit transactions (branch or ABM withdrawals, direct payment purchases, bill payments and pre-authorized payments), there's a $5 fee per transaction.

Play the market
with Warren Buffett

When the stock market slumped in 2000, value investing came back into style—and so did Warren Buffett. Ridiculed for not buying technology stocks during the boom years, Buffett was sitting pretty again. "We have embraced the twenty-first century by entering such cutting-edge industries as brick, carpet, insulation and paint. Try to control your excitement," the chairman of Berkshire Hathaway Inc. said in a recent letter to shareholders (www.berkshirehathaway.com).

Buffett, who's in his seventies, has an unabashedly old-fashioned approach that has served investors well. His holding company, Berkshire Hathaway, holds many different businesses—insurance, newspapers, shoes, furniture, jewelry, encyclopedias, soft drinks and razors—but no technology, telephone or Internet firms. If Buffett can't value a business over 10 years, he doesn't invest. "There are people who can analyze technology, but I can't," he said at his 1998 annual meeting.

From 1965 to 2002, Berkshire Hathaway's book value per share increased by 22.2 per cent a year. That's more than double the 10 per cent average annual gain in the Standard & Poor's 500 index (with dividends included). Berkshire Hathaway badly trailed the S&P in 1999, when technology was riding high (gaining 0.5 per cent versus

21 per cent for the index). But when tech stocks crashed in 2000 and the S&P index lost 9.1 per cent, Berkshire Hathaway's book value went up 6.5 per cent.

To get a piece of this phenomenal track record, you can buy a mutual fund that invests in Berkshire Hathaway shares. Your best bet is the AIC Group of Funds, whose founder Michael Lee-Chin reveres Warren Buffett as a god. The giant AIC Advantage and AIC Diversified Canada funds generally devote five to six per cent of their assets to Berkshire Hathaway.

Mutual funds, however, are required to limit their holdings of a single stock to 10 per cent at cost value. You may not find that enough. To get more exposure to Berkshire Hathaway, you have to buy the shares yourself.

I'm not suggesting you buy the Class A shares, which traded on the New York Stock Exchange for $76,000 (U.S.) apiece in August 2003 (more than a hundred grand in Canadian dollars). They've never split in almost 40 years. No, I'm proposing you buy the more affordable B shares, the Baby Berkshires, which sell at 1/30 of the price. They traded at $2,580 (U.S.) each on the NYSE in the same period (about $3,700 Canadian).

The company's holdings are so diverse that all you need are a few shares. I own three Baby Berkshires in my RRSP as a low-cost alternative to a U.S. mutual fund. They're a great buy-and-hold investment. I like Buffett's motto that his favourite holding period is forever.

Berkshire Hathaway believes in keeping overhead razor-thin. There's no legal, public relations or strategic planning staff at the headquarters in Omaha, Nebraska. The firm would have trouble fielding a softball team. "The company after-tax overhead corporate expense runs less than one per cent of operating earnings," says follower Robert G. Hagstrom in *The Essential Buffett* (John Wiley & Sons). Since mutual funds charge expenses of 2.5 to 3 per cent a year to investors, you can see Baby Berkshires are a cheaper way to play the U.S. market.

Another Buffett devotee, Robert P. Miles, makes the case for buying Berkshire Hathaway shares in *101 Reasons to Own the World's Greatest Investment* (John Wiley & Sons). "Like a mutual fund, an investor gets a low-cost basket of stocks along with the world's great-est investor with one purchase," he says. A purchase of Berkshire also gets you many benefits not available from a mutual fund, Miles argues:

- The chairman sits on the board of directors of three of the top holdings.

- Berkshire owns a portfolio of wholly-owned private businesses, which are just as diverse as the portfolio of publicly traded shares. Equities are only 25 per cent of its market valuation.

- Berkshire does not advertise.

- Berkshire helps successful entrepreneurs cash out by agreeing to be acquired. Its first choice of capital is to buy entire businesses.

"In the future, there will be years in which the S&P soundly trounces us," Buffett wrote in 2003. (His marvellously articulate let-ters to shareholders each year are posted at the Berkshire Hathaway Web site.) "That will in fact almost certainly happen during a strong bull market, because the portion of our assets committed to common stocks has significantly declined. This change, of course, helps our relative performance in down markets such as we had in 2002."

For the record, Buffett is still pessimistic about stocks. Despite three years of falling prices, he said in his 2003 annual report, "we still find *very* few that even mildly interest us. That dismal fact is tes-timony to the insanity of valuations reached during The Great Bub-ble. Unfortunately, the hangover may prove to be proportional to the binge."

Buffett also had some provocative comments about company boards. He will appoint as directors of Berkshire Hathaway only those who own millions of dollars' worth of company stock they pur-chased on their own. He pays his directors "a pittance" and won't provide liability insurance to directors (as do most boards), "not wanting to insulate our directors from any corporate disaster we may have."

How to earn income
with income trusts

Income trusts are a popular investment you might want to add to your portfolio during tough times. Think of them as a halfway house between riskier stocks and low-risk bonds or guaranteed investment certificates. Despite a spotty track record, income trusts are hot. There are a couple of hundred in the Canadian market, with a value of more than $60 billion.

Income trusts are a unique, home-grown product, made possible by our tax laws. There is nothing quite like them in the United States. "Normally, we take our lead on evaluating securities from Wall Street, but New York has little to teach us when it comes to assessing the merits of a particular income trust. We're pretty much on our own," says investment author Gordon Pape.

When you put your money into an income trust, you're buying a share of a commercial enterprise, similar to a share in a conventional corporation. But an income trust pays out most of its profits to investors—unlike a corporation, which can use the money it earns to reinvest in the business. An income trust, therefore, can be tough to manage since capital is tight.

The structural difference between trusts and corporations became an issue when then-Premier of Ontario Ernie Eves decided not to proceed with the planned sale of Hydro One, the province's electricity distribution business. Eves said Hydro One could become an income trust. The province would own the assets, but the cash flow generated by the assets would be paid out to Ontario's taxpayers. Income trusts work well for businesses that need little capital investment. But Ontario's power grid is aging and requires constant updating.

Income trusts not only pass through their cash flow to investors; they also pass through the tax breaks that would normally be claimed by a corporation in calculating its liability to the Canada Customs and Revenue Agency. Say, for example, you own units in a real estate investment trust like RioCan. Part of the payments you receive is sheltered by your share of the depreciation allowance on the properties the trust owns. This portion of the distribution is called "return of capital" and is not taxed in the year it's received.

"One person wrote to complain that he didn't want his capital back, he wanted to keep it invested," Pape writes in his *Internet Wealth Builder* newsletter. "Clearly, he did not grasp the concept. The trust is not really refunding your capital, it is simply passing on to you a tax deduction that it could claim itself if it were a corporation."

Many people switched into income trusts when markets tanked. Advisers had an obvious interest in encouraging this move, since it prevented clients from cashing out. Income trusts were one of the few high-margin products they could sell that investors wanted to buy.

But not everyone who buys this product truly understands it. Here are three important things to remember:

- Income trusts are equities, not fixed-income investments with a guaranteed payout.

- Most are small or medium-sized companies. Only a few (such as the Yellow Pages income trust) qualify as large, blue-chip securities.

- The businesses on which they're based may not be able to keep up the same steady cash flow from year to year.

Natural resources and energy firms are subject to market cycles, while real estate is susceptible to rising interest rates. The rising Canadian dollar hurt many income trusts, which price their products or services in U.S. dollars. There are many unpredictable events that can affect their cash flow and reduce distributions to investors. And, of course, the quality of the underlying assets may go down over time because of the lack of capital investment.

While it's true that income trusts provide stable income and some capital growth, there are no guarantees. Investors can also experience double-digit capital losses, as in the 1998 bear market.

The Scotia Capital Markets income trust index is a benchmark against which to measure your returns. Standard & Poor's and the Toronto Stock Exchange have created a more specialized index for energy trusts, and another for real estate investment trusts (REITs). In addition, Barclays Global Investors Canada Ltd. has launched an exchange-traded fund based on the S&P/TSX Canadian REIT Index. (Exchange-traded funds are similar to mutual funds, but have much lower management expenses.)

While investors are nervous about buying initial public offerings of stock, they're snapping up new income trusts. That has led to some unusual trusts based on restaurants, freezers and even beds (SCI Income Trust, the parent company for Simmons mattresses).

My advice: Choose carefully. Income trusts are difficult to analyze, so you should rely on recommendations from an investment adviser or other trusted source. Beware of income trusts that offer both high income and guaranteed repayment of principal. Some of these promises have proved to be unrealistic. An example is Pro-Ams Trust, which trades on the Toronto Stock Exchange (PAM.UN). Mulvihill Capital Management of Toronto raised more than $1 billion in March 2001, by offering an 8.5 per cent annual return through monthly cash distributions. These distributions were cut later to 6 per cent.

This type of trust guarantees capital by investing about half the proceeds in a strip bond. With the other half, it buys blue-chip stocks and tries to generate extra income with aggressive trading and derivatives strategies. But in a declining market, blue-chip stocks erode in value and the volatility needed for options trading isn't there. Investors get their money back, but not the income they hoped to achieve.

There's another risk with income trusts. You, the investor, could owe money to creditors if the trust were to go bankrupt and fail to pay off its debts. You could also owe money if the trust broke the law and had to pay claims for compensation. What's worse, you could be liable for more than the value of your trust units.

This is not a risk you face with shares of corporations, since limited liability is enshrined in the law. Canadians need new laws, giving those who invest in trust units the same protection against liability claims as those who invest in company shares.

While the liability risk is "very remote," it's a risk that should concern investors, says Toronto securities lawyer Stephen Erlichman. He uses the example of an energy trust that owns property in Alberta. There's a big oil spill and an environmental lawsuit, but the trust doesn't have enough assets or insurance to cover the claims. So why not take a shot at trying to get money from the unitholders? Lawyers may see this as a solution unless the law is changed to make unitholders invulnerable to claims.

"I suggest that no matter how remote the liability to unitholders may be, there should not even be an issue as to whether security holders could possibly be liable for claims against the trust," Erlichman said in a report to the Canadian Securities Administrators in 2000.

If your investment adviser hasn't said anything about the risk of unlimited liability, you can usually find a warning in the prospectus (under risk factors). Get a copy and read it to be sure.

Edward Jones, a large U.S.-owned brokerage firm, refuses to sell income trusts to its Canadian clients. "Unlimited liability is the reason," said president Gary Reamey. "People say it's a remote risk, but we're concerned that oil trusts can be hit with environmental lawsuits. We always ask whether an investment is in the long-term interest of conservative investors. Clients who want income can buy corporate bonds. For any perceived increase in income, why take the risk?"

With billions of dollars at risk, large pension funds can't take a chance on investing in securities that could expose them to unlimited liability. That's why income trusts are excluded from the S&P/TSX composite index. Standard & Poor's offers three separate indexes for income trusts, but keeps them out of the leading Canadian equity index.

"If income trusts were included in the S&P/TSX index, large investors that follow an indexing strategy would have to buy them," says Barbara Betanski, a trust analyst at Dundee Securities Corp. But pension funds have a responsibility under the law to safeguard members' savings. "They want to clear up the grey areas first," says the analyst. "They need everything in black and white before they buy."

No one I spoke to could cite an actual case where unitholders in a publicly traded trust were held liable for debts or damages. Still, everyone felt this could happen one day.

The Ontario government has promised to change the law so that investors in income trusts won't be responsible for damages—beyond their initial investment—if a trust goes bankrupt or loses a costly lawsuit. Alberta, too, is planning to close the loophole. If other provinces follow their lead, this could open the door to income trusts being included in Canada's key stock index, the S&P/TSX composite, and give a boost to share prices.

Income trusts are a fast-growth investment sector, representing six per cent of the total value of the Toronto Stock Exchange. Their popularity is easy to understand: They were one of the few investments posting positive returns in a bear market. Most income trusts provide yields clustered in the 9 to 11 per cent range. But the yield, by itself, can be misleading.

"A yield of 11 per cent implies that an investor who invests $100 will get $11 annually and $100 back at some point in the future," says Steven Kelman, a Toronto investment counsellor and author. "But with an income trust, you don't know whether the asset will be worth $100 down the road. If you buy an income trust that pays you 11 per cent for say 15 years, then stops paying—eliminating the $100 asset value—you will effectively have a total return of 7 per cent, reflecting the erosion of your capital over time."

Income trusts invest in income-producing assets, such as resources or real estate. Or they may be businesses where the revenues, after paying expenses, are distributed to unitholders instead of being put back into the company as capital expenditures. But trust distributions are not guaranteed and can be cut back when times get tough.

Sun-Gro Horticulture Income Fund, a peat moss grower, was forced to dip into its line of credit in 2003 to pay distributions after a later-than-normal planting season. The trust later cut its distributions and uncovered accounting irregularities. As a result, it traded at 20 per cent below its issue price at a time when trust values were rising. The yield went up to 12.2 per cent, reflecting the higher risk of the business.

Halterm Income Fund, which owns the largest container terminal on Canada's east coast, had to suspend payments to investors after the company lost two customers making up one-third of its container volume. The news shaved 72 per cent off the value of Halterm's units.

Think about investment trusts the same way you think about common dividends, Kelman says. The income is not a sure thing and may be cut or suspended. Do your homework and check the prospectus of any new trust you want to buy. For established trusts, you can check the annual and quarterly statements. All documents filed by Canadian public companies are available at the SEDAR Web site, www.sedar.com. (SEDAR stands for System for Electronic Document Analysis and Retrieval, and is the electronic filing system for the disclosure documents of public companies and mutual funds across Canada.)

There's a direct correlation between yield and risk. The higher the yield on an income trust at any given time, the greater the chance that it will not be able to sustain its current level of payments. "If income stability is important to you, focus on trusts that are currently yielding less than eight per cent," Pape says. If you opt for a trust with a higher yield, understand that you have a greater chance of a distribution cut down the road. If you are prepared to accept that risk, go ahead.

Understand what a company does and the business risks it faces. Look for stable distributions. Look at the company's debt to see whether interest rates are fixed or floating. If interest rates move higher, debt costs will rise, leaving less for distributions.

Finally, consider buying a mutual fund that invests in income trusts. You have lots of options. There were 40 Canadian income trust funds in 2003, up from 10 funds in December 1999. Mutual funds allow you to redeem your units any time at the net asset value. Funds also provide diversification, since your money will be spread among many income trusts. And you're delegating the risk analysis to a professional manager. Mutual fund managers tend to shy away from untested new issues on the Toronto Stock Exchange. Of the 10 income trusts most widely held by these funds, all had been around for at least five years.

As well as open-ended mutual funds, there are several closed-end funds that trade on the Toronto Stock Exchange. Closed-end funds often trade below their net asset value, which can frustrate investors when they want to sell their units.

If you want diversification, you can also invest in a real estate investment trust, or REIT. This is a pool of mature properties that distribute most of their rental income to investors. The CIBC World Markets Canadian REIT index showed an 8.7 per cent increase in the first six months of 2003, slightly less than the 9.1 per cent gain for the Toronto Stock Exchange/Standard & Poor's composite index. (You can follow the index at www.cibcwm.com; click "Industry Expertise," then "Real Estate," then "Insights," then "Canadian REIT Report.")

REITs offer potential capital gains, as well as stable income and tax advantages. You get more tax breaks holding them outside a registered retirement savings plan, since the depreciation (or wear and tear) on buildings flows through to investors. But if you invest only inside an RRSP, don't give up the opportunity to own REITs as a way to diversify your portfolio.

Some REITs, notably those in the hotel industry, took a hit in 2003 because the SARS outbreak in Toronto hurt tourism. For example, the

Legacy Hotels income trust, which owns 22 luxury and first-class hotels and resorts in Canada, said it wouldn't pay a second-quarter distribution to unitholders because of the impact of severe acute respiratory syndrome and other problems. That's why it pays to be diversified and buy several types of REITs. They're an interest-sensitive investment, meaning the price of your units could go down if interest rates go up substantially. But as long as the economy stays strong and interest rates low, the outlook for REITs is rosy.

Peace of mind investing with segregated funds

If you've been badly mauled by the bear market, you may be willing to pay a premium for segregated funds and sleep soundly knowing your capital is guaranteed. "Segregated funds have come back into vogue, now that people are seeing stock markets go down and stay down," says Cliff Oliver, a Toronto insurance broker. "Sure there's a cost, but the peace of mind is worth it."

Segregated funds are a life insurance product. The name comes from the fact the assets are held separately, or segregated, from those of the insurance company. In recent years, mutual fund managers have also started adding capital guarantees, insured by a life company, to many popular funds.

Older segregated funds offer a 100 per cent guarantee of your initial capital after 10 years (or when you die). But nervous industry regulators have forced insurance companies to cut back their generous guarantees. Most segregated funds now refund 75 per cent of your capital on maturity.

Some of these funds offer a reset feature, which allows investors to wait till stock markets are high and lock in these gains at any time. But the reset feature, if used, extends the maturity date when the capital guarantee kicks in.

I asked Rob Bell, senior vice-president of Morningstar Canada, for a profile of segregated funds in Canada. Here are some numbers:

- They represent just over 10 per cent of the fund universe. Assets in segregated funds are $49 billion, compared to $470 billion for mutual funds, labour-sponsored and other funds.

- The average management-expense ratio for Canadian equity funds is 2.9 per cent for segregated and 2.4 per cent for non-segregated funds. The average MER for Canadian balanced funds is 2.7 per cent for segregated and 2.2 per cent for non-segregated funds.

- The average annual return for Canadian equity and balanced funds, both segregated and non-segregated, is almost the same over most time periods. Segregated funds trail by up to half a percentage point, reflecting the higher costs.

"It looks like the extra insurance policy is worth it if you think we're heading into a Japanese-type market," Bell said. Japanese stocks were depressed for a decade and lost half their value. In such a case, segregated fund holders would end up ahead by getting back 75 per cent or 100 per cent of their original investment.

Segregated funds offer other benefits that can make the higher costs worthwhile for some people. Unlike mutual funds, they provide a death guarantee that covers 75 to 100 per cent of your capital when you die. The death benefit is attractive to older people or those in uncertain health. You can remain fully invested throughout your life, "without having to retreat into low-paying, ultra-conservative securities for fear of jeopardizing the value of your estate," say Gordon Pape and Eric Kirzner in *Secrets of Successful Investing* (Viking Canada).

Is it worth paying an extra half a percentage point a year for segregated funds? That depends on how much of a pessimist you are. Pape and Kirzner think it's highly unlikely that a well-diversified, conservatively managed equity fund will lose money over a 10-year period, especially now that stock markets have gone through a major correction. The chance of a bond or balanced fund losing money is even less. "We don't believe maturity guarantees are needed at all, except for the most speculative funds, and few investors are likely to be interested in those these days," they say.

Still, segregated funds can be useful for estate planning purposes. The assets pass directly to your survivors when you die, bypassing probate and costly probate fees. If you're the kind of person who buys insurance for everything, why not insure your investment portfolio, too? If the bear market comes back, you'll be happy you did.

Hedging some of your bets

Hedge funds are an enigma to the average investor. Either you've never heard of them or you've heard very bad things about them. But hedge funds gain appeal when stock markets turn sour. As their dreams of retirement and children's education retreat ever further into the future, people start to get tired of the same old buy-and-hold approach. That's where hedge funds come in, since they offer alternatives to traditional investment strategies.

"The universe of hedge funds is as broad and diverse as the universe of mutual funds," says Miklos Nagy, publisher of a bimonthly newsletter called *Canadian Hedge Watch*. (For highlights, go to www.canadian-hedgewatch.com.) You can get a list of current Canadian offerings (with links to the managers) at www.hedge.ca, sponsored by Montrusco Bolton Investments, a terrific resource for comparison-shopping investors.

There is no simple definition of hedge funds, Nagy admits. They are defined by their characteristics, including a non-traditional strategy, a focus on risk rather than reward, reduced correlation to traditional markets and a performance-based fee structure for managers.

These are the early days of alternative investing. Most money comes from professional investment managers and affluent investors.

Hedge funds are not suited to, and are often barred from, registered retirement plans, because they use high-risk strategies.

It's a challenge for investors to analyze a manager's strategy. Short-selling stocks is one of the tools. (This means they borrow shares they do not own and wait for the price to drop, so they can sell them at a profit.) Hedge fund managers can also borrow money, using leverage to intensify gains or exaggerate losses. And unlike mutual fund managers, they can put more than 10 per cent of the portfolio into a single holding.

"Selecting hedge funds is a much more difficult task than choosing mutual funds," says *Canadian Hedge Watch*. "Potential investors must either carry out due diligence for themselves or trust their financial advisers to narrow down and then select hedge funds."

A "fund of funds" structure helps reduce risk. Essentially, you hire an expert to check out each hedge fund manager and build a portfolio of hedge funds into one investment. The advantage of a fund of funds is having a professional manager looking after all investment and monitoring decisions for you, Nagy says. The disadvantage: "The fees are higher than traditional investing." You pay fees on each hedge fund, as well as to the fund-of-funds manager.

Let's be honest: No investment is a sure-fire thing. Hedge funds are designed to perform in bull or bear markets, but some managers are better than others. The results depend on which strategy they use and how skilled they are.

Sprott Hedge Fund LLP was a top performer in 2001 (up 64.2 per cent) and 2002 (up 74 per cent). From the fund's launch in November 2000, the fund manager Eric Sprott did a brilliant job of taking short positions in large U.S. stocks, such as GE, Microsoft and IBM, and long positions in gold, energy and income trusts. The fund grew so large that it was closed to new investors in July 2002 and a new clone fund was opened up.

Both Sprott hedge funds lost 25 per cent of their value when stock markets recovered in the first half of 2003. This was at a time when the S&P/TSX index went up 6.7 per cent. "We essentially cut our short exposure in half across all our long/short portfolios to roughly 40 per cent," Sprott explained in a quarterly report in June 2003, "in an effort to minimize volatility and short-term losses during what we believe to be a highly dramatic market upswing that seems excessive and unsustainable." His largest remaining short positions were in Canadian and U.S. financial institutions, housing and consumer products.

At least Sprott made money during the bear market. Many hedge funds showed the same negative numbers as stocks and mutual funds. That's not why you buy them and what you expect them to do.

"Mutual funds are highly correlated with the stock market, so there's a lot of market risk," says Steve Kangas, a consultant and managing editor of the Fund Library (www.fundlibrary.com), an Internet site for investors. "Hedge funds move differently from the market, but you're totally dependent on the manager's skills and talent. With hedge funds, you're trading off market risk for manager risk."

Financial advisers generally aren't up to speed on hedge funds, Kangas says. There are no formal courses they have to take and the category isn't big enough to support a full-time analyst.

Because of the potential for losing your shirt, you can't get into a hedge fund in most provinces unless you have a six-figure income and a net worth in the seven figures. And some managers, such as Sprott, insist on a $150,000 minimum investment.

There's pressure on securities regulators to open hedge funds to less well-heeled investors. But I think that would be premature until financial advisers get more training in hedge funds. We also need more transparency for do-it-yourself investors. Until then, if you don't have big bucks to invest, you have to sit on the sidelines or try some of the new hybrid investments.

Index Plus Tactic, for example, requires a $500 minimum investment. Your capital is guaranteed at maturity and you have the chance to earn higher returns with a fund-of-funds approach using 25 to 30 hedge managers. Classified as an annuity product, with investments protected up to $60,000 by a life insurance compensation fund, Index Plus Tactic is marketed by Desjardins Financial Security Life Assurance Co. and sold online at www.finactive.com.

GPR Hedge Fund Notes is a fund-of-funds product that trades on the Toronto Stock Exchange. There's a $5,000 minimum investment and your capital is guaranteed by Citibank Canada at maturity in November 2011. For information, go to www.triaxcapital.com.

For pessimists, gold hasn't lost its lustre

Investment experts often recommend keeping 5 to 10 per cent of your assets in gold stocks or precious metals funds. The reasoning is simple: Gold moves in the opposite direction to stock markets and the U.S. dollar. It helps stabilize a portfolio and protect it against disasters. But gold's role as disaster insurance came under question in the 1990s, when the price of bullion barely moved. Today, many popular commentators don't favour gold at all. "I used to be of the view that you should hold a little gold as insurance. But it's not something I do," says financial author Gordon Pape. "I see it as just another commodity, good for those who like to play commodities. It's only for aggressive investors. I wouldn't put any gold in a registered plan. It's too volatile."

Gold sank to $253 (U.S.) an ounce in August 1999, when stocks were surging. With the bursting of the technology bubble, gold climbed close to $330 an ounce. But it fell below $310 when the stock market rallied. This prompts the question: Is it too late to invest? Have I missed the cycle?

If you're a value investor, someone who prefers buying near the bottom rather than close to the top, a stock market rally is not the time to get into gold. Precious metals funds had a big run-up in 2002.

Some doubled in value. RBC Precious Metals Fund had a 153.1 per cent gain, AGF Precious Metals was up 103.8 per cent and Mackenzie Universal Precious Metals was up 89.7 per cent.

Over the five years to June 30, 2003, the Mackenzie Universal fund is the best performer with a 20.5 per cent average annual return. The RBC fund shows an 18.8 per cent annual gain and the AGF fund has a 12.8 per cent annual gain. One fund, StrategicNova World Precious Metals, has a 1.9 per cent annual loss.

Precious metals funds are volatile since they invest in junior mining companies as well as established firms. When the price of gold goes up 10 per cent, a gold fund may move up 30 per cent. Investors typically have one terrific year, followed by several flat or down years. The infrequent good times make up for the bad.

For example, the Royal Precious Metals Fund has an average annual return of 12.4 per cent over the 10 years to June 30, 2003. That's a very solid performance. But you can get goose bumps when you check out the fund's biggest gain in a one-year period (163.7 per cent) and the worst loss (45.3 per cent). The fund lost 10.2 per cent in the first six months of 2003, when the stock market rallied.

Market timers may want to stay out of gold. But it's always a good time to invest if you're a pessimist by nature and you're looking for a store of value in uncertain times. Those who prefer gold bars to gold shares should look at the Millennium Bullion Fund, which invests equal amounts in gold, silver and platinum at the spot price. The tiny fund ($8.6 million in assets) had a 14.7 per cent loss in the first six months of 2003, lagging the performance of the TSX gold and precious metals index (down 13 per cent). You can read the prospectus (and much else) at the Web site, www.bullionfund.com.

Advisers should reach out to jittery clients

When things are falling apart, do you know where your financial adviser is? Consider yourself lucky if you get a call from your stockbroker, mutual fund dealer, insurance agent or banker during a crisis. Many people are out there alone, feeling anxious and abandoned by an adviser who's missing in action.

Your investment representatives should be communicating with you. It's the least you can expect for the fees or commissions you're paying. If you're not getting phone calls, letters or personal visits, why aren't you demanding more? Instead of being cast adrift, you might as well fire your adviser and find another one. Or consider becoming a do-it-yourself investor.

I talked to a couple of independent experts about what clients should be getting from their advisers when stock markets collapse and portfolios get punctured. The answer: A heck of a lot of hand-holding.

"Smart financial advisers should be on the phone 12 hours a day, talking to people and seriously reviewing their accounts, making sure they're properly balanced for the individual," said author Gordon Pape. He knows it's not happening because he gets so much email from abandoned investors at his Web site, www.buildingwealth.ca.

Even when advisers do call clients, they're often just pushing a point of view. "Hang in there," they say. "The market will rebound. You just have to be patient." That advice may work if your portfolio is well diversified and worth holding onto in good markets and bad. But what about the stuff you own that should have been dumped when the bull market peaked in the spring of 2000?

It's never too late for you and your adviser to change your asset mix, Pape insists: "If the investor is too heavy in equities, I'd say rebalance." He suggested shifting from growth stocks to value stocks, or from growth funds to value funds. A bear market demands different investments, solid and boring things you may not have looked at before. Your adviser should be bringing them to your attention.

Kelly Rodgers is a self-employed investment consultant who helps affluent clients (with $1 million or more) find the right money managers. She, too, thinks investors should ask more of their advisers. "Those with accounts of less than $200,000 or $250,000 generally don't receive a lot of personal contact," she said. "They're lucky if they get an annual phone call at RRSP season to say, 'Hi, are you sending me more money?' Most of their contact is with administrative assistants."

Here's a checklist against which you can rate your investment adviser:

- Do you get statements on a regular and timely basis? Once a year doesn't make it.

- Do you have telephone or Internet access to your account?

- When you get your statement, can you easily understand it?

- Do you know the annual percentage rate of return on your entire portfolio?

- Do you know how well you're doing relative to accepted benchmarks?

Moving an investment portfolio is expensive and takes forever—and may get you no better results than you had before. To improve your odds of success with advisers, you have to ask the right questions. The input you give at the beginning of a relationship will yield a better output in the long run.

The Canadian Securities Administrators, an umbrella group for 13 provincial and territorial securities commissions, gets more complaints about investment advisers than anything else. Unsuitability—a mismatch between investor and investment—is the perennial beef. Clients blame advisers for pushing them into things that exceed their comfort with risk. But sometimes clients are at fault, because they don't make their investment needs clear.

In a booklet called "Choosing Your Financial Adviser," available from the CSA Web site (www.csa-acvm.ca), there's a checklist of questions to ask that will make you a better-informed buyer:

- What products and services do you sell? How are you paid? Do you face any conflicts of interest that may taint your recommendations?

- Do you specialize in a particular type of investment product (speculative securities, blue-chip stocks, mutual funds) or a particular clientele (conservative investors, people with high net worth, speculators, institutions)?

- What products are you or your firm registered to sell? How long have you been registered? Do you operate in other provinces? How many employees do you have?

- Do you provide advice and research, as well as trading? Do you have an internal research department that will give me reports? Do you offer educational seminars for clients?

- Have you or your firm been subject to any disciplinary proceedings in the past few years? What about the suppliers and others you're dealing with?

- Is the firm a member of a contingency fund designed to protect clients in case of insolvency? If so, what coverage does the fund provide?

- Can you give me references from clients? How big is your client list and what's the size of the average client's portfolio?

- How does the firm charge for its services? What commission rates or fees would a client like me expect to pay?

If you're buying mutual funds, make sure the adviser explains and itemizes fees. You'll find a checklist for fund buyers at www.investorism.com:

- What are the sales charges? Are they imposed up front or when I sell?

- If there's a deferred sales charge, does it apply to the initial price I paid or the market value? What's the deferred-charge percentage each year and when does it disappear?

- Can I withdraw 10 per cent of my investment each year without attracting a DSC?

- Is there an early withdrawal penalty in the first 60 or 90 days?

- How do I give directions to sell the fund: In person, by fax, by phone, in writing, by email? What time do I have to give my request for a same-day sale?

- What is the annual management-expense ratio (MER)? Can you show it as a percentage of fund assets and also in dollars and cents?

- Does the MER include an annual trailer fee paid by the fund manager to you or your firm? What is the percentage and the dollar amount?

- Do I pay extra advisory fees (on top of the MERs) for a managed portfolio of funds or wrap account?

- Is there an MER performance bonus when the fund exceeds its benchmark return? How much?

- Are you allowed to sell funds that don't pay sales commissions and/or trailer fees to distributors?

For example, ask the adviser if he could sell you a Phillips, Hager & North fund. "I've never heard of Phillips, Hager & North," is the wrong answer. Established in 1964, Vancouver-based PH&N is one of Canada's largest independent fund managers, with below-average management-expense ratios. An adviser who doesn't know about these funds is either new to the industry or prefers to sell products that pay better. In either case, you should look for someone else.

Many people would like to dump their advisers, but don't think they could find anyone better. They're cynical and distrustful of the whole financial services industry, as well they should be. "The industry has to change the way it markets to clients," says Barry LaValley, a former adviser who thinks the current approach is irrelevant and outdated.

Advisers have sold themselves as experts in picking stocks and mutual funds and one-size-fits-all investment solutions. The focus has been on products and performance. But when clients' accounts are shrinking, advisers have to come up with a new value proposition, something that makes their services worthwhile.

LaValley, who's in his late forties, has a 10-year-old son and a 75-year-old mother who's just started dating again. He's part of the sandwich generation, the group he thinks financial advisers should target by helping them connect to their deeper values and figure out what they want to do with the rest of their lives. Instead of financial planning, they should do life planning.

"We've treated money and its performance as an absolute," he said. "But the older you get, the more contextual you get. You relate your money more closely to what you're doing in your life." Financial advisers feel uncomfortable talking about issues that don't relate to money, so it won't be an easy transition. But LaValley suggests they bring in specialists in areas such as health and fitness, leisure and careers to work with baby boomer clients.

Financial considerations aren't the only barrier to Freedom 55. Many people find meaning and satisfaction on the job. Rather than looking forward to a life of leisure, they want to keep working at their own pace, reinventing themselves and finding new challenges. This desire has led to the growth of Web sites that are helping people redefine their mission in mid-life and retool for the next 20 or 30 years.

Joanne Fritz, www.notyetretired.com, offers advice for those looking to find jobs in retirement or start a post-retirement business, along with profiles of people who successfully passed up retirement.

Howard and Marika Stone, www.2young2retire.com, provide stories of 70 real people who have adopted new careers. The Stones, who left careers in publishing and writing in 1998 to start the Web site, think it's time to retire the word 'retirement' from your vocabulary. "Look it up: It means to withdraw or to retreat. Words can shape reality and it's time for this one to go," they say. "Doesn't 'renaissance' or 'graduation' better define your post-career life?"

Watch out for an adviser's conflict of interest

A writer friend in her late 60s, who had limited knowledge of investing, wanted my advice. Should she stay with her current investment adviser, who had switched to another firm, or find a new adviser? I looked at her portfolio, which was invested conservatively, and the documents she showed me. Everything seemed to be in order. Then, as an afterthought, she pulled out the "know your client" form that investors are supposed to fill out in consultation with their advisers. The form said she was an experienced investor who wanted to take the highest risks in order to get the greatest growth possible.

"Did your adviser consult you before filling this out?" I asked, wondering why he had created a profile that was more appropriate for someone half her age. No, she replied. Her adviser had not consulted her about the know-your-client form, nor had he even brought it to her attention.

I explained to her why it's important to have an accurate profile of your investment knowledge, experience and tolerance for risk. It can be used as evidence in case you have a dispute about whether the adviser has recommended an unsuitable investment.

If my friend had left the know-your-client form as it was, she wouldn't be able to argue later that an investment was unsuitable.

Her adviser had falsely identified her as an aggressive investor, letting himself off the hook for any future lawsuits or disciplinary action. Once I told her this, she immediately hired a new adviser.

The know-your-client rules are part of a regulatory system that is sadly outdated. It's based on products, rather than on relationships between investment advisers and their clients. That's why the Ontario Securities Commission put forward a new "fair dealing model" and created an interactive Web site (www.fairdealingmodel.com) to bring the concepts to life for average investors.

"The compensation system is not structured to promote fair dealing," said Julia Dublin, senior legal counsel for the commission, when talking about the conflicts of interest faced by investment advisers. On the Web site, there are several case studies of real-life compensation schemes that benefit advisers and hurt clients. One case study involves a firm with investment advisers who sell proprietary or house-brand mutual funds, as well as those managed by outside companies. The house-brand funds are more profitable for the firm, which in turn pays higher commissions to advisers selling these funds.

As well, advisers are encouraged to borrow money from the firm to acquire equity ownership. This creates an incentive for them to earn the highest possible commissions in order to pay off the loans. But clients suffer, because they pay higher management fees for house-brand funds than the industry standard.

In another case study, a mutual fund manager has an existing fund with relatively low costs for investors and low commissions for advisers. The company starts another fund that is identical, except for higher costs and commissions. Advisers prefer to sell the higher-cost fund, which gives them a bigger payback, not just up front but every year the client owns the fund. But investors lose out if they buy the recommended fund. It's exactly the same as another they could get more cheaply and doesn't perform as well (because of the higher costs).

Such abuses were highlighted in former Ontario securities commissioner Glorianne Stromberg's two hard-hitting reports on mutual fund regulation, released in 1995 and 1998. Disappointingly,

Stromberg was not given credit, though she's the one who got the ball rolling.

Why has it taken regulators so long to develop a fair-dealing model? This is only a proposal, which leads to a concept paper and more feedback. At the earliest, we could see new legislation in late 2004 or 2005, a decade after Stromberg's first report. "The issues have been flogged to death, but the solutions are long in coming," she told me. "Given the abuses the regulators know are taking place, how do they justify not moving ahead with the things they know are sadly lacking?" The know-your-client rules and suitability, in particular, should be cleaned up as soon as possible. "What are they waiting for?" Stromberg asked.

Frank is another investor who didn't recognize an adviser's conflict of interest. Now 67 and retired for 10 years, he got in touch with me because he didn't understand what was going on with his investments. His RRSP portfolio—invested two-thirds in mutual funds and one-third in bonds—was worth $175,000 and had dropped $12,500 since he had moved to a new investment dealer less than a year earlier.

Frank owned 13 equity and balanced funds, worth about $120,000, spread among several well-known managers (AGF, Trimark, Fidelity, Mackenzie and Templeton). Seven of the thirteen funds had deferred sales charges, ranging from four to six per cent and not maturing until 2008 or 2009. He would face substantial penalties if he sold the funds—a total of $7,878 in deferred sales charges—that would only compound his losses.

Why would a long-time retiree hold such a portfolio? He would have been better buying funds with up-front commissions (or front-end loads). The deferred sales charges (DSCs) were inappropriate for Frank, who would soon be taking money out of his RRSP to fund his living costs. These taxable withdrawals would not go as far if he had to pay a DSC each time.

To make things worse, Frank's adviser wanted to redeem some units right away and use the proceeds to invest in funds with no DSCs. (Most funds allow withdrawals of 10 per cent a year without penalty.) These redemptions would make Frank better off in the future—but they would help his adviser, too, since he'd earn twice the fees on the new fund units (one per cent annually, compared with 0.5 per cent before, paid for ongoing service to clients).

"I'm hoping it's a win-win situation for both sides," the adviser said about the higher fees. He told me he had made little money from Frank's portfolio so far and he had spent lots of time with him, talking at least once or twice a week on the telephone. But he hadn't explained to his client's satisfaction what he was doing with the portfolio. And once I explained, Frank moved on to another adviser.

One way to avoid conflicts with an adviser is to write down everything you want at the start of the relationship. This is called an investment policy statement and it's standard practice with large institutional clients. Having a written plan helps you stick to your principles when you're prone to euphoria (at the top of the market) and panic (at the bottom of the market). It's designed to take the emotion out of investing.

Here are some elements of an investment policy statement:

- What are you saving for: Retirement, post-secondary education or buying a home? Once you know where you're going and your investment needs, you can determine what rate of return will accomplish that goal.

- Does the risk you're willing to take match your goals? Say you need a 10 per cent return, but you don't want to invest in anything except GICs and short-term bond funds. Historically, these types of investments have not provided that high a return over the long run. You'll have to adjust your goals or your willingness to take risk.

- What asset classes and investment vehicles are most appropriate for your needs? You may want to prescribe certain limits—for example, no more than 65 per cent in equities; 25 per cent in bonds; and 10 per cent in cash. You could be more specific and say you won't buy certain types of investments, such as initial public offerings, junk bonds, commodities or emerging markets.

- What method will you use to rebalance the allocation when it gets out of whack? What benchmarks will the portfolio be measured against?

- If you use mutual funds, do you want primarily index funds, actively managed funds or a combination? Do you plan to pick individual stocks? Do you prefer growth or value stocks? Do you prefer government bonds or corporate?

- How important is minimizing taxes to you?

- What do you expect of the adviser? How often do you want to meet? What kind of information do you want to be provided? How much time are you willing to spend monitoring your investments?

Writing down these issues forces you to think out your investment strategies and stay on track. Once you and your adviser agree to the terms, you should sign and date the document and keep a copy on hand for reference. Although it's not a legal contract, it's an agreement between you, to be revised when appropriate. You and your adviser can go back to the investment policy statement for guidance and clarification if there's any misunderstanding or dissatisfaction with the portfolio in the future.

Investing in your business

As hard as you try to save for the future, you may come up short. One solution is to start a business while you're still working, a business that can generate a decent income when you're retired. Many of us already have a hobby that can be turned into a paying gig. Before we get to the hard facts—the type of ownership, the business plan, the sources of capital—let's spend some time on the soft stuff. Do you have what it takes to succeed in business?

Life as an entrepreneur is a mixed bag, say Margaret Kerr and JoAnn Kurtz, authors of *The Canadian Small Business Kit For Dummies* (John Wiley & Sons). Yes, there are advantages: You're free, you can be creative, you have new challenges and increased financial opportunities. And your job will be secure as long as you have a business. But there's a hefty list of negatives that may outweigh the positives. You may not make a lot of money. Worse, you may go bankrupt and lose not only your business but most of your personal possessions as well. You have to work really hard and you may not have a lot of free time. And you lose your paid holidays and employment benefits, unless you hang on to a job elsewhere.

You may have to put a lot of your own money into starting up the business. Even if you can borrow, you have to give personal guarantees that the money will be repaid within a certain time. You have to keep on top of changes in your field, the impact of new technology, economic fluctuations and new rivals coming in and taking away your customers.

Besides having the right temperament, you need the practical skills to start and run a business. Here's a checklist you can use to assess your personal strengths and weaknesses, taken from a U.S. Web site called the Business Owner's Toolkit (www.toolkit.cch.com):

- Sales skills: Pricing, buying, sales planning, negotiating, direct selling to buyers, customer service follow-up, managing other sales reps, tracking competitors.

- Marketing: Advertising, promotion, public relations, marketing plans, media planning and buying, copy writing, distribution channel planning, pricing, packaging.

- Financial planning: Cash-flow planning, bank relationships, managing credit lines.

- Accounting: Bookkeeping, billing, payables and receivables, profit and loss statements and balance sheets, tax preparation.

- Administrative: Scheduling, payroll handling, benefits administration.

- Personnel management: Hiring, firing and motivating employees.

- Personal business skills: Oral and written communications, presentations, computer literacy, organization.

- Intangibles: Ability to manage risk and stress, ability to deal with failure, ability to work alone, ability to work with and manage others, family support.

Rate your skills in these areas from one (low) to five (high). Then add up the numbers. If you score less than 20, you should reconsider whether owning a business is the right step for you. If your score is between 20 and 25, you're on the verge of being ready. But you may be wise to spend time strengthening some of your weaker areas. If your total is 25 or more, you're ready to start a business now.

Develop a road map for your business

Asaf Shad decided to strike out on his own when his employer, Retirement Counsel of Canada, was sold to Berkshire Investment Group. He started his company, Acquaint Financial Inc., with five employees, a Toronto office, a Web site (www.acquaintfinancial.com) and a focus on financial counselling and education for employees. "The key element is to have a business plan," said Shad, 26, who had an honours degree in commerce from the University of Toronto. "It takes a lot of time. Ours took six months. That's a full-time job in itself."

Lenders look for a business plan so they know the kind of risks they're taking. They want to see projections of income, cash flow and expenses. A business plan also provides a road map of where you're going and how you'll get there. As well as numbers, a business plan should include strategies for marketing, sales, operations and management.

Gary Lok, the small business adviser with the city of Toronto's Economic Development Office, has seen business plans written on napkins and other stray bits of paper. "Writing a plan is very easy, but gathering research takes up to several months," Lok says. "It's quite detailed and complex."

So where do you go for information? A good place to start is the Canada Business Service Centres, a cross-country network sponsored by the federal and provincial governments. (Call 1-800-567-2345 in Ontario or check the Web site, www.cbsc.org/ontario.) Each centre has an extensive and up-to-date reference collection, as well as information officers to help you navigate your way through all this data.

Toronto's Economic Development Office runs Enterprise Toronto, a CBSC network partner that handles 40,000 inquiries and 600 consultations a year. "We'll assess your idea," Lok says. "Then we'll guide you to information on your industry, your competitors, who your clients may be. Doing market research is the first step. And once you have a simple draft of a business plan, we'll review it for you." You pay nothing for these services (which would cost a bundle if you hired a consultant) because Enterprise Toronto exists to strengthen the local economy and, ultimately, boost the tax base. (Call 416-395-7403, www.enterprisetoronto.com.) Industry Canada's Web site, www.strategis.gc.ca, is another good resource. It contains two million electronic documents and more than 20,000 links to related business sites.

Much of what's available is generic information. It's not customized to your business. There's no one magical site that will do all the work for you. You have to do your own research and talk to people in the business you want to enter. That includes sitting down with potential competitors. "Many people think they have to keep their business a secret from competition. I disagree," Asaf Shad told me. "There is always information that you can share for mutual benefit."

David Chilton is the author of *The Wealthy Barber*, a popular personal finance book, and has published two successful cookbooks, *Looneyspoons* and *Crazy Plates*, by Janet and Greta Podleski. Later, he raised $1 million from a private investor for his frozen foods company, Crazy Plates Inc., using a 25-page business plan that had hardly any numbers in it. Chilton believes passion is key to a successful business plan. If you're not head over heels in love with what you do, then why would anyone want to lend you money? His point: Work on your business vision and values first. The numbers will flow out of your strategic planning.

The Royal Bank provides free advice for those writing a business plan at its Big Idea Web site, http://www.rbcroyalbank.com/sme/bigidea. "It is a common misconception that business plans are written for the sole purpose of obtaining financing," the bank says. "The most important reason for writing a business plan should be that it is an important tool for you."

A business plan lets you "operate" your business on a dry-run basis without financial outlay or risk, say Douglas and Diana Gray in *The Complete Canadian Small Business Guide* (McGraw-Hill Ryerson). "Many people do not venture out on their own because they become overwhelmed with the 'what if' syndrome," they point out. But with a comprehensive plan, you can anticipate "what if" problems and develop strategies to overcome them months before you start your business. You can walk through each stage of your business plan on paper and make many of your crucial decisions before you have invested any money.

Once you start writing your business plan, when do you stop? How much is enough? Business plans can be a few pages or up to 100 pages or more, says an interactive guide produced by the Canada Business Service Centres (CBSC), http://www.cbsc.org/ibp. "Although there are no hard-and-fast rules, many sources recommend that business plans should be between 10 pages and 25 pages in length," it says. "You can always provide more information if asked or you can attach more detailed background documents to your business plan."

The executive summary is the most important part of a business plan. People will read it first and it may be the only section they read. Keep the executive summary short (two pages at most) and highlight what is important in your plan. It should get the reader excited about your business.

One common mistake is to take a sample business plan and simply change the names and numbers. The problem with this approach: A good business plan should flow like a story, with the sections working together to demonstrate why the business will be successful. "Business plans which borrow too heavily from other business plans tend to be disjointed, with some sections contradicting others and some key issues left unaddressed," says the CBSC's interactive business planner.

You can find more than 60 sample plans at http://www.bizplans.com. This is the Web site of Palo Alto Software Inc., based in Eugene, Ore., which sells a $99.95 (U.S.) program, Business Plan Pro, which has been adapted for Canadian entrepreneurs. Show drafts of your business plan to others. This will give you useful feedback before you do the final version.

Off the dole and into business ownership

If you're out of a job and receiving employment insurance benefits, you can join a federally funded program that teaches you how to start and run your own business. The program, called self-employment assistance, is open to anyone who has been on employment insurance in the past three years. You can go back five years if you have received EI benefits during a parental leave. The ticket to admission is a good idea for your business, backed by research to show it can work.

"We have to determine if this is viable," says Kay Saunders of Jewish Vocational Service, one of seven agencies that deliver the program in Toronto. "People have to do more research than they think. They have to work their contacts. It's harder than many realize."

Don't expect to get in right away. Competition is fierce and many people have to apply two or three times before they're accepted. The prize, once you get in, is the opportunity to get federal income support for up to a full year while you polish your entrepreneurial skills. You receive up to eight weeks of classroom training, during which you prepare your business plan. Then you put that plan to work. During the following 10 months, you get at least an hour a month of counselling and support from an experienced business mentor.

Business plans can and do change when subjected to the harsh light of reality. There's the man who wanted to start a butterfly farm, hoping to use the butterflies as a teaching aid in high schools. After doing his research, he realized there was a more profitable market than education. He now releases swarms of butterflies at weddings, funerals and bar mitzvahs, getting $2,000 to $3,000 each time he appears. "He found a better way to market the product," says Ted Barton, a program consultant with SEDI, the agency that co-ordinates the self-employment assistance program in Toronto.

SEDI, which stands for Social and Enterprise Development Innovations, has compiled statistics on the self-employment assistance program since it started in Toronto in 1993. "We have assessed 7,500 businesses," Barton says, "and just over 5,000 people have entered the program. More than 90 per cent of these people actually started businesses and 85 per cent of them were still in business one year after the program ended."

What happens when people start a business without such support? While there are no hard-and-fast statistics, Barton says it's generally believed only 50 per cent of businesses are still operating one year after they start.

Graduates of the self-employment assistance program in Toronto have generated more than $100 million in revenue through the businesses they've started. Two-thirds of the businesses are in the service sector. Many people build on skills developed in former jobs or on personal experiences that show a market need.

Sherri Auger, for example, started a business that helps families with the practical details when a loved one is sick or dying. She got the idea after her mother unexpectedly died and her father was placed in a long-term care facility, both in the same week. Her experience as an only child working in a management job while facing family obligations led her to start Estate Matters Inc. (www.estatemattersinc.com), which helps organize tasks such as selling a house, filling out government forms, closing bank accounts and tracking down investment information.

Any type of business idea is eligible for the program. Only sex-based businesses and anything seen as exploitive would be ruled out.

To get more information and application forms, you can check with your local Human Resources Development Canada office. Anyone who has received EI benefits knows where that is.

Alternatives to the business bank loan

Where do I get money? That's the first question that pops into many people's heads when thinking about starting their own business. We've all heard stories about how the banks don't like lending money to small business, at least to start-up operations. In fact, you may not need a bank loan at all.

"I'd venture to guess that 50 per cent of all small businesses in Canada do not borrow money," says Susan Kennedy-Loewen, vice-president of small business banking at the Bank of Nova Scotia. You can use your own capital to start a business, especially if you have a lump-sum pension payment from a former employer to get you going. You can borrow from family and friends, or even total strangers who are looking for a way to invest in a business. You can lease equipment, cars, office or factory space, freeing up cash for other needs and enjoying tax benefits (since you can deduct the lease payments as operating expenses).

But at some point, you may have to ask the bank for a loan or a line of credit. What are your chances of being approved? Banks reject about one in ten loan applications, according to a 2000 survey of 10,000 small business owners by the Canadian Federation of

Independent Business (CFIB). You're more likely to be turned down for a loan if you have less than 10 years of business experience and fewer than 20 employees. Your chances of being financed are also lower if you're a female business owner or you're in the personal services sector.

And if your bank keeps changing account managers, watch out. The loan rejection rate for CFIB members who had the same account manager for three years was 7.1 per cent, compared with 22.8 per cent for those who had four or more account managers. (You can read the full report at www.cfib.ca.)

It's no coincidence that Scotiabank later started running TV commercials boasting about the staying power of its account managers. The CFIB is a powerful lobby group; banks respond to its concerns. In a later survey done in 2003, however, things had gotten worse for entrepreneurs. The CFIB said the loan rejection rate had gone up to 16 per cent (from 10.5 per cent in 2000).

Lines of credit and business loans are the main sources of financing, the CFIB found. About 71 per cent of small business owners had lines of credit and 41 per cent had loans. One in four owners used commercial and personal mortgages, personal loans, supplier credit and credit cards, while one in five owners used lease financing and account overdraft protection. "Love money," a loan from a family member or friend, was used by 11 per cent of owners (but 20 per cent of younger firms). Seven per cent received loans from a government agency or program, while five per cent relied on the factoring of receivables.

When it comes to interest rates, small businesses paid an average 1.5 percentage points above the prime rate on both loans and lines of credit. The smallest firms paid an average 1.83 percentage points above prime, while the largest firms paid only 0.85 percentage points more—a difference of almost one full percentage point.

In recent years, banks have introduced business credit cards with lower interest rates. Scotiabank, for example, has a Visa card for business with an average rate of prime plus two per cent and a 26-day grace period before interest is charged. "If you are too busy, you don't have to move the balance to your operating line to save money, since the rate is equivalent in many cases," says Susan Kennedy-Loewen, who has spent 20 years in banking and written a book, *The Canadian Small Business Handbook* (Key Porter).

Where do you go when the bank turns you down? Lynda Morris started her computer consulting business with a $3,000 loan. Two years later, Niclyn Computer Consultants had 300 clients, $70,000 in annual revenue and one full-time employee. Morris got the money she needed from Calmeadow Metrofund, a Toronto microlender, after being turned down by the banks.

"It was humiliating," she says about her banking experience. As a single mother living in a co-op housing development, Morris didn't have enough collateral to meet the banks' requirements. But as a graduate of the federal government's self-employment assistance program, she qualified for a Calmeadow microloan. She paid it back and later borrowed $10,000 from Metro Credit Union, which took over the Calmeadow portfolio in July 2000. The credit union lends $1,000 to $15,000 to graduates of a recognized business training program. The interest rate is prime plus six per cent (higher than what banks charge), plus an administration fee of six per cent of the amount borrowed. "We look to give out about $250,000 a year in the microloan program," says credit officer Susan Weekes.

Small businesses don't need a lot of money to get started. One study showed that half of all bank loans to small firms are for less than $50,000. Loans of that size have low margins, say Allan Riding and Barbara Orser in *Beyond the Banks: Creative Financing for Canadian Entrepreneurs* (John Wiley & Sons). Bank loan managers have to administer high volumes, often 80 to 120 accounts. The heavy caseloads mean they have little time to devote to each client, "so the ground is fertile for misunderstandings," say authors Riding and Orser, both business professors.

Maurice Chaput builds custom locomotives for full-scale model trains. He launched his business, Moe's Locomotive Works Ltd., in Flamborough, Ontario, with financing he received from a member of his model train club. He was enrolled in the federal self-employment assistance program, but that didn't help him get a bank loan. "The banks said, 'Show us six months of income.' They want security before they lend you money, but that's tough if you're starting a new business." Chaput invested $2,000 of his own money and expects to get $26,000 to $30,000 from his "angel investor." He'll start repaying the loan with interest once he gets a few orders.

Angels, also known as informal investors, are important sources of early-stage capital for businesses. Riding and Orser put together a profile after interviewing almost 300 informal investors. A business angel is typically a 47-year-old man, with previous small business experience and a big enough personal net worth (at least $1 million) to back other people's ideas. Most are university graduates and many have advanced degrees. They have succeeded as entrepreneurs and they're looking for their next success. They understand the risk of new business ventures.

While the average investment made by Canadian angels is slightly more than $100,000, angels often invest as little as $10,000. They're patient investors. "On average, for each dollar invested, informal investors expect to take $7 out of the firm six to seven years later," the authors say. This may seem high, but only two out of ten angel investments are profitable.

How do you find an angel? Study your own local networks. Get all the referrals you can from boards of trade, chambers of commerce or other business groups. Another approach is to meet as many local business owners as possible. It's likely that angels have invested in many of these enterprises. In time, these owners may be willing to refer you to the investors they know.

When it comes to start-up funding, keep your expectations low. You may not get a business loan and you may have to use your personal credit. "Start on a shoestring," advises David Trahair, a Toronto chartered accountant and consultant on financial management for small businesses. Keeping your overhead low means you'll be able to sit tight when clients don't pay right away—and they won't. Don't rent an office at first. Operate out of your home or use a client's space. Don't give up your day job. Work for yourself half the time and spend the rest of your time working for someone else.

"You can apply for a $50,000 unsecured line of credit over the phone from a virtual bank such as ING Direct," says Trahair, who has a free small business tool kit at his Web site, www.mywebca.com. "Or think about switching from a gold credit card to a no-frills card. The amount you save in interest (about eight to 10 percentage points) could make the difference between starting and not starting your business."

In the dot-com era, everyone wanted to get big quickly. The focus was more on financing than on running a business. But lenders are more cautious now. They're less willing to advance seed capital to those without experience and management skills. "Banks are almost doing you a favour by being so tough," Trahair says. "If someone gives you $200,000, you'll spend it on a huge marketing campaign. You're encouraged to be lazy when money is just handed to you."

Another alternative for small business financing is the Business Development Bank of Canada (BDC), a federal crown corporation that helps fund start-ups willing to accept BDC-sponsored training. "We offer not just money but consulting," says Steve Kirton, a Toronto area branch manager. "That combination makes us different from the banks." The Business Development Bank has a micro-business program that provides loans of up to $25,000 to new firms or $50,000 to established firms that need to get to the next level.

The BDC looks for sectors that are under-served by mainstream financial institutions, like knowledge-based industries with few fixed assets to offer as collateral. "Such businesses often run into difficulty obtaining term loans for critical uses such as research and development, permanent working capital and market development projects," Kirton says. For information, call 1-888-INFO BDC or check the Web site at www.bdc.ca.

Finally, you can get fixed-rate loans of up to $250,000 to finance the purchase or improvement of buildings and equipment, backed by the federal government. The money cannot be used to buy shares of other types of ownership in a business, to finance working capital (such as inventory or accounts receivables) or to buy real estate for resale. Banks, credit unions, and trust, loan and insurance companies all provide loans that qualify for a government guarantee under the

Canada Small Business Financing Act. For information on the program, go to Industry Canada's Web site, www.strategis.gc.ca/csbfa. Then apply to the lender of your choice.

Giving your start-up a head start

Should I incorporate my business? When and how? These are decisions every start-up must make. "I compare it to giving birth," says Benj Gallander in *The Canadian Small Business Survival Guide* (Dundurn Press). "A completely new entity is formed that must be ultimately responsible for itself." A corporation is distinct from the owner. It's different from either a proprietorship or partnership, which is identified as a legal part of the owner. Limited liability is the most important reason to incorporate. Since a corporation is its own being, debts incurred by the corporation are the responsibility of the business rather than the owners.

Lisa Wiseman, a registered nurse, incorporated her Toronto health-care business as soon as she started it in 1995. "I didn't even have any staff," she says. "I'd come up with a name and that's about it." Eldercare Home Health Inc. now has 65 caregivers on staff who help older people remain at home, rather than move to an institution. The average client is 90 years old. "Because of the kind of business I'm in, with the potential liability, I was advised that incorporation was a good idea," Wiseman says.

Her husband, Malcolm Marcus, is a partner in the health-care business. He also owns an entertainment company, in which his wife is a partner, which has made a computer-animated video for kids (*Cody's Crew*). After operating as a division of Eldercare Home Health for several years, Marcus incorporated his company to create new television projects. "I needed to make a break and do things differently," he says. Incorporation makes it easier to raise capital—*Cody's Crew* was entirely self-financed—and there are potential tax advantages.

On the minus side, incorporation means you're closely regulated. Complying with all of the government's rules is onerous and takes a great deal of time. And incorporation is costly. You're shelling out hundreds of dollars that could be used in the working capital of your start-up operation. Wiseman paid more than $1,000 to incorporate her company, using a lawyer. Her husband spent only $300 to $400 to incorporate his company and didn't use a lawyer. "I chose federal incorporation," Marcus says. "It was not that much different in cost from provincial incorporation and seemed like a better idea."

Companies that are federally incorporated can operate in more than one province, but they have to comply with both federal and provincial regulations. Marcus went to Industry Canada's Strategis Web site and used the electronic filing centre at www.strategis.gc.ca/corporations. He picked a name, Marcus/Wiseman Entertainment Inc., that wasn't taken by anyone else by doing an electronic search at www.businessnames.ca. "Online is a very good way to go," Marcus says. "I'd recommend it if you're doing a relatively straightforward incorporation."

You can also pick up business incorporation kits at bookstores. An example is Thomas O'Malley's *How to Form Your Own Corporation in Ontario Without a Lawyer for Under $1 a Day*, published by Hushion House, and sold for $29.95 at Chapters and Indigo stores.

Do-it-yourself works if your company has one or two shareholders. But if you have a more complex business structure from day one, "you might want to get your lawyer involved straightaway," says Susan Kennedy-Loewen, Scotiabank's vice-president of small business banking. Incorporation doesn't limit your liability completely. Most financial institutions demand personal guarantees for business loans, she says, to ensure they'll be repaid if the business goes under.

Another reason to incorporate your small business is to save money on taxes. "The decision to incorporate can be based on many factors, but the income tax advantage for small business corporations usually ranks as the top one," says accountant David Trahair. If you're a Canadian resident and you own a corporation, it's probably eligible for a low rate of tax on the first $200,000 of active business income. The combined federal and Ontario tax rates on the first $200,000 of business income is about 20 per cent. That compares with personal marginal tax rates of more than 45 per cent.

The federal government made a change in 2002, allowing a middle tax bracket for corporate business income between $200,000 and $300,000. But here's something to keep in mind: It's only a tax deferral. "Eventually, you will want to take this money out of the corporation. What good are tax savings if you can't spend them?" says chartered accountant Stephen Thompson, author of *Beat the Taxman: Easy Ways to Save Tax in Your Small Business* (John Wiley & Sons). "When you do, you may pay another tax on the corporation's payment to you. When you add these two taxes together, they will equal approximately what you would have paid if you had received the money directly without using a corporation."

Only the most successful small and home-based businesses need to incorporate, Thompson says. You must be in a position to leave the money you saved by paying a lower tax rate in the corporation. Here's his rule of thumb: If you need all the profit from the business to cover your living expenses, a corporation is likely not for you.

However, incorporating may be useful in giving you additional protection if you operate a business where the risk of accident or lawsuit is high—an important factor to keep in mind.

When trying to decide whether to use a corporation, there's one last thing to consider. "It's possible to transfer all or any part of a business operating as a sole proprietorship or partnership into a corporation at any time, tax-free," Thompson says. Wait until your business is established and you can determine if a corporation will be of benefit to you. Then, roll the business into the company at that time.

"Often the worst tax planning is to start up a business in a corporation that is losing money and you have no way of deducting those losses against personal income," he says. "It is better to keep the business outside the corporation until it starts becoming profitable."

Whether you're incorporated or not, you can deduct the same business expenses for tax purposes. You're allowed to claim costs you incur solely to earn business income—such as a home office, motor vehicle, meals, entertainment and accounting and legal fees—if you have the proper paperwork. That means hanging onto all business-related vouchers and receipts, and recording all your expenses in a journal. You must keep your records for at least six years after the end of the year to which they relate, according to the Canada Customs and Revenue Agency.

Most small business owners don't like to spend the time recording their business transactions. It distracts from what they believe really makes them money, their business. But a good record-keeping system can also make you money by saving tax dollars and helping you survive an audit, Thompson says. The easiest method is to create a separate envelope for each expense and revenue category. As you incur the expense or receive the revenue, put each receipt in its envelope. At the end of the year, total each envelope and enter the information on your tax return.

If you want to know more about how to incorporate your business and how to file a corporate tax return, you can find the answers at a federal government Web site, www.businessgateway.ca. It provides a single access point to all the government services and information needed to start, run and grow a business. The site also has some useful tools, such as a calculator that helps you decide whether to buy or lease your business equipment, and financial ratio calculators that help you evaluate the performance of your business and identify potential problems.

part four

Saving for Retirement
In and Out of an RRSP

If you're going to save and invest for the future, you're better off doing it in an RRSP. That's because of the generous tax benefits the government provides to those who are saving for retirement. Not only can you deduct the contribution against your income, but you can also let your money grow untaxed for all the years it stays in the plan. That's an awesome one-two punch.

But don't lose your perspective. Many people contribute to an RRSP just to get a juicy refund in the spring. This is short-term thinking. Never make the mistake of assuming that all the money in your registered retirement savings plan belongs to you. The government is giving you a tax deferral, not a permanent tax holiday, and will get its due eventually.

Since you're going to pay taxes on your RRSP one day, why not change your strategy? Think about reinvesting your refund—rather than frittering it away—or borrowing from the bank to increase your contribution. This may be a sacrifice at first, but you'll have more left in the retirement plan once the taxes are paid and you're living off the money.

I'm a believer in RRSPs—and not only as a way of saving for retirement. Because I started in my twenties, I was able to take money out during both my maternity leaves. This helped fill the gap between what we needed to live on and what I received in employment insurance benefits. I did it in the days when a maternity leave was only four months. If you plan to take an extended one-year parental leave, an RRSP will come in especially handy.

Think of the RRSP as a tax-advantaged way to save money. It's your decision when to withdraw funds and for what purpose. Some people take a sabbatical and use their retirement plan to finance the time off work. Others go back to school, subsidizing their tuition fees with tax-free money from their RRSP under the lifelong learning plan. I'll talk more about this in a later chapter.

You can make it easier on yourself by contributing to an RRSP all year round, instead of waiting till January or February to get a tax refund for the previous year. Even better, you can ask the tax department to lower the amount of tax withheld from your pay because you're contributing to an RRSP. This means you won't get a refund, but you'll have more money to spend because your tax is prepaid. Stand by for an explanation of how to get Ottawa to deduct your RRSP at source.

Of course, I recognize there's no panacea in the world of personal finances and no one-size-fits-all solution. If you prefer to save in other ways, such as devoting yourself to paying off your mortgage more quickly, that's okay too. The satisfaction of owning a valuable asset free and clear when you retire may be worth more to you than having a retirement fund (especially if you already have a good employer-paid pension). In this section, I examine the pros and cons of paying off a mortgage instead of investing in an RRSP.

Finally, you never know what the future will bring. Don't knock yourself out saving for a retirement you may never experience. You may continue working at a reduced pace well into your sixties or even your seventies. Because we're going into an era when there will be a shortage of skilled labour, you should have no trouble negotiating with your employer to stay on the job, if that's what you want to do.

I know I plan to keep going for as long as I can. My golf isn't good enough that I'd want to play every day. Maybe I'll write personal finance books for 80-year-olds. With luck and good health, I may never need to cash in that RRSP after all.

Design your own timetable for RRSP investing

Are you saving enough for retirement? How much do you need to save in an RRSP and how much outside an RRSP? Are there better ways to save for retirement, such as buying a home or paying off debt?

Let's start with the premise that RRSPs are oversold in January and February. There's too much advertising and media hype and way too many public opinion polls sponsored by financial institutions. All this creates an artificial sense of urgency to get your money into a registered retirement savings plan before the March 1 deadline.

With all the pressure, it's understandable that some people think about RRSPs only near the deadline. They throw in any money they have on hand and choose investments that look good at the time. After this seasonal chore is completed, they go back to their real-life concerns. The result: Too little attention is paid to increasing the size of contributions and improving the rate of return. For many Canadians, retirement saving is a once-a-year affair.

True, once a year is better than never when it comes to planning for the future. But why let the financial industry dictate your timing? Why not do things on your own schedule?

Get one thing straight. There's no such thing as an RRSP contribution deadline. No longer do you face a "use it or lose it" scenario with each year's limit. The rules allow you to catch up on missed contributions. So, if you do nothing by March 1, you can carry forward the amount you could have contributed for use in future years. That's a comforting thought if you have other financial priorities. You can postpone your retirement saving and make it up later. You don't have to make your full contribution every year.

"Retirement funding rests on the premise that you will build up a fund over the course of your career," say Bruce Cohen and Brian FitzGerald in *The Pension Puzzle: Your Complete Guide to Government Benefits, RRSPs and Employer Plans* (John Wiley & Sons). This means you can contribute to an RRSP in many different ways. Here are three options:

- Start early and stop or scale back later, while you raise a family or pay off a mortgage. Because you started young, compound growth will build up your savings during the contribution holiday.

- Wait to contribute until you're middle-aged and have more money to spare than in the cash-strapped years after completing your education.

- Contribute a steady amount every year. Even a relatively modest amount will add up to a princely sum if you stick with it for your entire working life.

Here's an example of three people who end up in the same place with their RRSPs. Ali contributes $1,000 a year from age 20 through 29, then stops. Ben contributes $553 a year for his full career. Charlie delays saving until he's 45, then invests $2,893 a year. Assuming they earn eight per cent average annual compound growth, they all retire at age 65 with RRSPs worth about $250,000. So it doesn't matter when you start—and after you factor in inflation, RRSP procrastinators like Charlie have an easier time investing $1 than eager beavers like Ali.

The moral: Stop thinking about an RRSP contribution deadline. What you have is a deadline each March 1 (or thereabouts) for writing off an RRSP contribution on the previous year's tax return. If you carry forward the contribution to a year in which you have more income and you're in a higher tax bracket, the RRSP deduction will be more lucrative for you.

Reinvest your tax refund

Suppose you put $1,000 into a registered retirement savings plan. Does that mean you're saving $1,000 for your retirement? Nope. You still have to pay tax on the money when it comes out of the plan. "You're hoping you'll be in a lower tax bracket when you take money out of the RRSP," says financial educator Talbot Stevens.

But that's a gamble. How do you know you'll pay less tax when you retire? You may have enough income from pensions and savings to keep you in the same tax bracket—or lift you up to the next level. In addition, Ottawa may raise existing taxes down the road. There's already a clawback on the Old Age Security pension. If your net income is above $57,879, your OAS pension will be reduced. If it's above $94,148, your pension will be eliminated. Governments may introduce punitive new taxes when the wealthy boomers start retiring after 2010.

It's a different story when you invest money outside an RRSP, using tax-paid dollars. Your original investment is not taxed or clawed back when withdrawn. This means you're committing the full $1,000 to your retirement goal.

If you expect tax rates to rise in the future, you're better off investing for retirement with after-tax money. You have more control. "After-tax income is all that matters," Stevens says. "We only own after-tax dollars, where income taxes have already been paid." But if you prefer to invest for retirement with an RRSP, you have a way to reduce the impact of taxes later on: Reinvest your tax refund.

Do you find that advice hard to swallow? You probably think of your tax refund as a reward for putting money aside for retirement. What's the incentive to go the RRSP route if you give up your refund, too? But a tax refund you spend generates no retirement income. It increases your current standard of living at the expense of the future. Reinvesting your entire tax refund can increase your RRSP retirement income by 30 to 45 per cent, depending on your tax bracket. Let's look at how this works, using a 30 per cent tax bracket:

- You contribute $1,000 to an RRSP and reinvest your $300 tax refund. You now have $1,300.

- If you cashed in the RRSP immediately, the after-tax value would be 70 per cent of $1,300, or $910.

- By committing $910 to your retirement goal, instead of $700, you're increasing your RRSP funds by 30 per cent.

What you do with your tax refund "is an overlooked parameter that has a huge impact on the size of your retirement fund," Stevens points out. He has three other tax refund strategies—gross-up, top-up and catch-up—which all involve borrowing money to invest in an RRSP.

With the "gross-up" strategy, you borrow an extra $400 to get your $1,000 contribution up to $1,400. Then you use your $420 tax refund to pay back the loan right away. Your after-tax commitment is now 30 per cent of $1,400, or $980—almost the same as if you had invested $1,000 in a non-registered plan. But you'll probably end up with more retirement dollars because of the RRSP's tax-deferred growth.

With the "top-up" strategy, you borrow enough money to make your maximum annual contribution. Suppose you have a $5,000

RRSP limit and you have only $1,000 to contribute. You borrow $4,000 and get a refund of $1,200, which you apply against the loan.

With the "catch-up" strategy, you borrow enough to make up for your unused RRSP contributions in the past. If you have contributed only $1,000 for the past five years, you take out a $20,000 loan to make up for what you missed earlier. You get a tax refund of $6,000 and pay back the remaining $14,000 over several years.

Borrowing for RRSP makes sense

Can't come up with the money for an RRSP contribution? Consider borrowing from a financial institution that offers RRSP loans at low rates. This can be a smart thing to do, even though interest paid on these loans is not tax-deductible (as it is when you borrow to invest outside an RRSP).

Suppose you can make a $5,000 RRSP contribution one year, but you've saved only $2,000. You're debating whether to contribute $2,000 to the RRSP or to borrow an extra $3,000, repayable in 12 monthly instalments, at an interest rate of 6.5 per cent. Let's assume your marginal tax rate is 40 per cent and you earn 5 per cent on the money invested in your RRSP.

- You make a $2,000 RRSP contribution, you get an $800 tax refund and you earn $100 interest in your RRSP. You're ahead by $900 in one year.

- You boost your contribution to $5,000, using $2,000 of your own savings and a $3,000 loan. You get a tax refund of $2,000 and you earn $250 in your RRSP.

- You're ahead by $2,250, but your net gain is $2,143 when you deduct the $107 of interest paid on the loan. That's still more than double where you would be if you had relied on just your savings.

■ Your borrowing cost can be less than $107 if you use your $2,000 tax refund to pay down the $3,000 loan as soon as the cheque arrives.

If that $3,000 you borrowed stays in the RRSP for 25 years, earning compound interest of five per cent, it will grow to more than $10,000. "That's a pretty good return from a single loan," says Gordon Pape, who uses the example in his *2003 Buyer's Guide to RRSPs* (Viking Canada). Of course, you'll pay tax on the money when it comes out of the plan, but you'll enjoy years of tax-sheltered compounding.

No matter what tax bracket you're in, your return from borrowing for an RRSP will be greater than if you fail to make your full contribution. That's assuming you borrow at commercial rates and you repay the loan within one year. In the second year, the carrying cost (6.5 per cent) will be higher than the interest the money earns inside the RRSP (5 per cent), and there will be no more offsetting RRSP tax deductions.

I'm talking here about a smaller RRSP "top-up" loan. If you take out a larger "catch-up" loan to make up for previous years when you didn't contribute the maximum or anything at all to an RRSP, you might take 10 years or more to repay the money. Here's an example of how you can benefit, taken from Talbot Stevens's booklet, *Dispelling the Myths of Borrowing to Invest* (www.talbotstevens.com).

■ You have $20,000 of unused RRSP contribution room available and you're in a 40 per cent tax bracket.

■ You borrow $20,000 and get an immediate tax refund of $8,000, which you apply to the loan. That reduces the balance to $12,000.

■ If you pay an interest rate of eight per cent, you will discharge the loan in 10 years with annual payments of $1,656 a year (or $138 a month).

■ That $20,000 you borrow will start growing inside your RRSP right away. If you get a four per cent return, it will be worth $29,610 after 10 years.

Surprisingly, the catch-up loan strategy often makes sense even when the cost of borrowing is substantially higher than the investment returns earned inside the RRSP. Suppose, instead of borrowing, you use $1,656 of your annual cash flow to contribute to an RRSP. After 10 years, you'll have only $20,680 in your RRSP, assuming you spend the tax refunds. Even if you add the refunds to your RRSP, you'll have slightly less ($28,950) than if you had borrowed ($29,610).

"The catch-up loan approach can be best because it forces a higher level of commitment to your retirement goal," Stevens says. Remember, the RRSP loan rates you see advertised may be for a one-year term only and can jump considerably for longer terms. Also, you may get the best loan rate only if you switch your RRSP (and other business) to the lender.

Let Ottawa deduct your RRSP at source

Borrowing is a way to contribute to an RRSP if you're short of money in February. But there's another way that doesn't cost you a penny in interest. The federal government will help you budget for your RRSP contribution. All you have to do is write a letter or fill out a special form to submit to Canada Customs and Revenue Agency, asking your employer to withhold less tax from your income.

If the request is approved, your employer will give you more money in your take-home pay to account for the expected tax saving from your RRSP contribution. You won't get a tax refund after you submit your tax return showing the RRSP deposit, but you'll have the satisfaction of knowing the proper amount of tax is deducted from your paycheque. You won't be giving the government an interest-free loan of your money, to be refunded at a later date.

Here are the steps to take:

■ Submit a written request to your local Canada Customs and Revenue Agency office. (The addresses are listed in the "Government" blue pages of the telephone book, under "T" for tax.) The letter says you want to give your employer permission to reduce the tax deducted at source. Enclose proof that you're making regular RRSP contributions.

■ Instead of a letter, you can fill out a tax form called "T1213: Request to Reduce Tax Deductions at Source For Year(s)," which can be obtained from a local tax services office or by calling 1-800-959-2221. You can also print the form from the Internet (go to www.ccra-adrc.gc.ca, then to Search, Forms and Publications; type in "T1213").

■ Don't include any RRSP contributions deducted from your pay by your employer (say, for a group RRSP plan). Make sure your income tax returns are up to date and you don't have a balance owing to the government.

■ Send the completed form, along with supporting documents, to the Client Services division of your local tax office.

■ Wait (up to two months) for your request to be approved. CCRA will then issue a letter of authority to your employer for a specific tax year.

Suppose you want to make stepped-up regular contributions to an RRSP, starting on January 1, 2004, in order to take advantage of the higher RRSP limits that go into effect for that year. Ideally, you should have submitted your T1213 form to CCRA in September 2003, leaving enough time for the 60-day approval process and for your employer to revise its payroll deductions. You don't have to wait till the beginning of the year, however. You can ask to change the source deductions at any time.

There's a similar strategy you can use if you get a bonus from an employer and want to contribute the money to an RRSP. You ask the government to let your employer reduce source deductions on the lump-sum amount. This means the tax savings that result from your RRSP contribution are effectively prepaid—and you won't get a tax refund later on.

Minimize taxes on RRSP withdrawals

You put money into a registered retirement savings plan and you get regular statements showing how well you're doing. Don't be tempted to think the money is yours. It's not. Remember, the real value of the RRSP is what you end up with after you pay the taxes that weren't deducted when the money went into the plan.

The first thing to know is that the government lets you take money out of an RRSP with little or no tax in special situations. Here's a list:

- Death of a spouse: You can designate your spouse as beneficiary of your RRSP by filling out a form with the institution that holds your plan. If you do this, the money in the plan can be transferred to your spouse's RRSP or RRIF (registered retirement income fund) with no taxes payable after you die.

- Dependent child or grandchild: If you have no spouse or your spouse dies first, you can name a financially dependent child or grandchild as your RRSP beneficiary. The child or grandchild's income must be below the "basic personal amount" on the tax return ($7,634 in 2002).

- Marriage breakdown: If you're separated or divorced, and there's a court order or written separation agreement relating to property division, you can transfer funds directly to your spouse's RRSP or RRIF without paying tax. You must be living apart at the time. In all cases, a "spouse" may include someone with whom you've lived common-law for at least a year or with whom you've had a child.

- The Home Buyers' Plan: If you're buying a principal residence, you can withdraw up to $20,000 from your RRSP (up to $40,000 in total from both spouses' RRSPs) tax-free and interest-free. The plan, launched in 1992, was amended in 1999 so that people who borrowed from their RRSPs to buy a home can do so again, as long as they haven't owned a home in the previous five years.

- Lifelong Learning Plan: If you're going back to school to upgrade your skills, you can borrow up to $10,000 a year from your RRSP tax-free and interest-free. You can withdraw up to $20,000 in total each time you participate, which can be more than once in your lifetime, and repay the money over a 10-year period. You must be a full-time student, taking a program of at least three months at an eligible educational institution.

- RRSP maturity: You must wind up your RRSP no later than December 31 of the year in which you turn 69. As an alternative to cashing in the plan and paying tax, you can transfer the assets tax-free into a registered retirement income fund (the most popular option) or an annuity. With a RRIF, you must make taxable withdrawals each year, according to a government formula, starting in the calendar year after the plan is set up. With an annuity, you receive regular payments from a life insurance company for a specified period of time. There are no tax breaks on RRIF or annuity income.

Suppose you want to get money out of your RRSP if there's a financial emergency. Try to wait for a time when your income is low (you've been laid off your job or you've taken a leave of absence). This will minimize tax on your RRSP withdrawals.

If you're married or living common-law and you contribute to a spousal RRSP, you can take money out of the plan of the lower-income spouse. But be careful about dipping into that spousal plan, unless there's a gap of at least three years between the last contribution and a withdrawal. If not, the amount withdrawn is attributed back to the spouse who made the original contribution and taxed as income at the full rate.

When you withdraw money from your RRSP, the trustee is required to withhold tax at source: 10 per cent on the first $5,000, 20 per cent on the next $10,000, and 30 per cent over $15,000. You can minimize the impact by making a series of small withdrawals from your RRSP, instead of a single large one.

Say you want to take $20,000 from your plan. You will have $4,000 deducted if you withdraw the money at once. Or you can ask for four instalments of $5,000 each and have only $2,000 withheld in total taxes.

But remember, this is not a real saving. You'll pay the full amount of tax owing on RRSP withdrawals at your marginal rate when you file your next tax return. With only 10 per cent withheld at source, you may be shocked when you're hit with big taxes on the RRSP income the following year. And if you withdraw a large amount, your income for that year will rise and you may find yourself in a higher tax bracket as a result.

As you get older, lower your debt

Contribute to an RRSP or pay down the mortgage? Assuming you can't afford to do both, which is the better option? "The younger you are, the more you should lean toward your RRSP," says Toronto adviser and chartered accountant Kurt Rosentreter, author of a book on tax-smart investing. "The older you are, the more you should lean toward getting rid of debt."

The RRSP works better if you start early. Your tax-sheltered money won't grow as quickly if you wait till you're middle-aged. As you get closer to retirement, your goal should be to pay off all credit cards, retire any investment loans and discharge all your consumer loans and mortgages.

Not owing any money when you retire will give you three huge advantages, says Gordon Pape in *Retiring Wealthy in the 21st Century*:

- Interest payments are a drain on what will likely be a reduced income flow when you retire. You may have to compensate by reducing your standard of living.

- Loans are more difficult to pay off after you retire. If your income drops, you'll find it harder to put aside money to reduce your outstanding principal.

- Carrying debt into retirement puts you at risk. Any sharp upward move in interest rates would increase your monthly costs and put an additional strain on your retirement budget.

With a fully paid-up house, you'll eliminate a major cash drain on your retirement income. Just think of how much money goes into your mortgage payments now. And if you're mortgage-free when you stop working, you can downsize to a smaller home or move to a lower-cost community and use the capital gain to provide retirement income. Another benefit of paying down a mortgage early is the sense of security it provides. This may be more valuable to you than the extra money available at retirement from an RRSP.

Paying down a mortgage is a tangible investment. You know the interest rate and exactly how many dollars of interest you save by accelerating your payments. But RRSP investments carry some risk and uncertainty. Your expected return depends on the direction of the economy, interest rates and stock markets.

Another risk with RRSPs, as I just pointed out, is that you don't know what your tax rate will be when you retire and start taking money out of the plan. Nor can you anticipate any income tax penalties you may face, such as clawbacks on your old age security pension.

But there are a couple of arguments in favour of RRSPs: cashability and diversification.

"By using extra cash to reduce the mortgage, you are eliminating (or at least reducing) liquidity," says York University finance professor Moshe Milevsky in his 1999 book, *Money Logic* (Stoddart). ("Liquidity" means "how quickly assets can be converted into cash.") By paying down the mortgage instead of investing in an RRSP, you sacrifice a degree of liquidity. "In an emergency, it's quite simple to cash an RRSP, notwithstanding the negative tax consequences of early redemption," Milevsky says. "It's far more difficult and undesirable to sell a house in an emergency."

Diversification refers to the process of adding new types of investments to a portfolio. It raises the odds that when one asset decreases in value, another will increase in an offsetting fashion. By paying down your mortgage, you are effectively increasing the percentage of assets held in the "house" investment. But Canadians typically have too large a proportion of their assets tied up in their house, Milevsky says. "Most probably should work to decrease the level of that investment through diversification, by purchasing other investments," in his view.

The RRSP home buyers' plan seems to offer the best of both worlds. It allows you and your spouse to take out $20,000 each from an RRSP to make a down payment on a first home, thus lowering your mortgage payments. But many financial commentators think young people should ask their parents for help with a down payment, rather than lose valuable years of tax-free growth in an RRSP.

"This will devastate your plan in the early years," Rosentreter says. "Most people use the home buyers' plan when they're 25 and take 15 years to pay back the money. Now, they're 40 and they have only 25 years to build the RRSP back up again."

Garth Turner, an author who once favoured real estate, now expects financial assets (such as stocks and bonds) to grow more quickly than residential housing in the next decade. "If you withdrew $5,000 from your RRSP and didn't repay it for 30 years, assuming a 10 per cent rate of return, you'd have $85,000 less in retirement," he says in *The Little Book of Financial Wisdom* (Key Porter).

Turner's example of the damage done by raiding your RRSP is less dramatic when you assume a lower rate of return on your investments. Since I'm a believer in using conservative scenarios, I'd reduce his 10 per cent return to a more realistic 6 per cent. In that case, your $5,000 RRSP withdrawal for a house down payment, if not paid back, would give you about $30,000 less in retirement.

Borrowing to invest can be risky business

Most homeowners try to get rid of the mortgage as quickly as possible. You pay a hefty amount of interest over the life of the loan—and mortgage interest is not tax-deductible in Canada, as it is in the United States. So it makes sense to work on paying down the mortgage, even if it means not contributing to an RRSP for a while.

You can start an RRSP while young and scale back later, letting compound growth build your savings during the contribution holiday. Or you can pay down the mortgage first and contribute to an RRSP later, borrowing money if necessary to catch up on unused contribution room from previous years.

Some financial advisers have a different idea. They point out that interest on money borrowed to invest is tax-deductible, but interest on RRSP loans is not deductible. Their advice: Get rid of the mortgage and take out a new home equity loan to buy investments outside an RRSP. This makes the mortgage tax-deductible.

But here's the key. To claim the interest as an expense, you must invest in assets that pay you a return greater than the interest you pay on the loan. That means buying stocks or equity-based mutual funds, since the interest on GICs or bonds is below the lending rate.

Garth Turner, a well-known stock market bull, discounts the risks of borrowing to invest. He even tells people to cash in some of their investments each month to cover the interest-only payment on the home equity loan. Equity funds will give you substantial capital growth—despite the fact you've removed money to cover the financing charges—if you hold them for five years or more, he says. Five years is overly optimistic, in my view. If you borrow to invest, give yourself a 10-year window to cover the loan costs and build a nest egg, too.

Fraser Smith, a retired financial planner from British Columbia, is the latest advocate for making your mortgage interest tax-deductible. In a self-published book, *The Smith Manoeuvre* (sold at his Web site, www.smithman.net), he advises setting up a home equity line of credit. Each time you make a mortgage payment that reduces the principal, you should borrow back and invest the monthly principal reduction in an equity portfolio.

If you have a $200,000 mortgage at seven per cent, you can turn almost half the mortgage interest expense into tax-deductible interest this way, he says. You will do even better if you use the tax refund to pay down the mortgage, then immediately borrow the money again to invest. He also advises cashing in term deposits, Canada Savings Bonds and any other paid-up assets to reduce the mortgage, then borrowing back the same amount to replace the assets. But Smith reduces his credibility (as does Turner) by assuming a 10 per cent annual investment return. Many economists expect lower returns in the future.

I think borrowing to invest is a risky strategy. The stock market dips can make you too nervous to continue, especially if you're carrying a big loan at the same time. You need strong willpower and a financial adviser you trust before dipping a toe in these choppy waters.

Using RRSP to pay down mortgage no panacea

Suppose you have $50,000 in your RRSP and you owe $50,000 on a first mortgage on your home. Wouldn't it be nice to use the RRSP to fund the mortgage? You can do this, since your RRSP is allowed to hold a mortgage on any Canadian real estate owned by you or an immediate relative. But is it a worthwhile strategy? Only if you're a very conservative investor.

Here's how it works. You put the $50,000 mortgage into the RRSP as a "contribution in kind." Then you remove $50,000 in cash tax-free, which you use to pay off the financial institution. As a result, you will be paying mortgage interest to yourself, not to a bank, and earning higher rates than you would get on a low-risk investment.

While the RRSP-mortgage combo looks tasty, you may be disappointed when you try to take a bite. You'll face fairly strict rules set by the federal *Income Tax Act* and the financial institution that administers your RRSP—even though it is your money. Here are the things you can and can't do:

- You can't give yourself a special deal on rates. They must be comparable to what you'd get from a regular mortgage lender.

- You must insure the RRSP mortgage against default. There's an insurance premium of 1.25 to 2.5 per cent, depending on the size of the loan as a percentage of the home's value. For a $50,000 mortgage, that translates into an insurance cost of $625 to $1,250, which is usually tacked on to the mortgage principal. (Ontario residents also pay eight per cent provincial sales tax on the insurance, which adds $50 to $100.)

- You must pay the other costs of applying for a mortgage, such as appraisal and legal fees—let's say $1,000 up front—plus ongoing annual costs.

- You must have a self-directed RRSP, which has an administration fee of $100 to $150 a year.

- The RRSP trustee will charge a separate mortgage administration fee, which won't be less than $50 a year and could run up to $375.

You can pay these annual fees directly or take the money out of your RRSP, using pre-tax dollars. But that reduces the size and potential growth of your tax-sheltered retirement fund.

This strategy won't work unless you have enough cash in your RRSP to fund the mortgage. If your plan has at least $50,000, but it's locked into long-term guaranteed investment certificates, you won't be able to move until the GICs come up for renewal. Stocks and mutual funds can be cashed in more easily, but you may not want to sell when their value is down. Don't forget to include commissions and sales charges, which will reduce what may be an already shrunken investment.

You have to decide what to do with the mortgage payments once they get into your RRSP. If you let the money accumulate for a few months before being reinvested, that could hurt your returns. And with a large mortgage in your RRSP, you won't be able to take advantage of other investment opportunities as they arise. Remember, this is a long-term relationship.

Given all these negatives, why do it? Here are a few reasons:

- There's the emotional satisfaction of cutting out the middleman.

- Parents get the chance to help out adult children who might otherwise have trouble financing a home.

- You have the chance to earn a higher return on your retirement savings. Mortgages tend to pay two percentage points more in interest than long-term guaranteed investment certificates.

- Once retired, you may be reluctant to put your RRSP funds into the stock market or mutual funds.

There's no point in doing an RRSP mortgage to save money. If you can afford to pay more each month, you should shop for the highest commercial rate you can find. But keep in mind that you're not allowed to price your mortgage higher than what's available in the market at the time of set-up.

"The goal of an RRSP mortgage is to make it last as long as possible, and to be as costly as possible, so you can maximize the transfer of wealth into your tax-deferred retirement plan," says Garth Turner in *The Little Book of Real Estate Wisdom* (Key Porter).

He advises going with the longest amortization period possible, such as 25 years. Go with a monthly-pay mortgage, instead of a weekly or biweekly one, to pay it off more slowly. If you already have a mortgage in place on your home, you can create an RRSP mortgage as a second one, which boosts the interest rate even further. But this will cost you more in mortgage insurance.

If you default on your payments, your RRSP mortgage ends up taking ownership of your house (which must then be sold off). "Your RRSP, according to the rules, can finance real estate, but it cannot own it," Turner says.

There's an alternative to this strategy. You can hold an arm's-length mortgage in your RRSP without the restrictions that apply to a loan to yourself or a family member. A mortgage broker or lawyer may be able to find you a second mortgage at a premium rate. Check with your financial institution first, since each has different rules about what kind of investments you're allowed to hold in an RRSP.

Tapping into RRSP for small business equity

You have a small business that needs money to grow and expand. You also know people who want to help but can't put their hands on ready cash. Friends and family may have thousands of dollars tied up in their registered retirement savings plans. Wouldn't it be nice if you could offer them a chance to invest in your company by swapping shares for tax-sheltered cash?

Well, it's possible. But don't expect it to be easy. John Bulloch knows how hard it is to use RRSPs for equity financing. As founder of the Canadian Federation of Independent Business (CFIB), he lobbied Ottawa in the early 1980s to make small business shares an eligible RRSP investment. The rules, introduced in 1986, say RRSP investors cannot own more than 10 per cent of the shares of any small business, unless they deal at arm's length with the company and own less than $25,000 worth of shares.

Bulloch later left the CFIB and started Vubiz Ltd., an electronic learning company that has clients in Canada, the United States, Britain and Mexico. "I never thought I would use this provision," he told me. While he managed to line up $200,000 of new investment for Vubiz through friends' RRSPs, he was shocked to find that many investment dealers were unfamiliar with how to handle small business shares in RRSPs. Some wouldn't touch the shares at all.

Moreover, the tax department provided little information to the investment community—or the general public—on the subject. There's nothing at popular government Web sites, such as Industry Canada's www.strategis.gc.ca. All that's available online is an 11-page interpretation bulletin, IT-320R3, at the Canada Customs and Revenue Agency's Web site, www.ccra-adrc.gc.ca. (Search for "qualified RRSP investments.")

Unless you're a tax lawyer, you'll get a headache trying to decipher the bulletin, which is definitely not user-friendly. "We're the first to agree this is a little bit complicated," says Colette Gentes-Hawn, a CCRA spokeswoman. "But we need specific rules to ensure fairness."

The investor must use a self-directed RRSP and the RRSP trustee (usually an investment dealer) must check out the small business to make sure the share value is reasonable. Once the business is approved as an RRSP investment, the investment dealer will release RRSP funds and swap them for shares.

It can be time-consuming to get the approvals, Bulloch warns. Investors who advance funds to a company may have to arrange bridge financing from a bank while waiting for RRSP funds to be released. Vubiz's first RRSP investment took nine months to be completed. The second took three months, while the third was done in three weeks. (Bulloch cut off RRSP investments after the first $75,000, though he had commitments for more. It was taking too much of his time.)

In fairness, Bulloch notes, it's not easy to establish the value of shares in a private company. He solved that by offering shares to investors at the same value that he paid for his own shares. This measure should be used only for second-stage financing (rather than start-up capital), he says, since the value is easier to establish.

It's too bad the government has failed to publicize a useful tax measure that could help small businesses in Canada raise equity. If you're interested, shop around for an investment dealer that understands the rules.

RRSP flip can deliver added tax refund

You can get a tax refund each year without putting any new money into your RRSP. This little-known strategy involves buying a labour-sponsored venture capital fund with money that's already inside the plan.

Labour-sponsored funds invest in small and medium-sized Canadian businesses, many of which are in their early stages and haven't yet gone through a public offering. The government gives you an incentive—in the form of rich tax credits—to buy these high-risk funds.

For a $5,000 investment, you get $750 back from the federal government. You may also get another $750 from the provincial government, depending on where you live. (In Ontario, investors can get up to $1,000 if they invest in a more risky kind of labour fund that finances research in universities and hospitals). Unless you hang on to your labour fund units for eight years, you'll have to repay the tax credits you received.

If you're a patient, long-term investor and don't mind devoting some of your retirement plan assets to more-speculative investments, you may want to investigate the RRSP flip. Here's the drill:

■ Use assets in an existing RRSP to acquire a labour-sponsored fund. Do this before February 28 or March 1, the deadline for getting a refund on your previous year's tax return.

■ File your tax return, attaching the receipt for the labour fund contribution. In a month or two, you should get your tax assessment and refund cheque.

■ The most you can invest is $5,000 a year, meaning you get back $750 in most provinces (and $1,500 to $1,750 in Ontario). These tax credits are non-refundable, so you must have enough taxable income to cover them.

You can spend your tax refund if you like. But if you want to invest the money you get back, here are a few suggestions from Winnipeg tax author Evelyn Jacks:

■ Contribute to your spouse's RRSP or one for your children, as long as they have earned income.

■ Contribute to a registered education savings plan for your child. This means you can get the Canada Education Savings Grant. The federal government will give a 20 per cent rebate, up to $400 a year, on your RESP contribution.

■ Pay back any loans you took out to buy an RRSP. Or repay money withdrawn from an RRSP under the home buyers' plan or the lifelong learning plan.

Jacks likes the idea of flipping RRSP assets into labour funds so you can generate money for other financial planning needs. (This investment should not be made without discussion with your financial adviser, she says.)

RRSP flips are trickier for older people. They can transfer labour fund units held in an RRSP to a registered retirement income fund, but can't buy new labour fund units once they reach age 69 and convert their RRSP to a RRIF. However, they can buy labour funds and hold them outside an RRSP at any age.

When you do the RRSP flip inside a spousal RRSP, either spouse may claim the labour fund tax credit. However, only the contributor can claim the tax deduction.

There are several dozen labour-sponsored funds to choose from, with new ones being launched all the time. Many funds have a strong focus on technology, a narrow approach that increases your risk exponentially. Stick to labour funds with a more diversified approach.

We need a new way to look at fund fees

Mutual funds were the favourite RRSP investment for many years. But the bear market made investors anxious, confused and hesitant to buy more funds. In November 2002, a survey by RBC Financial Group found almost three-quarters of respondents "in a state of investment inertia," too stunned to review their RRSP portfolios or make any changes. More than half (51 per cent) owned mutual funds in a retirement savings plan. But 41 per cent didn't know what type of funds they held and 36 per cent weren't sure of the current value of what they held.

I sense a growing public anger and distrust. Many people feel betrayed by what they see as a gap between what the mutual fund industry promises and what it delivers. It starts with the assumption of never-ending growth, the incessant optimism shared by virtually everyone selling mutual funds. Bearish predictions don't help sales.

Another assumption underlying the industry is that there are superstar managers, who can deliver excellent results in good markets and bad. But while everyone talks about Warren Buffett, "the Wizard of Omaha," it's hard to identify superstars on the Canadian scene. Investors have learned that no manager stays on top consistently and shines in all types of market conditions. That's why you need different investment styles in your portfolio.

If fund sellers can't pick the superior managers, then why pay for their advice? That's another question investors are asking themselves. Advice is bundled into the cost of mutual funds. Financial advisers receive sales commissions and a share of the annual management fees paid by fund investors, whether they provide good service or not.

And why do management fees and expenses constantly go up, even when funds get bigger? Why aren't there discounts because of economies of scale? Managers didn't cut costs during the bull market of the 1990s, nor did they cut costs once the bear market began in March 2000.

I think the industry will come under pressure to change when investors wise up to the fact that costs are eating up their meagre returns. We need a new way of looking at the fund's management-expense ratio (MER), normally shown as a percentage of assets. A $100 million fund that deducts $2 million in costs has a two per cent MER.

Suppose that $100 million fund goes up six per cent a year, a pretty good return in current market conditions. After the two per cent MER is deducted, investors get a four per cent return. In other words, they lose one-third of their gain. And if the fund earns only four per cent before costs, the MER consumes half of the gain. Now doesn't that put a different spin on the damage that high costs can do?

In fact, a two per cent MER is on the low side for equity funds. Many have MERs that exceed 2.5 per cent. According to a Morningstar Canada study in 2003, the average expense ratio for mutual funds sold in Canada had grown to 2.62 per cent, up from 2.02 per cent in 1995. Specialized funds—such as labour-sponsored funds, hedge funds and life insurance segregated funds—have MERs that may exceed four per cent.

"You're going to see MERs trending down," says David Chilton, a big fan of mutual funds when his best-selling book, *The Wealthy Barber*, came out in the late 1980s. Today, he's worried that high costs are eroding their advantage—especially with lower-cost rivals, such as exchange-traded funds, now on the scene. He thinks the bear market will force investors to become more cost-conscious. "There aren't many industries that will voluntarily lower prices when no one is complaining," he says.

If you think mutual funds have become money-hungry marketing machines, you're not alone. John C. Bogle, founder of the giant fund manager Vanguard Group Inc. (based in Valley Forge, Pennsylvania), thinks marketing has replaced management in the mutual-fund driver's seat. "The art of persuasion has crowded out the art of performance," he argued in a book published in 2000, *Common Sense on Mutual Funds* (John Wiley & Sons).

Bogle, known as Jack, is a crusty septuagenarian who calls himself an outcast in the industry he helped shape for almost 50 years. To understand his argument, consider this paradox. Why is it often more profitable to own shares of fund managers like Investors Group than to own the funds they manage? The way the industry is structured, he explains, there's a "profound conflict of interest" between fund managers and investors.

Mutual funds are owned by investors—but there are so many investors, and they're so spread out, they don't exercise working control. Instead, control is vested in an external management company that provides essential services—such as investment advice, distribution, marketing and administration—in return for an annual fee. Fund managers take investors' money (without their consent) to pay for advertising. Then they reap the benefits as the assets roll in. "A dollar in profits for the management company is a dollar less for the mutual fund shareholders. It's as simple as that," Bogle says.

Vanguard, founded in 1974, is one of the biggest U.S. fund managers. It specializes in buy-and-hold index funds that replicate market averages. The only U.S. fund firm that manages its own affairs on a cost basis, Vanguard boasts razor-thin expenses, as low as 25 cents on $100 in assets.

A Canadian investor organized a letter-writing campaign in 1998 to put pressure on Vanguard to come north. "John Bogle is the only advocate for the investor in the entire mutual fund industry. We sure need the likes of him up here," said Bylo Selhi (whose name, based on the famous investment advice "buy low, sell high," is a pseudonym). The campaign went nowhere, but Bylo's not unhappy. "With all the low-MER Canadian-based index funds, Canadian-based exchange-traded funds (ETFs) and U.S.-based ETFs that are now available through

Canadian brokers, there's also less *need* to own Vanguard funds than there used to be," he says. Check out his Web site (www.bylo.org), a veritable encyclopedia of helpful stuff on investing, MERs and low-cost alternatives.

Here's my advice: Start asking everyone in the industry when MERs will come down. And start calculating how much of your return is being eaten up by costs. That's a first step in becoming more militant on this issue.

A *Toronto Star* reader had a different way of looking at fees—as a percentage of the fund's return over and above the relevant index. "I tell friends to think of it this way: In these days of rising prices, suppose there was an additive to put in your car's tank with each fill-up that would increase your car's mileage by 10 per cent ($4 on each $40 fill-up). Sounds good, right? Now, if I tell you the additive costs $6 at each fill-up, how many treatments of the additive are you likely to purchase?" he said.

Index and exchange-traded funds treat RRSP ennui

Do you suffer from RRSP ennui? It's a new disease I made up, a feeling of boredom and disgust with the available investment choices. RRSP ennui has a well-known symptom, which you may recognize. In January or February, you contribute to your plan by parking cash in a low-interest savings account or money market fund—and delay making a decision on the investments until a later date.

But there's a danger in waiting. You may forget to check back with your RRSP until you get an annual statement. At this point, you realize you've earned almost nothing on your savings—and it's time to make the next year's contribution. Another problem with procrastinating is that you won't know when to switch out of cash. If the stock market has already moved up, you think you're too late. If it's pulling back, you're nervous that it will fall more. There's never a right time.

Finally, you're ready to invest for the long term. But what if the top-ranked fund you invested in before is down in the dumps, performing more poorly than its rivals? Maybe it's time to stop picking fund managers and pick indexes instead.

Consider whether you agree with this statement: "I believe that some actively managed funds will beat the index, but I do not believe that it is possible to consistently pick the winners in advance." If so, you're a candidate for buying index funds, those that try to do no more than mirror the benchmark stock and bond averages in different investment categories. If you buy index funds, you can take much of the emotion out of investing. You won't remove your money from sinking funds just before they begin to rebound and put your dough into zooming funds just before they stall.

You have lots of choices. There are dozens of traditional index funds and also an abundance of newer exchange-traded funds (ETFs), which tend to have lower management expense ratios. While index funds have MERs ranging from 0.5 per cent to one per cent, the Barclays iUnits S&P/TSE 60 index fund—which trades on the Toronto Stock Exchange under the symbol XIU—has a management expense ratio of just 0.17 per cent. The iUnits bond index fund has an MER of 0.25 per cent.

Will ETFs put extra money in your pocket? You can try out different scenarios using the MER impact calculator at the iUnits Web site, www.iunits.com. I compared the Templeton International Stock Fund (MER of 2.71 per cent) with the iUnits MSCI International Index RRSP (MER of 0.35 per cent). Here's what I found:

- If you invest $10,000 in both funds for 20 years at a pre-cost return of six per cent, you end up with $32,071.

- The MER on the Templeton fund after 20 years is $13,420, leaving you with a net return of $18,652.

- The MER on the iUnits fund after 20 years is $2,280, leaving you with a net return of $29,791.

This example assumes both funds have the same returns. I did another comparison, building in a higher gain for the actively managed fund than the exchange-traded fund. Here's the result:

- If you invest $10,000 in the AIC Advantage Fund at a pre-cost return of eight per cent, you end up with $46,610 after 20 years.

- The AIC fund's MER of 2.41 per cent adds up to $17,826 over 20 years, leaving you with a net return of $28,783.

- If you invest $10,000 in the iUnits S&P/TSE Canadian MidCap at a pre-cost return of six per cent, you end up with $32,071 after 20 years.

- The iUnits fund's MER of 0.55 per cent adds up to $3,449 over 20 years, leaving you with a net return of $28,622.

In this example, the exchange-traded fund lags behind the actively managed fund (by $161 after 20 years), despite its much lower MER. That's because of the wide gap of two percentage points in performance. Will you be lucky enough to pick a fund that beats the index by so much and for so long? If you doubt your skills (or your adviser's skills) in finding these star performers, you may be better off with the index fund.

You pay commissions to buy and sell exchange-traded funds and you need to open a brokerage account. The iUnits calculator assumes you pay a discount brokerage commission of $28 to buy and sell exchange-traded funds. That's a bit misleading, because it ignores the higher commissions charged by full-service brokers. But as an offsetting factor, the calculator excludes any up-front or deferred sales charges paid by mutual fund investors.

So, if you're suffering from RRSP ennui, check out exchange-traded funds. You'll find a wide range of choices at the Web site of the American Stock Exchange, www.amex.com. They're an investment you can stick into your retirement plan and ignore. That's my idea of excitement.

Don't let your RRSP payments go astray

This is the story of two people whose RRSP contributions went astray in late February. Both were upset to learn they missed the deadline to get a tax deduction for 2002. Luckily, the financial institutions agreed to backdate the receipts once I got involved, so the clients got their tax refunds after all.

It's always a bit frantic from mid-February to early March, even in a slow RRSP season. The deadline-induced rush to contribute to a registered retirement savings plan means there's enough transaction volume that things can get overlooked. In both cases, the clients were not told about their missing RRSP contributions in a timely way. This made things worse when the problems became known.

Debbie, the first person I heard from, planned to find another financial adviser because of the RRSP snafu. She had met with her investment representative on Feb. 22. "I didn't have enough money for an RRSP contribution, so we discussed doing a contribution in kind," she says. A contribution in kind works well if you're short of cash and own investments outside a tax-sheltered plan. You can move these investments into a self-directed RRSP to get a tax deduction, but you pay tax on any gain in market value since the purchase.

Since Debbie had purchased a $20,000 corporate bond two months earlier, she decided to contribute a $12,000 chunk of the bond to her plan. She was looking forward to getting enough money back from the government to paint her house. On March 22, she called to ask about her tax receipt. Only then did she get the news that her contribution was too late to make the March 3 deadline for the 2002 tax year.

Debbie's investment representative refused to speak to me. She worked with Edward Jones, a U.S. brokerage firm that has opened 570 offices in Canada since 1994, with 250 of them in the Toronto area. Luckily, the Canadian head office took the complaint more seriously. "As soon as this came to our attention, we addressed it," said Don Burwell, head of compliance for Edward Jones. A contribution in kind is fairly simple, he told me, and the delay was not the client's fault. Burwell was satisfied that Debbie had given instructions to transfer the assets before the deadline.

I also heard from a man in a similar predicament (who didn't want his name used). Short of cash for an RRSP contribution, he had agreed to take out a loan for a spousal plan with ING Direct, the Dutch-owned online bank. He had spoken to a customer service representative by phone on Feb. 24 and had sent his application form by registered mail on Feb. 25, along with a void cheque to allow monthly deductions from his account.

On Feb. 27, he got a call from ING saying there were problems with his loan application. He thought they were straightened out during the conversation. "The call entailed long waits/holds and some annoyance at not having been provided the correct advice in the first place, because we had followed those instructions to the T," he said.

A month later, he called ING looking for his tax receipt and found no contribution had been made on his behalf. This came as a shock. It seems he was so frustrated by his Feb. 27 conversation he told customer service "it did not really matter if the RRSP went through or not." He didn't recall saying that, but the company records all conversations with clients and had it on tape.

Still, how could a representative decide unilaterally to close his file after all the time and effort he had spent? "Wasn't she obliged to advise us that she was 'junking' our RRSP application so we could have made alternative arrangements?" the man asked.

The RRSP loan was pre-approved based on the man's financial situation, said Andrew Ross, communications director at ING Direct. The company didn't know until later the loan was for a spousal RRSP, which entailed checking the wife's credit rating as well. "There was miscommunication on what was required," Ross said.

The moral: Don't wait till the last weeks of February, especially if you're doing something out of the ordinary with your RRSP. But if you miss the deadline because of a company's mistake, there's hope. You can get your receipt backdated if you put up a good fight.

Focus on enjoying life now, rather than later

Freedom 55. Wouldn't it be nice? London Life Insurance Co. owns the name (even calling its Web site www.freedom55financial.com) and has helped popularize the dream of early retirement. Why slave at a job you dislike till you're 65? By the time you get out from under, you may be too old and tired to have any fun.

Those who retire in their mid-60s and drop out of the rat race are not always happy with their decision. Disillusionment rates are sky-high for retirees. In one U.S. survey, 41 per cent of retirees called it the most difficult adjustment of their life and said they still struggled with the monotony, boredom, lack of purpose and lack of intellectual stimulation that traditional retirement offers.

"Most people don't really want retirement as we know it," says Mitch Anthony, author of *The New Retirementality: Planning Your Life and Living Your Dreams…at Any Age You Want* (Dearborn Trade). "What they want is the freedom to pursue their goals and interests. They want to call their own shots. They want to do what they want, when they want and where they want. They want change from the rut that their life of employment has become." He stresses the importance of finding work you love rather than focusing on retirement. "I think retirement is a failed social experiment," he said.

"Retirement was designed to be a one- to two-year bridge to the grave, not a 25-year journey. The first thing I like to encourage people to do with their financial life planning is figure out something they're passionate about, because passion is a greater payoff than a paycheque."

In Canada, early retirement has become a reality for many people—partly because of widespread corporate downsizing. The average retirement age has dropped to 61.5 for those in the private sector and 57 for those in the public sector. Two-thirds of Canadians now retire before the full CPP/QPP age of 65. "People generally have more money now, so they're more interested in early retirement," says Ian Markham of Watson Wyatt Worldwide, a Toronto-based benefits planning firm.

So how do you decide when to retire? As a first step, you can ask your employer about the age at which you can draw an unreduced pension. Suppose you're 60 years old and have 30 years of service with your company. You're offered a defined-benefit pension of $30,000 a year if you retire.

Take the money and run, Markham advises. If you stay till age 65, you likely won't get enough extra pension entitlement to justify losing $30,000 a year. That's especially true if your salary remains flat. "People often continue to work—they like the job or they're not ready to retire—and still gain financially in nearly all cases," he says, referring to the salaries they earn. "But they may not see any increase in the value of their pensions."

Another thing to remember: We're entering an age when there will be shortages of skilled workers. The number of people retiring in Canada is projected to increase from 239,000 in 2001 to 426,000 by 2026, according to the Urban Futures Institute in Vancouver. "Employers will be thinking longer and harder about letting people go, realizing they will be harder to replace," says Markham, who believes early retirement plans will shrink dramatically.

Ask your employer about "phased-in" or gradual retirement programs. You may be able to work out a deal in which you retire but continue to work on a contract basis with your old company because your skills are in demand. Another option is to negotiate a reduced-hours package, while maintaining your full pension contributions.

If there's nothing at your current workplace, speak to a few corporate recruiters. They're often on the lookout for seasoned pros to place in short-term contracts with companies that are reorganizing or going through a lengthy search for a new executive. "If you're fit, if you have energy and keep up to date with technology and new business developments, age no longer is a factor. Experience is in," says a corporate recruiter, who has parachuted in people well into their seventies for temporary placements.

Of course, many people haven't saved enough to finance early retirement—or retirement at any age. The median value of RRSPs for people in the 45-to-55 age group is just $30,000, say authors Ranga Chand and Sylvia Carmichael in *Is Your Retirement at Risk?* (Stoddart). As Canadians' life expectancy has risen, "it's possible we could be living 30 years in retirement. Where's the money going to come from? And what if there's a bear market at the start of your retirement? Our research shows that could lead to a 40 per cent drop in income."

Chand wrote the book as a wake-up call for people to start saving for retirement. "Get on autopilot when you're young," he says, "and you'll never have to think about retirement again." But the alternative may not be so bad either. "People are living healthily for longer, so many workers might not be averse to staying on the job for a few more years," he writes. "A great number of them might even welcome such an outcome, which would give them a chance not only to accumulate more savings for retirement, but also to remain a productive part of society for longer."

You may want to work with your current employer beyond age 65, depending on the company's retirement policy. You can apply for and receive your CPP pension at age 65, or you can choose not to apply for CPP and keep contributing until age 70. Your CPP pension will be adjusted upward by 0.5 per cent a month for each month after your sixty-fifth birthday.

For information on all your retirement options, check with your employer first. You may have access to pre-retirement courses or one-on-one counselling sessions with a financial planning firm. Also, check with Human Resources Development Canada about your Canada Pension Plan entitlement (or the Quebec government if you're eligible for the Quebec Pension Plan). HRDC has set up a Web site, Work-Life Balance in Canadian Workplaces, http://labour-travail.hrdc-drhc.gc.ca/worklife, with a wealth of information about the issues of an aging work force. A key study, "Collective Agreements and Older Workers in Canada," shows what unions have negotiated and what you can aim for in your negotiations with employers in non-unionized firms.

Running a business is a common choice among people who have retired or who switch careers in mid-life. Often it's a small business in a rural setting, says Donna Messer, owner of a career-counselling firm in Toronto. She talks about a retired service manager at Xerox Canada Inc., who bought a bed and breakfast establishment, and another retired executive from Rolls-Royce Ltd., who operates a fishing lodge. Some older people switch into financial planning because they have a strong interest in managing their own money— and can work with others their own age who haven't saved enough for retirement.

part five

Financial Planning and Your Extended Family

Financial planning is all about trying to anticipate what may happen in the future and making preparations in advance. You never know what life will throw at you, but there are a few certainties in most people's lives—aging, illness and death. If you plan for these contingencies, you won't be caught off guard.

Does this kind of talk upset you? You're not alone. You want your loved ones to stay healthy and you don't want to think about a time when they're not around. Moreover, it seems morbid to arm yourself with financial tools to use when someone is ill or dying. That's why many people never get around to having the crucial conversations with family members or making any plans for the future. They're too intimidated.

It's important to talk to your parents about their financial affairs, but you may find yourself rebuffed when you try. Older people are often reluctant to discuss their finances with their children. Sometimes, the best way to start a conversation with your parents is to talk about your own plans for the future. You mention you've done your will recently or you've reviewed it to see if any changes are needed. Have they done their own wills and updated them? If not, maybe they'd like to consult the same lawyer you used or maybe you can get a referral to a lawyer in their community.

If the conversation is going well, you can broach the next topic. You tell your parents that along with your will, your lawyer drafted a power of attorney. What's that? It's a document in which you appoint someone to manage your financial affairs or make decisions about your health care if you can't act for yourself. Is that a good thing to do? Sure, it is. Here's a copy of the form you signed so they can look it over.

My own father was never receptive to this kind of talk. He made his preparations and didn't want to discuss them, even with his wife. But after he died, my mother moved to Toronto from Montreal. That meant her will had to be redone, a perfect opportunity to open a discussion about what she wanted. My brothers and I also made sure to get a power of attorney for health care and for finances.

Now that's all taken care of, we're dealing with more difficult stuff. She's shaky on her feet and we want her to use a walker. She says never. Her memory isn't what it used to be, so we insist she gets her pills dispensed by the nurses at her retirement home. She says she can do it herself. We're bargaining with her all the time to get more help and she's trying to hang on to her last shreds of independence.

You may be coping with changes in your parents' lives and capabilities, too, while facing the challenges of bringing up children still living at home. At the same time, you're working at a demanding job and trying to fit your caregiving responsibilities into the limited time you have on evenings and weekends. It's a tough balancing act.

In this section, I'll tell you how to negotiate with your employer for a more flexible schedule and more time off during the day. Hint: Get your co-workers to buy in before you approach the boss. I'll talk about a type of trust that helps provide for disabled children after the parents have gone. I'll also look at the reverse mortgage, which appeals to older people who are house-rich and cash-poor. It's not the panacea it appears to be and the ads don't tell you everything you need to know.

Along the way, I'll zero in on how to protect elders from fraud and make sure they get the government benefits to which they're entitled. Finally, the funeral: Do you want to plan it in advance and do you want to prepay as well? If that's not staring death in the face, then what is? Read on if you dare.

Elder care is a looming workplace challenge

In the 1980s and 1990s, Canadian employers were under pressure to help workers who were starting families. Today, there's a new workplace challenge, one that could cost business dearly in terms of absenteeism, low morale and lost productivity. Many workers are caring for elderly relatives, who are living longer than ever—but often in poor health and with little community support.

Some people will quit their jobs. The stress of family caregiving, combined with work demands and responsibility for children living at home, will cause burnout. "In Canada, 32 per cent of people with conflicts between their work and home life turned down or chose not to apply for promotions and transfers and considered quitting—or actually quit—their jobs," said Roy Romanow, who headed a commission looking into the future of health care in Canada. "Families are often caught between paying for care in an institution like a nursing home, paying for home care or losing income because giving care at home is competing with their job."

The lack of support for unpaid caregivers discriminates against women, Romanow's preliminary report noted. Most caregivers are women and they're usually the primary caregiver (even if a man is also giving care). And there's a growing tendency in Canada to shift care of older people from hospitals to a lower-cost home setting.

Elder care is not yet on the radar screen for many companies. The Conference Board of Canada surveyed 1,528 private and public organizations in 1999 and found fewer than half (43 per cent) had implemented even one program to help employees dealing with elder-care issues. Information and referral programs were the most common initiative, adopted by 37 per cent of Canadian companies. Only six per cent of companies had such services in 1989. But few organizations offered financial assistance for caregivers, respite care or emergency-care programs. Companies said they hadn't heard from employees of the need for such benefits.

Employees are reluctant to talk about caregiving responsibilities in the workplace, said Raynia Carr, program manager of family matters at Warren Shepell Consultants, which handles about 7,000 requests for dependent care each year under employee assistance programs. "There's still a stigma about elder care, because it doesn't operate on the employer's time clock. You get a call at the office saying your mother has fallen and broken her hip and you have to stop doing everything and run," she pointed out.

Companies have to train middle managers and give them the latitude and flexibility to help people solve work-life conflicts. "Elder care is episodic in nature—unlike child care, which is more intense," says Nora Spinks, president of Work Life Harmony Enterprises, a consulting and research firm in Toronto. "With elder care, absences are totally unpredictable and there's no early warning system. People need to step out of the work force and step back again. Employers will have to be more flexible around those career breaks and absences."

As caregiving needs increase, employees will demand more of their employers than a phone number to call for resources in the community. "Expectations will escalate," Spinks says. "Employees will want case co-ordination, case management, intense consultation and assistance in dealing with situations where there are no services to purchase."

Beyond referrals, employers and employee assistance programs can offer workplace seminars on elder care. These work best when they're interactive and allow employees to share tips about caregiving. "The best solution-finders are often those who've had the same problems," Raynia Carr said.

Some companies allow employees to charge their family care leave against their sick leave credits. Ask your employer if this is an option, assuming you don't need to use the sick leave you've accumulated for your own medical care. "This flexibility measure may be a sign of an evolving situation whereby family-related responsibilities are increasingly acknowledged as being as important as health-related needs," says the federal government study on collective agreements and older workers.

Help your parents plan for aging

Karen Henderson spent 14 years looking after her father as he grew more ill and sank into dementia. Frustrated with her inability to find the support she needed, she set up a company called Caregiver Network Inc., a resource centre for adult children and seniors facing elder care (caregiver.on.ca). "We plan for vacations, we plan for children's education, but we don't plan for aging," she says.

For the first time in history, a significant portion of the population is entering middle life with one or more parents still alive. Statistics Canada's 2001 census data shows fewer seniors living in health-care institutions. There are several million unpaid caregivers in Canada, working to keep elderly relatives out of long-term care facilities. Resentments are quick to build up, especially when the burden of care falls unequally. Some siblings take over and feel oppressed, while others complain about being kept out of the loop.

Henderson advises families to hold meetings and create agendas. Let everyone talk and make decisions together. If that proves impossible, hire an objective third party as facilitator. Ask parents about their wishes before a crisis hits, rather than making guesses later. "Recognize the speed at which chaos can descend from a fall or an unexpected medical event or diagnosis," she advises. Falls are the leading cause of injuries in people age 65 and over. They lead to loss of independence for the elderly and more stress for caregivers.

Your parents may be getting older, but doing fine on their own. Then you notice some troubling signs. Their personal hygiene starts to slip or their home isn't as clean as before. They forget birthdays or holidays or special occasions. They've always managed their own finances, but now they're not paying bills promptly, or they're neglecting income-tax payments. You worry about interest charges and tax penalties, collection letters and withdrawal of essential services.

This is the time to talk to your parents about their changing needs—not when a crisis forces you to make decisions and guess what they want. But how do you initiate the conversation? What should you do if you're held back by feelings of denial, dread and a desire to preserve the status quo? I asked caregiving experts how to get family members to open up and plan for the future. "Always say what you want in the other person's terms," said Mary Ellen Tomlinson, client services director of Senior Care Options Inc. in Toronto, who gives workplace seminars. "For example, justify your need for information by your parents' need for fast action in a crisis."

Don't mention money at first, since that's a sensitive issue. Start with health care, Tomlinson suggested. Record your parents' health card numbers and medication files. Ask how long they've been taking their drugs and why they're taking them. Go with your parents to meet their doctors and pharmacists. You can help them ask the right questions and put the answers in writing. If necessary, you can request a geriatric assessment by a specialist.

Take the same approach with finances. Gather information (such as account numbers for savings and investments) and meet the people in the financial institutions who are looking after your parents' money. Again, emphasize your need to handle things quickly in an emergency. For example, what if your dad has a stroke or a heart attack when he's 69? This is the deadline for converting a registered retirement savings plan to a registered retirement income fund or annuity. Your dad could miss the deadline and pay unnecessarily high taxes on his RRSP unless he hands over decision-making authority to a family member.

Patty Randall of British Columbia, author of a book about caregiving, tells the story of her dad's savings account that had earned no interest since he retired in 1972. She finally reviewed his banking in 1996 and was appalled to think how much money he could have earned in the 24 years. She confronted the bank representative and was told, "Many seniors have accounts like this still. They don't seem to like change." She blamed herself for not paying closer attention to her parents' banking affairs.

In her self-published book, *Let's Talk: The Care Years* (Trafford), Randall talks about taking precautionary measures to simplify banking matters:

- Have authorization forms on file so you can get access to information about the status of your parents' accounts by telephone, fax or computer. That's because caregiving-related dollars are often needed on the spur of the moment and must be handed over quickly.

- Ensure that all your parents' cheques (old age pension, disability, interest) are directly deposited to the proper accounts.

- Obtain an access card linking a parent's account to one of your own accounts for easy transfer of money, bill payments and special needs.

- Set up easy payment methods for regular bills (utilities, newspaper subscriptions, insurance policies) through an automatic debit system.

- Apply for a credit card to use exclusively for caregiving expenses, in order to help take some of the financial burden off your parents. A designated card also helps keep track of costs for income tax purposes and for reimbursement from health insurance plans.

No matter what you say, your offers of help may be rejected. "Try to understand your parents' reluctance to accept your assistance," says Barbara Jaworski, director of work-life solutions for FGI, an employee assistance provider in Toronto. "Any loss of independence can be difficult, and help signals the loss of independence. Recognize it's their choice whether they will accept or reject offers of help. Take the lead from your parents. Try to let them maintain control of their own destiny, provided that their health or safety isn't threatened."

If a parent refuses to talk, consider bringing in an outsider—a trusted family friend, family physician or social worker—to mediate. That's a solution favoured by Karen Henderson of Caregiver Network Inc. "You may have to leave the room," she advises adult children. "Proceed slowly. Let your parent think it was their idea. If siblings cannot agree, hold a separate meeting and hash out the solutions. If necessary, consider a mediator for this meeting as well."

Henderson devotes a section of her Web site, www.howtocare.com, to what's called The Conversation. She's realistic and knows that, sometimes, adult children hit a wall. What to do if a parent refuses all help, even though he or she is at risk (but is still deemed competent)? "The caregiver can only stand by and wait until something happens—a fall, a fire—which necessitates medical or other intervention. This is called 'dignity of risk' and it's a situation no one wants to face," Henderson says.

If you find yourself in the position of not being able to get a discussion going, don't despair. Talk to health-care, financial and legal experts about the issues, so you can be as prepared and informed as possible. And keep looking for opportunities to begin the critical conversation with your parents. It's never too late.

Don't forget to appoint power of attorney

Adult children need to ask their parents this question: "If you get sick and can't speak for yourself, who will speak for you? We're not talking about just finances here, but also about personal care—where you live, what you eat, your hygiene, safety and medical treatment. Chances are you'll never lose your ability to speak for yourself. But in case you become incapacitated, who will be your advocate and substitute decision-maker?"

You can appoint someone to act on your behalf, in writing, through a document called a power of attorney for personal care. (This document goes by different names, depending on the province where you live.) You must sign and date the document if it is to be valid. As well, two witnesses must be present and must co-sign the document in your presence and in the presence of each other. The person you appoint as substitute decision-maker can't act as a witness and neither can his or her spouse or partner. The witnesses can't be under 18 years old and can't be your spouse, partner or child.

Now we've gotten all the legal formalities out of the way, let's talk about how you choose your health care advocate. Obviously, it will be someone you trust. You can't choose someone who's paid to provide you with personal care, such as a nurse, or someone under 16 years of age. If you appoint two or more people to act together on your behalf, they must agree before making any decisions for you—unless you state in the document that they can make decisions separately.

Toronto lawyers Les Kotzer and Barry Fish have seen families torn apart by poor planning or lack of planning. In their book, *The Family Fight: Planning to Avoid It*, they provide questions for parents to ask when drafting a power of attorney for personal care. For example, if you have one child who lives in your city and one child who lives far away, will it be inconvenient to make both children act together? If you appoint three or more children, will you require unanimity? Or will you allow the majority to decide? If so, will two strong children overpower a weak one?

Think twice before appointing all your children to look after you, Fish and Kotzer advise. Physical location is important, since the health-care advocate should live nearby and be able to arrive quickly in a crisis. You should pick a health-care agent who you feel is most dedicated to you and will be the most likely to carry out your wishes. "It's not an easy job, so don't think that you're hurting someone's feelings by not appointing him or her," they say. Do all the children want the responsibility? Do they have the maturity and ability to carry out the duties that will be required—getting access to medical records, dealing with doctors, making decisions about nursing home admission?

There are ways to ensure that your surrogates exercise their powers responsibly, says lawyer Tom Carter in his book, *Your Health Care Directive* (Self-Counsel Press). You can require your substitute decision-maker to report to certain people on a regular basis and keep written records of any decisions made. You can ask your family doctor to get involved. Many doctors are happy to spend time reviewing these documents and answering questions about the medical issues that arise.

You can express your beliefs about medical treatment in writing. Pretend you're writing a letter to someone and use it as a way to capture the key elements of your values. Show your statement to the person you're thinking of choosing as an advocate and ask if you've made yourself clear. Include your statement in the power of attorney for personal care when both of you are satisfied.

After you've completed the document, give it to the person you've appointed or keep it in a safe place at home. Many people carry a wallet card that gives details on their substitute decision-maker.

In Ontario, you can get a free wallet card and a guide to advance care planning from the Ministry of Citizenship (www.gov.on.ca/citizenship/seniors, 1-888-910-1999).

Who will manage your money if you can't?

Once parents participate in a conversation about health care, they may be more open to discussing their finances. The question to ask: "Who will manage your money if you are alive but cannot make decisions for yourself because you're physically or mentally infirm?"

The person you name should be someone you trust, who understands your personal values and will follow your instructions. If you haven't left detailed instructions, he or she will make decisions based on what is in your best interest and will stand up for your wishes.

To appoint a substitute decision-maker for finances in Ontario, the document to use is called a continuing power of attorney for property. "This is a powerful document," says Toronto author Sandra Foster in her *Estate Planning Workbook* (John Wiley & Sons). "It gives someone else the power to make any decision you could make (except decisions related to estate planning, such as writing a will). Naming the wrong person to act as your attorney or representative could lead to major abuses of this power."

The alternative is to let an official of the provincial public guardian and trustee look after your finances if you're incapacitated and can't make your own decisions. This means your immediate family or those close to you have no automatic right to manage your finances on your behalf—at least, not without obtaining court approval.

Someone you appoint as your power of attorney for financial decisions will perform duties that may include locating assets and debts, collecting income, paying bills, managing investments, filing tax returns, signing legal documents and maintaining accurate records of activities done on your behalf. These duties end when you're no longer incapacitated or when you die. The executor named in your will takes over after your death to wrap up the estate.

If you name more than one person and don't say how they should make their decisions, the law says they must make all their decisions together (that is, unanimously). You might want to specify how disagreements will get resolved. If no one is available, you can name a trust company as your substitute decision-maker for a fee. Friends and family members usually go unpaid, but you can build in a fair price for their work if you want to do so.

There's a good chance your power of attorney won't be recognized by your bank. Financial institutions generally require you to sign their own legal forms, regardless of any other documents you have prepared. Similarly, your documents may not be accepted in the United States. "The more remote the area, the greater the chance of rejection," say Douglas Gray and John Budd in *The Canadian Guide to Will and Estate Planning* (McGraw-Hill Ryerson). They advise snowbirds who winter down south to pay $100 to $200 (U.S.) to get a power of attorney drawn up by a local lawyer.

Before naming a financial surrogate, you should make sure that he or she is willing to accept the responsibilities. Les Kotzer and Barry Fish recall a situation where a client appointed one of his adult children to carry out his wishes, but neglected to consult the person in advance. Alas, the person refused to act when the time came. The other children would have been happy to take over their father's finances, but it was too late to name them. You can find stories of how poor planning can tear families apart at the two lawyers' Web site, www.familyfight.com.

Husbands and wives should have their own continuing power of attorney for property. One document can't carry out the function for both spouses. A marriage licence does not allow spouses to act for each other if one becomes incapable. "This is a false comfort," say Kotzer and Fish. "A marriage licence confers no such authority."

Don't play favourites when making a will

We've talked about initiating discussions with parents about a power of attorney for health care and for property. It's also important to ask if they have a will. Tell them you want to make sure everything is covered, while making it plain you're not looking for details on who's been left what.

Wills are needed to answer two questions, says estate planning lawyer Barry Fish: Who looks after what you've got when you die? (That is, who will be your executor?) And how is your property distributed?

When it comes to choosing someone to manage their affairs, parents should check with children first to see if they're willing to do the job. Being the executor can be tough and time-consuming. You have to find the assets, pay the bills and hand out everything that is left to the beneficiaries according to the instructions in the will.

Lawyer Tom Carter didn't know what executors were up against until he worked as a trust officer for a trust company. (Trust companies are routinely named as executors in wills.) He often went into people's homes and searched for important papers inside drawers, housecoat pockets, envelopes, boxes and cupboards. His job was to make sure that a crumpled-up savings bond, a diamond ring, a stock certificate or a $1,000 bill wasn't tossed out inadvertently with the trash. "If this seems like a lot of work for a trained professional like a trust officer, what about the person who has never done anything like this before and has to try to squeeze it all in between getting the children to school and going to work?" he asks in *Wills Guide for Canada* (Self-Counsel Press).

Some people, because they can't think of the perfect person to be their executor, never get around to signing their wills. Carter calls this condition "executor anxiety." Since it's a big responsibility, parents should name more than one executor and have one or two back-up choices. The executors can hire accountants and lawyers to help with any complicated issues.

As for distributing assets, parents should treat children equally unless there are special circumstances. "All children should share in your estate regardless of their income and position," says Toronto estate lawyer Edward Olkovich. Parents who play favourites risk leaving a lifetime of pain for children who carry the burden of feeling unfairly treated.

"You can treat them unequally while you are alive," Olkovich says, giving the example of a daughter who lives with older parents and takes care of them. The parents may be justified in giving her their home. But they should inform their family while they can, and deal with any problems the other children may have.

Barry Fish, too, is sensitive to the needs of caregivers. He tells the story of two siblings, Joan and Steven, whose mother had a stroke and required full-time care. Joan lived with her mother for many years, while Steven went on with his life. It was understood among family members that Joan would get the house when her mother died, in return for the sacrifices she had made over many years. But the will did not grant Joan the special recognition she had expected. Everything was divided equally between the two children. Steven wouldn't release his interest in the home, but hired a lawyer and insisted on enforcing all his rights under the will. Joan felt exploited by her brother. She later refused to attend the wedding of Steven's daughter, with whom she was very close. The moral: Fairness is dictated by family circumstances, which may change as parents get older and sicker.

Parents can reward a care-giving child with money or personal items during their lifetimes—along with a letter explaining their reasons for doing so. They can name the caregiver as beneficiary of a life insurance policy or make a special gift in their wills.

Parents can also recognize inequalities created when they pay university costs for some children and not others. They can make compensating gifts during their lifetime to those who didn't get an education or leave money in their wills.

But before conferring a special benefit, parents may wish to have a discussion with the child first. Some children may prefer not to have the recognition, Fish says, in order to avoid confrontation with siblings.

Booking off for
family problems

A family member needs emergency care and you want to take time off to help. What do you tell your employer? First, find out whether you're entitled to emergency leave under the law covering your workplace or under a union or employment contract. These provisions aren't always publicized. You may be surprised to see you have some leeway to book time off for health issues involving your immediate family.

Quebec and British Columbia provide five unpaid days a year for obligations related to childcare, while New Brunswick provides three days of unpaid leave. In British Columbia and New Brunswick, this also applies to responsibilities involving other members of the employee's immediate family. In Newfoundland and Labrador, employees can take a combined total of seven days of unpaid sick leave or family responsibility leave in a year. And in Ontario, those who work for a company that has at least 50 employees are allowed up to 10 unpaid days a year to deal with an urgent matter involving a close relative.

Unpaid emergency leave is not the same thing as sickness or bereavement leave, which is often part of a workplace policy or paid benefit plan. You can't be penalized if you take emergency leave, but your employer can ask for proof that you're eligible.

Starting in January 2004, Canadians will be able to collect up to $413 a week for six weeks under a new compassionate leave benefit announced in the federal budget of February 2003. You can qualify for this benefit if you're caring for a gravely ill or dying spouse, child or parent—you must have a doctor's note—and you're eligible for employment insurance or EI. This means you must have accumulated 600 insured hours in the previous 52 weeks. You can't be self-employed.

This leave can be shared with other family members. For example, three siblings can each take two weeks off from work to spend time with a dying parent. The federal government will pass new laws to protect employees' jobs under the Canada Labour Code. But most employees are covered by provincial labour codes, so the provinces have to follow suit. Some provinces already provide unpaid family care leave, so they will have to integrate their benefits with the new EI-paid family care leave.

If you don't qualify for a family emergency leave or you've exhausted your paid or unpaid days off, that's when you may find yourself negotiating with your employer for more flexibility. Many companies offer flex-time arrangements. You work a set number of hours, but you have an adjustable hour or two at either end of the workday. You can ask for a temporary shift into part-time work or telecommuting, where you work at home and stay connected by telephone or the Internet.

How do you convince your boss to let you have a flexible work arrangement? You'll need to make a strong case, put it in writing and be prepared to sell it. Decide what type of arrangement you want. Then write a proposal that outlines how the work will get done and how you will deal with co-workers' concerns.

Before you pitch your boss, go to co-workers or clients with whom you feel comfortable talking about your plans, says Jacqueline Foley in her self-published book, *Flex Appeal: An Inspirational Guide to Flexible Work for Mothers* (Out of Our Minds Press). These people will be affected by your new arrangement. Approaching them before you make the change will show them you care about the impact it will have on them and encourage their buy-in. It also ensures you can go to your boss with a proposal that has practical ideas for staying connected to your co-workers and helping your clients.

A written plan forces you to come up with good answers to the tough questions your boss is likely to ask. If you find it daunting to write a proposal, you can buy a template called Flex Success at a Web site called Work Options, www.workoptions.com. For $29.95 (U.S.), you have four flexible options to choose from: job sharing, compressed workweek, part-time and telecommuting. Foley interviewed more than 100 mothers who had moved from full-time work to a flexible arrangement. Many of them swore by the Flex Success template, saying it had helped them create a professional proposal and negotiate what they wanted.

The key to success is gathering proof that flexible hours work for the employer, as well as for you. Start with examples within your company, if they exist, and include testimonials from the relevant manager about how the arrangement is working out. Then add a summary of the research you have found in support of flexible work arrangements in general and, if possible, the specific arrangement you're proposing.

You can find many of the backup articles and statistics you need at a Web site sponsored by the federal government, Work-Life Balance in Canadian Workplaces, http://labour-travail.hrdc-drhc.gc.ca/worklife. You'll find surveys by well-known academics, which show the stress people face trying to juggle the needs of their families with the challenge of earning a living. Among the highlights:

- Dual-earner families now outnumber single-earner families by three to one. And lone-parent families represent 10 per cent of all families.

- More than 70 per cent of all dual-earner families have both parents working full-time. In many of these families, the parents work different hours or days of the week.

- Only about 33 per cent of the work force works standard hours (Monday to Friday, 9 a.m. to 5 p.m.) in a standard job at the employer's workplace.

■ While the standard workweek is about 40 hours a week, about 25 per cent of workers work 50 hours a week or more (counting overtime, travel and office work brought home).

■ About 66 per cent of full-time employed parents with children report they are dissatisfied with the balance between their job and home life.

■ For every Canadian whose personal or family circumstances are interfering with performance at work, there are five Canadians whose work and work circumstances are interfering with their family and their life.

In an Ipsos-Reid survey in April 2003, 1,000 Canadians were asked what they wanted from their work lives. Which of eight options would they choose as the top indicator of success in their own careers? Three out of ten people picked work-life balance as the pinnacle of workplace achievement, ahead of job challenge (14 per cent), level of responsibility (12 per cent) and advancement opportunities (10 per cent). Organizations will have to accept this new norm of career success, says noted business professor Linda Duxbury of Carleton University in Ottawa. It's in their best interest to take whatever measures they can to accommodate employees' responsibilities outside work, because balance among employees can be strongly linked to the bottom line.

For many people, working flexible hours means working less and a cut in pay. You have to plan how you'll accommodate yourself to a lower income. Start by making a list of all your monthly expenses, Foley advises, from video rentals to alcohol. Make sure to factor in any savings you make from working or commuting less (such as fewer meals eaten out and less money spent on clothes and dry cleaning). Then if you need to start cutting, start with the smaller items on your list. If cutting these doesn't go far enough, you may have to reduce something significant, such as your mortgage, car expenses or groceries. "Only you can decide what you're willing to trade off," Foley says.

Henson trust ideal for disabled children

"What will happen to my child after I'm gone?" All parents agonize about this when their kids are young. But the question lingers for parents of disabled children, who may never become self-sufficient adults. The key is to leave enough money to provide for these special children, but without taking away the government benefits they receive.

Setting up a trust in a will is a common estate-planning tactic. But for disabled children, it's important to use a special trust called a Henson trust. It's named after Leonard Henson of Guelph, Ontario, who provided for his disabled daughter Audra, using a trust with assets to be paid at the discretion of the trustees. This meant she didn't own the assets.

Henson was trying to bypass a provincial rule that said disability support payments would be reduced by the income received from an inheritance. The Ontario social services ministry challenged the will and lost in court. A subsequent appeal by the government was dismissed in 1989. This established the principle that an absolute discretionary trust, known as a Henson trust, preserves the right of a child with disabilities to receive benefits.

Since that court decision, "lawyers in the know have used Henson Trusts across Canada when making arrangements for disabled beneficiaries," says John Poyser, a partner with the Winnipeg law firm of Inskter, Christie, Hughes and co-chair of the wills and estates Section of the Manitoba Bar Association. It's important to word the trust properly. The document must stipulate that the disabled child has a life interest in the assets, but does not control or own them. This means he or she can continue to collect full benefits from the government.

Some lawyers use a disability expenses trust, which in Ontario allows a child to inherit up to $100,000 without penalty. This doesn't go very far if the parent dies when the child is still young. A disability expenses trust is also too limiting. Funds can be used only for expenses directly related to the child's disability, such as specialized medical care or a wheelchair. With a Henson trust, there are no restrictions on how much can be left to the child or how it's paid out for his or her benefit.

Ottawa lawyer Ken Pope says he has seen parents try to create their own options to protect the inheritance. For example, they place the money in the hands of a trusted family member or friend in a secret trust. Such an arrangement leaves the beneficiary with no recourse if the trustee goes bankrupt or loses the money through divorce or bad financial management. And, if the arrangement is discovered, the province can take legal action to get access to the money on behalf of the disabled person to offset disability support payments.

The choice of a trustee is critical to making the plan work, since the trustee has absolute and unfettered discretion. "It must be someone you trust, as there's a potential for abuse," Pope says. Brothers or sisters may have a conflict of interest, but they can be appointed to administer a trust with someone outside the family—a close friend or professional trustee (if the assets are more than $250,000).

If parents don't have enough money to leave behind, life insurance is an effective alternative. An insurance policy can be paid into an absolute discretionary trust for the child.

Besides writing a will and setting up a trust, parents should also prepare a comprehensive life plan for a disabled child. Future caregivers need to get a complete picture of the person: likes and dislikes, friends, education, preferred activities and particular means of expression. The quality of life the child will have after your death is determined by the life planning that goes before. "You can write a letter of intent, a wish list, and keep it outside the trust agreement," says John Dowson, a financial adviser in Newmarket, Ontario, who specializes in estate planning for people with disabilities (www.life-trust.com).

Preparing for the big chill

Elly Elder, 81, has planned her funeral and paid for it in advance. She wants to make it easier for her family when the time comes. "My daughter will have no difficulty finding the information and knowing what I want," she says. An active member of a consumer group that advocates dignified funerals at a moderate cost, Elder wants to keep things as simple as possible. She's arranged with a Toronto funeral home for a plain unlined container, with no embalming or visitations. Her body will be cremated and her remains will go into a plastic box, leaving her daughter to decide where to put them. At a later date, she wants a memorial service at her church—again, to ease pressure on the family.

This type of funeral costs about $1,000, a fraction of the $5,000 cost of an average Canadian funeral. Cemetery fees and crematorium costs add to the bill. Elder decided to pay in advance because the money she'd set aside for her funeral was earning such a low interest rate at the bank. She was afraid her family might have to make up the difference if funeral costs went up.

Paying in advance for a service can be risky. What if the company goes out of business or steals the money held in trust? In Ontario, prepaid funerals are protected by a compensation fund run by the

Ontario Board of Funeral Services (which is made up of eight funeral directors and five members of the public, all appointed by the province). "I felt perfectly safe prepaying because of the compensation fund," Elder says. Her contract guarantees the final price won't be higher than the prepaid amount. And if the cost is lower, the extra will be refunded to her estate.

With the exception of Newfoundland, every province has legislation dealing with prepaid funerals. Any funds paid are held in trust by the funeral home or a provincial organization, with the interest credited to you or your estate. "Make sure the contract doesn't simply state that the funds to be held in trust by the funeral home will only be applied toward the actual cost of the funeral," advise Douglas Gray and John Budd in *The Canadian Guide to Will and Estate Planning* (McGraw-Hill Ryerson). This could mean if there's a shortfall, the family or the estate might have to make up the difference.

Any prepaid contract should specify that surplus funds held in trust go back to the estate. If there's a change in plans and the funeral home does not carry out the service as arranged, the funds held in trust (plus the accrued interest) should also be returned to the estate. Some provinces allow the funeral home to hold back a portion of the prepaid funds as a fee (up to 20 per cent in British Columbia, for example, and up to 10 per cent in Ontario to a maximum of $200).

The total value of prepaid funerals in Canada exceeds $1.5 billion. The average customer is 65 years old—with most between 55 and 75—and they do it because they want to save money. People generally pay less for a pre-arranged package, because they have time to shop around and can negotiate a better deal when they don't have to deal with the grief and time pressures of an abrupt death. Also, many of us seem more willing to spend money on a loved one's funeral than we would on our own (the guilt factor).

Prepaying also offers tax benefits. If the funeral home sets things up according to the federal Income Tax Act, the interest earned on money in an "eligible funeral arrangement" or EFA is not reported as income for tax purposes—and not included in the estate's income if used for funeral costs. The income must stay in an EFA until you die to remain tax-free. And it will be invested conservatively by the funeral home, not in anything that could make you rich.

"In the long run, income from an EFA will probably end up being used to offset inflation in the cost of the goods and services provided by the funeral home," say lawyers Margaret Kerr and JoAnn Kurtz in *Wills and Estates For Canadians For Dummies* (John Wiley & Sons). That's assuming you live for long enough after planning your funeral for interest and inflation to have a noticeable effect.

The interesting thing about EFAs is how much you're allowed to put into them—up to $15,000 for funeral services, up to $20,000 for cemetery services and up to $35,000 for both. That's a lot more than the average cost. "Here's what we think," say Kerr and Kurtz: "If you've got $35,000, forget the funeral. Throw a great party while you're still around to enjoy it."

When pre-arranging a funeral, it's not necessary to prepay as well. You may be unsure of your future plans. Why cut off the possibility of moving to British Columbia because you have a prepaid contract with a funeral home in Toronto? Prepaid plans can be cancelled at any time with a written request to the funeral home. Moving elsewhere is easier with a pre-arranged funeral that's not prepaid. The funeral director can transmit your wishes to the funeral home you choose in another location.

Pre-arranging is a sensible and considerate thing to do. Your family knows your wishes in advance and won't be forced to make tough decisions while in an emotional state. "You accept that death will occur. This is one trip you are going to make," says Pearl Davie, president of the Federation of Ontario Memorial Societies, which has 51,000 members. "Your survivors are relieved of enormous stress that's guilt-related. They won't say, 'Let's give Mom a big fancy funeral because we forgot her birthday last year.'"

Memorial societies, staffed by volunteers, don't own or operate funeral homes, cemeteries, crematoriums or monument companies. They help members pre-arrange a simple funeral at a fixed price with designated funeral homes. Telephone advice is also provided. (For information, go to www.myfuneralplan.org in Ontario and www.afuneralinbc.com in British Columbia.) They recommend you discuss your choices with your family and keep written instructions attached to your will.

Not only memorial societies endorse planning in advance. Mainstream funeral homes have also embraced the idea, which they call "pre-need." Michaele-Sue Goldblatt is one of two full-time social workers at Benjamin's Park Memorial Chapel, a Jewish funeral home in Toronto, who helps customers with planning. "There are as many reasons to pre-arrange and pre-fund as there are people in the world," says Goldblatt. "But I'd single out three main reasons: Peace of mind, freezing the cost at today's prices and arranging convenient payment terms."

Payment terms are almost impossible to arrange at the time of a person's death. Funeral homes perform a service and want to be paid right away. Many families pay with a credit card, at interest rates of 18 to 20 per cent, while waiting for the life insurance to be paid or the will to be probated. But with prepaid contracts, funeral homes give you up to five years to pay the full amount.

Goldblatt likes to visit customers at home to talk about preplanning funerals, where she can spend time dealing with their unconscious fears and anxieties. "You should be treated courteously and sensitively, without feeling any pressure," she tells customers. "Whether you pre-fund or not is irrelevant. Pre-arranging is the first step and we recognize that not everyone goes ahead."

In some provinces, funeral homes operate independently from cemeteries and crematoriums. So you may have to make separate arrangements to pre-arrange or prepay. A new Ontario funeral act will strengthen consumer protection by expanding the licensing of funeral directors to previously unlicensed casket retailers and monument builders. This is good news, since it means that all players in the bereavement sector will be covered by the compensation fund.

At the time of death, the family can find out from the funeral director about any benefits and grants that may be available to subsidize costs. Here's a list of the resources that may be available, courtesy of Douglas Gray and John Budd:

- Life insurance: To complete the claim, a proof of death certificate is required from the funeral director and/or the medical practitioner.

- Accidental death insurance: This may be provided under an automobile association membership or a credit card (if the cost of the plane, train, boat or bus trip was charged to the card).

- Canada Pension Plan: If you contributed to CPP for the minimum qualifying period, you will get a lump-sum payment for funeral costs sent to a lawyer or family member. Also, your spouse or any dependent children may be eligible for a monthly pension.

- Veterans' allowances: The federal veterans' affairs department provides means-tested benefits to armed forces veterans who are already receiving a pension or allowance. The Last Post Fund helps veterans who don't have the money to pay for a funeral.

- Company and union benefits: Check with your employer.

- Workers' Compensation: Benefits are available if the death is work-related.

- Compassionate travel or bereavement fares: Policies vary from airline to airline, but you usually have to pay the full fare and claim a rebate later. Discounts are usually only on economy class fares.

Look out for fraud aimed at seniors

Les Henderson is fascinated by frauds. He admits to being taken in a few times over the years. "So I'm stupid, eh? Well, I thought if I'm stupid, I bet there are a lot of other people who are being taken in, too. So I started to do research and found, yes, there's a colossal problem. But most people never come to the point where they say, 'I'm dumb, I'd like to report it.' They're afraid of being told they should have known better."

His research led to an encyclopedic 600-page book, *Crimes of Persuasion* (Coyote Ridge), and a Web site, www.crimes-of-persuasion.com. Con artists would be challenged to find anything that hasn't found its way into Henderson's vast database of information. Among the many subjects he covers: Telemarketing operations, investment scams, business and employment opportunities, loan brokers and credit repair agencies, unauthorized telecommunication charges, Ponzi and pyramid schemes, chain letters, fraudulent diet programs, modelling agencies and the Nigerian advance fee fraud.

The author, who's in his mid-40s and lives in Azilda, Ontario (outside of Sudbury), has never worked in law enforcement. His background is in investment and insurance sales and financial planning. He goes into more detail than I've seen elsewhere about how scams work and why people get taken in.

He's particularly insightful about the way telemarketing fraudsters prey on the elderly. Older people are home during the day, trusting, lonely, sometimes mentally infirm or debilitated with grief over the loss of a spouse. If they fall for a fraudulent prize promotion or charitable solicitation, they may be too embarrassed to report the crime. They're afraid they'll be considered incompetent to handle their own financial affairs.

Fraudulent telemarketers will often target older citizens, knowing they may have significant assets from a lifetime of saving. Once seniors make their first purchase or contribution, they commonly receive five or more calls a day from high-pressure telephone salespeople. Often they get trapped in a downward spiral of repeated victimization, as they grow increasingly desperate to recoup their losses. They dread revealing the full extent of their losses, fearing their well-meaning children will take away their last measure of independence.

As elders lose their savings, even comfortable lifestyles collapse. "The impact of fraud on elders can be profound and life-altering," says Henderson, who set his book in larger type for older readers. "Fraudulent telemarketers not only rob their victims of hard-earned financial assets, but also of their human dignity. Elder fraud victims often find their trust shattered. They doubt their judgment. They feel isolated, depressed, angry and ashamed. These violations of trust, compounded by the subsequent uncertainty about paying bills, often lead to illness."

Most of the fraud affecting the elderly is done through telephone and door-to-door sales pitches. But as more seniors get onto the Internet, fraud operators are stalking them there, too. To complain about telemarketing, call PhoneBusters (1-888-495-8501, www.phonebusters.com). Operated by the Ontario Provincial Police since 1993, PhoneBusters is the central agency in Canada that collects information on telemarketing, advanced fee fraud letters and identity theft complaints—and disseminates the information to law enforcement agencies. Look here for data on new scams, arrests and convictions.

Reverse mortgages
fraught with pitfalls

Lower interest rates are poisonous for senior citizens, whose cost of living seems to rise as quickly as their GIC returns fall. As a result, older people may be seduced by the siren song of the reverse mortgage. It's heavily promoted by the Canadian Home Income Plan, the leading national provider, as an alternative to cashing in investments and paying tax on the reduced value. What is the downside of a reverse mortgage? People want to know what's not disclosed in the company's newspaper advertisements and ubiquitous TV commercials featuring financial author Gordon Pape.

Let's look at a fictional couple, Jean and Jerry, living in Toronto in a house worth $400,000. They're 70 and 72, the average age when people take out a reverse mortgage. (You have to be at least 62 years old to qualify.) With a CHIP reverse mortgage, they can get a lump sum payment of $120,000—or 30 per cent of the value of their home—to spend as they please.

Before they get the cash, Jean and Jerry have a few bills to pay. They need a home appraisal ($150 to $200) and independent legal advice ($250 to $400). Plus, there are CHIP closing costs of $1,285. Still, they have the comfort of staying in the home and neighbourhood they know so well, with the support network they've built up there. They won't have the pain of uprooting, moving and downsizing.

A reverse mortgage requires no repayments. The interest compounds and is added to the balance of the mortgage, and the interest rate is higher than on a conventional loan. The CHIP mortgage had an interest rate of 7.25 per cent in 2003, compared to a one-year term mortgage available at about 4.5 per cent from major lenders, or prime rate (4.75 per cent floating) on a secured revolving line of credit. And unlike a conventional mortgage that carries a fixed rate, CHIP resets the rate on its outstanding reverse mortgages every year. This gives homeowners little protection if there's an upward trend.

Assuming the CHIP rate stays constant at 7.25 per cent, Jean and Jerry will owe $240,000—or twice the amount they received—in 10 years. This is how a rising-debt mortgage works. (Using the rule of 72 that applies to compound interest, you take the interest rate and divide it into 72. That gives you the time it takes for your assets to double if you're investing, or your debt to double if you're borrowing.) So if Jean and Jerry sell their home in 10 years, they'll have to pay $240,000—not the initial $120,000—to get rid of the reverse mortgage.

Of course, their $400,000 home probably will increase in value. But if there's a real estate crash and it's worth only $225,000 in 2013, that's all they have to pay back. CHIP guarantees the amount owed on a reverse mortgage will never exceed the fair-market value of the home. That's why it lends conservatively, advancing just 10 to 40 per cent of the home's value.

Jean and Jerry may be lucky enough to live to age 90 and 92 in their own house. If they die 20 years after taking out the CHIP reverse mortgage, they will owe $480,000 (assuming a constant 7.25 per cent interest rate). This means there will be little, if any, money for the children and grandchildren after the house is sold—unless the couple has other assets in their estate.

Jean and Jerry don't care about providing for survivors. They want more money to spend while they're alive. But there's another risk they face. What if they don't stay in their home until they die? If they buy another house, they may be able to take the mortgage with them. But it's more likely they'll move into a long-term care facility or a rental apartment. Since the reverse mortgage is designed to last until they die, Jean and Jerry will have to pay a penalty to get out. They'll face a penalty of six to eight months' interest, which could be in the $5,000 range, if they decide to sell within the first three years. Afterward, they'll face an interest-rate differential penalty.

About half the people who take out a reverse mortgage choose to get out early, says CHIP senior vice-president Sian Owen. They usually leave the program after five to seven years, moving across the country to be with their children or going into a long-term care facility. In such a case, the penalty is in the $500 range.

There's a larger cost, however—the lack of flexibility for seniors who need to tap their home equity for unforeseen expenses. Suppose Jean and Jerry use their $120,000 reverse mortgage windfall to boost their lifestyle. They can't resist the temptation to visit faraway places and leave the harsh winters in Canada. Before they know it, the money is gone. But as they get older, their health starts declining. They have to hire a live-in caregiver or renovate the house to make it wheelchair-accessible. Where does the money come from to pay their medical bills? Sure, they can sell the house. But their debt will have grown substantially—and what they get after discharging the mortgage may be too little to meet their needs.

Few seniors want to encumber their houses once they understand how CHIP really works. The company has only 5,600 clients, despite the constant advertising and a history of lending since 1986. "Our advertising encourages self-education. If people are asking questions, that's what we consider to be our success," Owen says.

Unfortunately, most people don't get to read the small print until they sign up for a reverse mortgage. CHIP's 17-page legal document, sent to me by a *Star* reader, lays out a lot of information that's not included in the ads or at its Web site (www.chip.ca). For example, you can't rent out all or part of the house without written consent—and only for six months within any 12-month period. You must hire a licensed property manager and provide copies of all contracts and agreements if requested. You must keep the property in good repair, pay property taxes and maintain insurance coverage. What happens if you don't? The lender may demand immediate payment of the entire balance owing.

A reverse mortgage is not for you—or your parents—if you're not comfortable with the idea of having a rising debt level or you're concerned about estate depletion. Homeowners who intend to make regular interest payments should consider cheaper alternatives, such as a home-secured line of credit. "Mortgage-free seniors should first look at the other options to unlock home equity or enhance retirement income before considering a reverse mortgage plan," says Ron Zaporzan, manager of advanced financial planning support for Investors Group.

CHIP's legal document will be made more accessible once it is translated into plain language, Owen told me. I hope that happens soon, since more transparency is needed for a company whose goal is education. If you want independent information, check the Web site (www.reverse.org) set up by the National Centre for Home Equity Conversion Mortgage, a U.S. non-profit group with no ties to the reverse mortgage lending industry. For Canadians, I'd suggest buying or borrowing from the library a comprehensive book on reverse mortgages and other options, *Have Your Home and Money Too* (John Wiley & Sons) by P.J. Wade.

Get the government benefits you deserve

Every working Canadian should become familiar with the Canada Benefits Web site, www.canadabenefits.gc.ca. It's an excellent starting point to pinpoint information about federal and provincial benefit programs, ranging from employment insurance to public pension plans to social assistance. Launched in November 2001 with federal government information, the site was expanded in January 2003 to include links to provincial and territorial information.

You're given several ways to navigate the site. You can use a keyword search, check an A-to-Z benefits index or click on a "life event," such as unemployment, retirement, home ownership, divorce, health and tax concerns and dealing with death. You can also personalize your search by registering with a "Benefits Finder" option. After answering 11 simple questions, including your age, you're given links to government programs that could relate to you or may interest you.

I tried the Benefits Finder option and was given information about eight programs:

- Child care and family programs (Canada Child Tax Benefit, Canada Educations Savings Grant, Registered Education Savings Plan and Maternity, Parental and Sickness Benefits under the Employment Insurance program).

- Education, learning and training programs (the Lifelong Learning Program that lets you withdraw money from your RRSP to finance education for you, your spouse or common-law partner).

- Health and wellness programs (the Ontario Drug Benefit's Special Drugs Program that covers the cost of certain outpatient drugs used in the treatment of specific conditions).

- Housing and rental programs (the RRSP Home Buyers' Plan and the mortgage loan insurance program funded by Canada Mortgage and Housing Corp.

As well, I was told about a program that may interest me—the ability to split Canada Pension Plan credits on divorce or separation. Not relevant for me right now, but thanks anyway.

The reason it's important to check on your access to benefits: If you don't apply, you may not get what you deserve. Many people don't realize this is how many government programs work. They think they'll get the Canada Child Tax Benefit when they give birth and they'll get the Old Age Security pension when they turn 65. Nothing is automatic. You have to ask and send relevant documents.

The longer you wait to apply, the more you risk losing out since many benefits are only retroactive for 11 months. This applies to the Old Age Security pension, the Guaranteed Income Supplement for low-income seniors, the Survivor's Allowance for people age 60 to 64 whose spouse or partner has died and the Canada Pension Plan. (Quebec Pension Plan rules are different. Its benefits are retroactive to July 1998.) In the case of the little-publicized Survivor's Allowance, it's estimated that fewer than half of those eligible are receiving it.

The extent of unclaimed benefits in Canada is so large that it's now perceived as a business opportunity. Dan Palladini of Montreal has created DetectaPension, www.detectapension.com, a service that tracks down missing corporate pensions or unpaid federal government benefits on behalf of low- or modest-income seniors. If he finds them extra money, he takes a cut—25 per cent of the increase over 12 months. If the amounts stay the same, there's no charge.

Palladini, a logistics expert who stopped working at 59, said the idea sprang from research he did tracking down his pension from a company he once worked for that was sold overseas and closed its Canadian office. He told the *Montreal Gazette* that many Canadians—widows and divorcees, for instance—might not be aware that their spouse was a past contributor to a company pension plan from which they might now be entitled to benefits.

Richard Shillington, an Ottawa-based social policy analyst, doesn't like the idea. "In a better world, there'd be no market for people charging a fee to get governments to give you what you deserve," he says.

Actually, there was method in Ottawa's apparent madness when it designed its retroactivity rules in the mid-1960s, says Mary Janigan in a *Maclean's* magazine article. "It did not want crafty seniors to pocket federal payments like the Guaranteed Income Supplement (GIS) for the low-income elderly—and then turn around, years later, and apply for their CPP plus interest in a tidy lump sum. After all, those seniors might not have been eligible for low-income programs if they had been collecting their CPP. So, to close the door to possible abuse and to relieve strain on the program itself, Ottawa selected an across-the-board method that was most convenient for its bureaucracy."

Shillington was working with needy people at a Toronto community group when he noticed that many seniors were not collecting their pensions. Back in Ottawa, he peppered the human resources department with freedom of information requests on delayed payments to the elderly. He estimates that 382,000 eligible pensioners did not receive the GIS in 1998 alone, saving the government about $500 million in benefits. Since his revelations, HRDC, working with the Canada Customs and Revenue Agency, has stepped up and expanded its efforts to reach eligible low-income seniors.

Later, Shillington found out about internal documents from Human Resources Development Canada showing that 20,924 elderly Canadians were no longer eligible for part of the money deducted from their paycheques for the Canada Pension Plan. Some seniors forget about CPP contributions made while working in jobs held decades earlier or never think to draw on a spouse's pension after death. A Toronto lawyer with a legal-aid clinic for low-income seniors plans to launch a lawsuit against the federal government on behalf of some low-income seniors to get retroactive benefits. Graham Webb, a lawyer with the Advocacy Centre for the Elderly in Toronto, said: "We have clients who just didn't know they were entitled to the pension and they didn't apply until their eighties."

The moral: Find out the government benefits you qualify for and apply for them. Do it earlier rather than later, since your ability to get retroactive payments may be extremely limited. If you have trouble filling out the application forms, get help from a local community clinic or legal aid lawyer.

Develop Good Money Habits

You want to pay more attention to your personal finances. Every January, you make a New Year's resolution to spend less on credit and save more for the future. You talk about finding a good financial adviser, someone who can communicate in language you understand. And every day, you plan to get organized and clear up the clutter of papers on your desk.

So what's stopping you? Obviously, there's still a job to do—or you wouldn't be reading a book like this.

You may have a mental block when it comes to money. Although you want to take control, you're awed by the scope of the task. You don't know how or where to start, so you put it off until tomorrow.

There are other emotions that come into play when you delay: The fear of losing discretionary dollars spent on non-essentials (restaurant meals, cigarettes and booze, health clubs and hair treatments); the guilt of finding out exactly where your money goes and why you spend more than you earn; and the anxiety of discovering that no matter how hard you try, you'll never get ahead of the game.

I'm here to say you **can** get ahead of the game, but you have to stop sitting around waiting for the play to start. Pick something and do it. You don't have to begin with a major improvement. A small success will give you the quick payback you need to get motivated.

Find a chapter in this book that speaks to you and follow the advice. For example, look at ways to cut your car and home insurance costs, such as raising your deductibles. Once you have that mastered, try something else. Dump the credit card you currently use and shop for one with a lower interest rate or fewer service charges. With a few victories under your belt, you can muster up the courage to apply for an RRSP catch-up loan or buy an exchange-traded index fund.

"Big projects look daunting; smaller ones feel easier," says David Posen, author of *The Little Book of Stress Relief* (Key Porter). He talks about the "Swiss cheese" method—it's like taking small bites out of a big piece of cheese instead of trying to eat it all at once.

Here's his advice about learning the art of doing it now:

- Make a list of all the things you've been putting off. Make it a long list.

- Pick one item on the list to address this week.

- Choose a time this week to do it. Assemble the things you'll need for the job.

- Set a kitchen timer for one hour. Just get started—no interruptions, no breaks, no distractions.

- And don't forget to reward yourself at the end.

Motivational experts urge you to set ambitious goals for yourself and put them down in writing. Your goals become more concrete and you work harder to get to your destination. But this approach doesn't work for everyone. It can be intimidating.

This year, I joined a marathon running group for the first time. Never having run more than 10 kilometres before—and finding that painful—I couldn't handle the idea of running 42.5 kilometres. It was much too grand a goal. Instead, I made a commitment to turn up each week for the longer runs. Since a marathon was unthinkable, I focused on the distance at hand—13 kilometres, then 16 kilometres, then 19 kilometres—and kept putting one foot in front of the other.

That was enough to propel me to the starting line of the marathon a few months later.

To me, success in life comes in increments. You work on getting one thing right, then you move on to the next thing. As long as you concentrate and give yourself time, you should be able to complete the tasks you set for yourself. One bit of business builds on another and so on. Eventually, you get to a better place.

The lofty goal you post on your refrigerator—say, accumulating a $1 million RRSP by the time you turn 50—may turn you off. Big numbers can be mind-boggling. File them away in the back of your brain and don't let them immobilize you. You have to devote your attention to the steps along the way. Take time to enjoy the scenery.

Do you procrastinate because you think you're not a good investor? Those who say they're not good investors do buy houses and cars and home entertainment systems. They are investors in the here and now. "We are all investors," says Mitch Anthony, author of *The New Retirementality* (Dearborn Trade). "The key that differentiates us as investors is whether we invest in the present or the future."

The key is to find balance. If you invest everything in the present, you have nothing in the future. If you invest everything in the future, you may be missing the opportunity to enjoy the present. By investing in the present and the future, you have a chance of satisfaction both now and then.

Baby boomers have been reared on instant gratification, what Anthony calls "eating the marshmallow." If you invest in tomorrow by paying something out of each paycheque, no matter how small the amount, you develop a powerful habit of waiting for the second marshmallow. Even $20 a week can grow to a six-figure retirement fund with the power of compound interest.

What you do with that $20 a week isn't nearly as important as your decision to save it in the first place. Many financial advisers look down on Canada Savings Bonds, for example, but they're a fine choice. A study of CSBs, released in October 2003, found they outperformed other investments more than 60 per cent of the time over periods of one to 15 years. And in the five-year period, Canada Savings Bonds were the top performers with a 5.2 per cent return, outpacing the average Canadian equity fund (1.5 per cent), the average Canadian bond fund (4.9 per cent) and the S&P/TSX composite index total return (0.5 per cent).

The crucial part of the exercise is developing good habits—the habit of saving, the habit of getting yourself organized, the habit of checking your paperwork regularly, the habit of looking out for trouble before it lands on your doorstep. Habits can be learned at any age and can be your armour against the nasty surprises life throws at you. Instead of being knocked off stride, you just pick yourself up, dust yourself off and start all over again.

So here's my advice: Don't put this book on the shelf right away. Find an area you want to improve and get started. That's the best return on your investment.

Web Site Directory

PART ONE: SAVING ON CARS AND HOUSING

www.caa.ca: Canadian Automobile Association, publishes an annual survey of new car driving costs and a template for calculating your own costs. Also publishes Autopinion, an annual survey of more than 20,000 members on reliability of different models.

www.oee.nrcan.gc.ca: Natural Resources Canada, Office of Energy Efficiency, tips on driving and maintaining your car and cutting greenhouse gas emissions.

www.climatechangesolutions.com: Pembina Institute for Appropriate Development, success stories on how individuals and families can cut energy costs and pollution.

www.climatechangesolutions.com/individuals/transport/tools/cpoolmap. html: List of van pool, car co-op and ridesharing programs across Canada.

www.autoshare.com: AutoShare, Toronto-based car sharing service.

www.goforgreen.ca: Go for Green, a national non-profit charity that sponsors the "walking school bus program," an alternative to driving kids to school.

www.kanetix.com: Kanetix, a comparison shopping resource for auto and home insurance.

www.insurancehotline.com: The Consumer's Guide to Insurance, insurance quotes from more than 30 companies online and by phone (416-686-0531).

www.insurance-canada.ca: Information for consumers and insurance professionals on insurance-related topics.

www.fsco.gov.on.ca: Financial Services Commission of Ont., annual survey that asks customers of four dozen auto insurance companies how happy they are with claims settlement procedures.

www.vicc.com: Vehicle Information Centre of Canada, part of the Insurance Bureau of Canada, looks at claims history of different makes and models of cars.

www.carcostcanada.com and **www.freeinvoiceprices.com**: Information on car dealers' invoice costs as a benchmark for negotiating a fair price.

www.canadianblackbook.com: Information on wholesale prices of cars, helpful when negotiating a price for a trade-in and buying or selling a used car privately.

www.dealfinder.org: Dealfinder Inc., a service that helps you negotiate a deal to buy or lease a new car and take delivery at your local dealer, for an up-front cost of $149.

www.lemonaidcars.com: Phil Edmonston, author of the Lemon-Aid new and used car guides, gives updates on vehicle safety, maintenance and legal issues.

www.alldata.com: ALLDATA LLC, free summaries of auto makers' technical service bulletins, which are useful if you're trying to find out if your car is covered by a secret warranty.

www.camvap.ca: Canadian Motor Vehicle Arbitration Plan, provides dispute resolution for manufacturers' defects in new vehicles or those going back four model years, with less than 160,000 kilometres. You don't have to be the original owner.

www.canadiandriver.com: Canadian Driver magazine, offers new and used car reviews and buying advice.

www.tc.gc.ca and **www.nhtsa.dot.gov**: Safety-related problems and recalls from Transport Canada and the National Highway Safety Administration in the United States.

www.ucda.org and **www.omvic.on.ca**: Free complaint mediation from the Used Car Dealers Association and the Ontario Motor Vehicle Industry Council.

www.landlordselfhelp.com: Landlord's Self-Help Centre, non-profit agency providing free information and advice to small-scale landlords.

www.cmhc.ca: Canada Mortgage and Housing Corp., government agency that provides mortgage insurance for buyers with less than a 25 per cent down payment. Also publishes an online guide to renting a home, aimed at both tenants and landlords.

www.quickenmortgage.ca: Calculator that helps you decide whether it makes sense to break your mortgage, sponsored by the Mortgage Alliance Co. of Canada.

www.amortization.com: Mortgage software seller gives 10 reasons why you need to ask your lender for an amortization schedule.

www.milevsky.com: Paper by Moshe Milevsky, a finance professor at York University's Schulich School of Business, on how you're better off renewing your mortgage annually rather than every five years ("Mortgage Financing: Floating Your Way to Prosperity").

www.gemortgage.ca: GE Mortgage Insurance Canada, private company that provides high-ratio mortgage insurance for those without a 25 per cent down payment.

www.xceedmortgage.com: Xceed Mortgage Corp., private lender that supplies up to 100 per cent of the purchase price to buyers with no down payments.

www.chba.ca: Canadian Home Builders' Association, provides free online guide to home renovation.

www.renomark.ca: Quality assurance program for contractor members of the Greater Toronto Home Builders' Association.

PART TWO: GETTING YOUR FINANCES IN ORDER

www.piac.ca: Public Interest Advocacy Centre, a non-profit consumer group that does good research on financial services.

www.fcac.gc.ca: Financial Consumer Agency of Canada, publishes interactive cost of banking guide and a useful twice-a-year publication, Credit Cards and You.

www.cba.ca: Canadian Bankers Association, provides information about banking and financial services, including a series of 15 free information booklets on basic issues..

www.cdnpay.ca: Canadian Payments Association, sets rules for the orderly conducts of Canada's cheque clearing and settlement system.

www.obsi.ca: Ombudsman for Banking Services and Investments, handles complaints that have been turned down by the company's ombudsman.

www.cfson-crcsf.ca: Centre for the Financial Services OmbudsNetwork, helps consumers with complaints and steers them to the right place.

www.privcom.gc.ca: Privacy Commissioner of Canada, looks into complaints about violations of customers' privacy and publishes results online.

www.moneysense.ca: *MoneySense* magazine, has credit card calculator that lets you see how much it costs to carry a balance at different interest rates.

www.equifax.ca: Equifax Canada Inc., one of the biggest credit bureaus in Canada, sells online credit reports at www.econsumer.equifax.ca.

www.tuc.ca: TransUnion Canada Inc., another large credit bureau, sells online credit reports at www.tuscores.ca.

www.creditbureau.ca: Northern Credit Bureaus Inc., a smaller credit bureau that sells online credit reports.

www.iquiri.com: iQuiri Inc., which is not a credit bureau, sells online credit reports from Northern Credit Bureaus in Quebec.

www.strategis.gc.ca: Industry Canada's portal to consumer and business information, publishes Dealing with Debt: A Consumer's Guide.

www.creditcounsellingcanada.ca: Credit Counselling Canada, a national association of non-profit credit counselling agencies, which helps you locate one near you.

www.indebt.org: Ontario Association of Credit Counselling Services, whose largest member is the Credit Counselling Service of Toronto, www.creditcanada.com.

PART THREE: INVESTING IN TOUGH TIMES

www.csb.gc.ca: Canada Savings Bonds and Canada Premium Bonds, current rates and those from past years.

www.fcidb.com: Federation of Canadian Independent Deposit Brokers, helps you locate a firm in your area that specializes in guaranteed investment products.

www.fiscalagents.com: Fiscal Agents, a Toronto deposit broker, has a calculator that lets you compare GIC rates and returns.

www.berkshirehathaway.com: Information on Warren Buffett's holding company, Berkshire Hathaway Inc., with complete text of his annual letters to shareholders.

www.sedar.com: System for Electronic Document Analysis and Retrieval, the electronic filing system for the disclosure documents of public companies and mutual funds across Canada.

www.cibcwm.com: CIBC World Markets, investment dealer that set up an index and publishes reports on Canadian real estate investment trusts (REITs).

www.canadianhedgewatch.com and **www.hedge.ca**: Information on hedge funds for Canadian investors.

www.fundlibrary.com and **www.morningstar.ca**: Information on mutual funds for Canadian investors.

www.bullionfund.com: Millennium Bullion Fund, an RRSP-eligible fund that holds equal amounts of gold, silver and platinum at the spot price.

www.buildingwealth.ca: Author Gordon Pape answers readers' questions and offers a free archive of more than 1,000 Q & A's going back to 1999.

www.investored.ca: Investor e-ducation Fund, spun off by the Ontario Securities Commission, to provide basic information to rookie investors.

www.csa-acvm.ca: The Canadian Securities Administrators, publishes a booklet, Choosing your Financial Adviser.

www.investorism.com: Activist Joe Killoran's checklist for mutual fund buyers.

www.fairdealingmodel.com: Ontario Securities Commission's concept paper on restoring the balance of power between financial advisers and clients.

www.toolkit.cch.com: Publisher CCH Inc., provides a checklist to assess your personal strengths and weaknesses as an entrepreneur.

www.rbcroyalbank.com/sme/bigidea and **www.cbsc.org/ibp**: Tips on writing an effective business plan from Canada's largest bank and the Canada Business Service Centres.

www.cfib.ca: Canadian Federation of Independent Business, collects information and writes reports on how to get better treatment from banks.

www.trahair.com: Chartered accountant David Trahair provides accounting and financial tips for small businesses.

www.bdc.ca: Business Development Bank of Canada, helps fund start-up businesses that are willing to accept training.

www.businessgateway.ca: Business Services for Canada, a portal to all the government information and services needed to start, run and expand your business.

PART FOUR: SAVING FOR RETIREMENT IN AND OUT OF AN RRSP

www.talbotstevens.com: Talbot Stevens, president of a financial education firm in London, Ont., has a number of articles published online about RRSP strategies.

www.ccra-adrc.gc.ca: The Canada Customs and Revenue Agency, which has a form you can print from the Internet with a request to reduce your tax deductions at source.

www.smithman.net: Fraser Smith, retired financial planner, explains how to make your mortgage interest tax-deductible as an alternative to an RRSP.

www.bylo.org: Toronto man who uses the pseudonym Bylo Selhi has an archive of articles on investing and how to keep costs low.

www.iunits.com: Barclays Global Investors, sells index funds called iUnits that trade on the Toronto Stock Exchange, has a calculator that helps you see the impact of management-expense ratios.

www.amex.com: American Stock Exchange, offers a wide variety of exchange-traded index and sector funds.

labour-travail.hrdc-drhc.gc.ca/worklife: Human Resources Development Canada's Web site on work-life balance and aging workforce issues.

PART FIVE: FINANCIAL PLANNING AND YOUR EXTENDED FAMILY

caregiver.on.ca and **www.howtocare.com**: After taking care of her elderly father, Karen Henderson dispenses helpful information to seniors and their adult children.

www.gov.on.ca/citizenship/seniors: Free wallet card and guide to advance care planning from the Ontario Ministry of Citizenship.

www.familyfight.com: Lawyers Barry Fish and Les Kotzer collect and publish stories about how families are torn apart by bad planning or failure to do anything.

www.myfuneralplan.org and **www.afuneralinbc.com**: Memorial societies in Ontario and British Columbia, dedicated to simple, low-cost funeral arrangements.

www.crimes-of-persuasion.com: Les Henderson's encyclopedic guide to fraud and how scams work.

www.phonebusters.com: PhoneBusters, operated by the Ontario Provincial Police, collects information on telemarketing and other frauds aimed at the elderly.

www.reverse.org: Information on reverse mortgages from a non-profit U.S. group with no ties to the lending industry.

www.canadabenefits.gc.ca: Information about benefit programs available from the federal and provincial governments.

www.consumerinformation.ca: Information about fraud, finances and spending smarter from Canadian governments and non-profit groups.

Index